THE
FAMILY
and the
UNIFICATION
CHURCH

edited by
Gene G. James

Conference series no. 15
First edition
© 1983
Unification Theological Seminary
Barrytown, N.Y. 12507

Printed in the United States of America
Library of Congress Catalog Number 83-80638
ISBN 0-932894-17-8

Distributed by
The Rose of Sharon Press, Inc.
G.P.O. Box 2432
New York, New York 10116

Cover by June Kiburz

CONTENTS

Introduction

I

The essays in this book are grouped into four sections. The articles in the first section, "Conflict and Commitment," deal with: (1) the conflict that has arisen between members of the Unification Church and their parents, (2) factors which tend to generate commitment to the Church, (3) conflicts which arise for members in carrying out their commitments to the Church. The articles in the second section, "Contrasts and Comparisons," compare Unification thought and practice regarding marriage and family to that of the Hutterites, New Christian Right, American Muslim Mission, and the Marriage Encounter and Parenting for Peace and Justice movements. Unlike the articles in the other sections which were written by professional sociologists, psychologists, theologians and philosophers, those in the third section "Responses to Challenges" were written by members of the Unification Church. The conflicts and commitments discussed from an external point of view in the other sections are thus dealt with from within in this section. The articles in the last section, "Theological and Philosophical Assessments," describe and evaluate the theological and philosophical assumptions and consequences of Unification doctrines of marriage and the family. In the remainder of the Introduction I provide brief summaries of the articles, emphasizing common issues, and pointing out the respects in which the authors seem to agree or disagree with one another.

II

It is ironic that the Unification Church, which stresses the importance of the family more than perhaps any other religious group, has been widely attacked for destroying the family. What accounts for this? Why have parents been so opposed to their children joining the Unification Church? Why has it been singled out from the many new religious groups and considered the archetypal cult? David Bromley and Anson Shupe, authors of the classic studies of new religious groups, *The New Vigilantes* and *Strange Gods,* address themselves to these questions in the first article in Section I, "The Archetypal Cult: Conflict and Social Construction of Deviance." Their answer to the last question, framed in terms of social conflict and labeling theories, is that the reasons are to be found as much in the beliefs and attitudes of those who have attacked the Church as in its practices. They conclude that the stereotypical image of the Church held by those who have attacked it, in fact, bear "little resemblance to reality."

The primary thesis of Kenneth Ambrose's article "Function of the Family in the Process of Commitment Within the Unification Movement" is that there is a "progression of the seeking individual, from close personal ties with members of the Unification movement, to commitment to the group, to acceptance of the ideology of *Divine Principle* and matched marriage . . . by Rev. Moon." According to Ambrose, marriage then serves as an additional reinforcement of commitment to the group and *Divine Principle.* The fact that members of the Church have frequently abandoned "careers, education and in some cases, their families of orientation," generates additional commitment. People remain committed to the Church, he concludes, because to leave it would be not only to renounce one's former beliefs, it would be to cut off oneself from one's friends and perhaps even one's immediate family.

Ambrose's thesis that personal attachments and commitments to the group precede acceptance of the teaching of the *Divine Principle,* contradicts the position maintained by Frederick Sontag in the 1981 article, "The God of Principle." Sontag writes:

Most who are outside the movement do not realize that the initial conversion of new followers takes place by continued study of the Principle through repeated lectures that go into greater and greater detail. . . . The primary confrontation takes place between the individual and the Principle. . . . Of course, the personal attraction of the members whom the novice meets, or the lecturer . . . has a great deal to do with conversion as is true in all religious movements, just as disappointing personal relationships have much to do with members leaving. Still, the Principle as the path to God forms the core of their religious experience.[1]

So strong is the appeal of the Principle, says Sontag, that "more than one ex-member has left the church through forced deprogramming, or due to some practical disillusionment, but has still maintained that he or she 'believes the Principle.'"[2]

The disagreement between Ambrose and Sontag may reduce to nothing more than the difference in occupational biases of sociologists who stress non-cognitive, and philosophers who stress cognitive, reasons for action. However, if it is true that most of the people who join the Unification Church do so knowing that it may alienate them from their friends and families, they would not seem to be the kind of individuals who would remain in the Church because of personal relationships even though they are no longer convinced by its teaching.

Eileen Barker, in the third article of Section I, also seems to emphasize belief as the primary factor which brings about division between church members and their parents. She says:

While much of the press reporting on "The Church That Breaks Up Families" is sensationalizing rubbish, there is no doubt that many parents have suffered considerable anguish on learning that their (adult) child has become a Moonie. It is also true that many a Moonie has suffered considerable anguish from his parent's inability to understand his point of view. . . .

Barker does not think the fact that Church members and their parents feel alienated from one another should surprise sociologists or historians of religious movements. "It is almost a sociological law that those who hold strongly to a belief system which radically challenges a generally accepted status quo will have to isolate themselves from those with whom they disagree, at least in the early stages of a movement's development, and this will frequently lead to familial estrangement." This claim, it should be noted, is consistent with Bromley's and Shupe's thesis that the major reasons parents think their children have been brainwashed and are being held against their will is their inability to find common areas of belief and the communal lifestyle of Church members.

The primary concern in Barker's paper is with the conflicts which arise within church members' commitments. Since Unificationism is a missionary religion, members who have families may find themselves torn between furthering the work of the Church and fulfilling their obligations to their families. There is thus a tension between their commitment to bring salvation to all people and their commitment to their family. This tension could, of course, be avoided if they were a separatist group such as the Hutterites who live apart from the larger society seeking primarily their own salvation. But this would mean abandoning the Unification belief that salvation can only be obtained through international social action.

Barker also thinks the fact that Unificationists strive to make their marriages "God-centered" can create tensions between marriage partners. Although this practice encourages one to look for those features in one's partner that God loves, it can also "lead to a denial, or a lack of facing up to . . . very real problems . . . regarding which negotiation may be necessary . . . " However, in her concluding remarks, Barker makes clear that in pointing out problems in Unification marriages, she does not intend to imply that they are "any less successful than those in the wider society. On the contrary what evidence there is suggests that by several criteria (such as the divorce rate) they could if anything be more successful."

III

Timothy Miller's article compares the family organization of the Unification Church with that of the Hutterites. He finds that even though Hutterites differ from Unificationists in pursuing primarily agrarian lives apart from mainstream society, both they and Unificationists employ a social pattern which he calls "families within families." This is a pattern in which biological families are looked upon as units within a larger family, the community of believers. This kind of organization structure, he maintains, has been a very durable one that has conferred great stability on communities which have utilized it. The Hutterites, who developed out of the Anabaptist movement which antedated the Reformation, have survived to the present with relatively few changes in their lifestyle. This is, of course, not as likely to be true of Unificationists who are much more involved in the larger society. However, Miller believes that the sense of family within the Unification Church may be one of the most important factors accounting for the "internal unity . . . in the movement, especially . . . when confronted with external threats such as deprogramming or government harassment."

Miller also argues that parents who feel they have lost their children to the Unification movement "fail to realize that what is happening is actually an affirmation of family values, not a rejection of them." This suggests that if there were more of an effort by parents to understand the values of their adult children who join the Unification Church, there might not be the radical alienation which exists between some parents and their children. This sometimes happens and in those cases, Miller points out, "old family ties remain intact."

Donald Heinz maintains in his article that many people today see political institutions as excessively remote, impersonal and bureaucratic. As a result they are turning elsewhere to find meaning and identity. In particular they are turning to what Peter Berger and Richard Neuhaus call "mediating structures," i.e., institutions which stand between the individual's private life and large public institutions. These are such groups as the neighborhood, family and church. Liberalism, Heinz believes, has been blind to the importance of mediating structures. One consequence is that "rights of the individual are defended against mediating structures, e.g., the child against the family, sexual license against neighborhood values." Heinz agrees with Berger and Neuhaus that mediating structures are essential for a vital democracy and sees the New Christian Right and the Unification Church as trying to strengthen them. Both, he thinks, are trying to restore what they believe is the divine order of things. Moreover, both see the family as playing an essential role in this order.

The most significant difference between the New Christian Right and the Unification Church, in Heinz's opinion, is that because the latter originated in Korea and contains some non-Christian elements, it does not have as great an access to the shared symbolism and political institutions of our society. It follows, he believes, that "at no time in the foreseeable future will the Unification movement be in a position, as the New Christian Right may be, to engage in attempts at coercive reform." Unificationists must content themselves with "expressive social action." However, he questions whether this would be true under different circumstances. Thus, he asks in closing: "If the Unification movement had sufficient political power and access to the American tradition and symbol system, would it attempt to mobilize its theological idealism into social reality through political action rather than ethical modeling?"

Na'im Akbar, a psychologist who has been greatly influenced by the ideas of the American Muslim Mission, compares their conception of the family with that of the Unification Church in the third article in Section II. Both groups, in his opinion, rightly think of the family as a natural organization ordained by God. The family, he argues, should not be conceived of as merely an organization to nurture children or provide companionship, although it does both of these. It is also the chief agency through which we are socialized and, if functioning properly, provides us with lifelong emotional support. Since he thinks the last of these one of the most important functions of the family, he attacks both Freudians who see aggression as a natural part of family life and Behaviorists who recommend manipulative techniques of child-rearing. The primary differences which Akbar finds between the American Muslim Mission and the Unification Church are: (1) Muslims in America no longer practice arranged marriage, a distinctive feature of the Unification Church, (2) unlike Unificationists who advocate interracial and intercultural marriage as a means of bringing about world unity, Muslims encourage marriage within the black community to help restore the black racial pride which has been eroded by slavery and oppression. However, like Unificationists, Muslims believe that the family is the primary place people learn brotherhood which is necessary for world peace. Akbar therefore concludes that Muslims and Unificationists differ more with regard to means than goals.

Jane Flinn's article "Three Models of Family: Marriage Encounter, Parenting for Peace and Justice, Blessed Family" is an examination of three contemporary movements to strengthen the family. She says that unlike the Moral Majority which offers only a "mishmash of platitudes rather than a coherent model for family life," these are organized attempts to provide daily guidance and group support to people trying to cope with the problems of family life. Although she praises Worldwide Marriage Encounter, she believes that its stress on sharing "tends to ignore the complementary need for privacy, autonomy, the dignity of being allowed to cope with one's own problems." Since the Parenting for Peace and Justice movement teaches democratic methods of conflict resolution, nonviolent techniques, and ways of overcoming sexism, it is as oriented toward society as the family. This is also true of the Blessed Family approach of the Unification Church. The Parenting for Peace and Justice movement, Flinn believes, has been rather successful in eliminating sexism from members' marriages. Unification theory, she states, also "suggests the possibility of equal and flexible roles for men and women." However, it has been less successful than Marriage Encounter in eliminating sexism. The Blessed Family still "tends to have rather traditional sex roles, a reflection perhaps of male-dominated Biblical and oriental societies." On the other hand, the Blessed Family has made genuine progress in overcoming cultural biases and racism.

IV

The article by Hugh and Nora Spurgin describes how they became members of the Church, provides an exposition of the Unification doctrine of marriage and the family by practitioners of the doctrine, and explains the role their beliefs play in their marriage and the rearing of their children. Both, it should be noted, indicate that they joined the Church because of their study of the *Divine Principle*. Since Nora is a former Director of the Church's Family Life Office and Editor of the *Blessing Quarterly,* which publishes articles to help members meet the challenges and responsibilities of marriage, her contribution to the discussion draws upon her wide experience in this area. The Spurgins do not attempt to hide the fact that conflicts of the type described by Barker occur in Unification marriages. To the contrary, they point out that Unificationists are likely to face more problems than most other married couples, e.g., different cultural and racial backgrounds. They also have the same practical problems other couples have such as "personality conflicts, financial problems, child-rearing problems, etc." Finally, the Spurgins candidly admit that although "our common faith is a great source of strength . . . we also go through crises and tests of faith . . . "

Tom Walsh draws on the work of the philosopher Alasdair MacIntyre to provide a framework for explaining the Unification practice of celibacy before marriage. Celibacy may be said to be a virtue for members of the Unification Church because it is a voluntary action in compliance with a standard intended to further a community ideal. Its function is to enable the individual to perfect his or her character as a prerequisite to marriage and the practice of "true family." The goal of celibacy in the Unification Church is thus not to denigrate the body or eliminate the passions. Its goal is the sublimation of desire so that one can give undivided love to God and service to mankind. Understood this way, Walsh maintains, the practice of celibacy is a form of self-realization. However, since it involves service to others and preparation for establishing an ideal family, it also has a social dimension. Unificationists, Walsh states, live in what Stanley Hauerwas calls a "story-formed community." They view all their actions in terms of man's fall and God's plans for restoration. They therefore see celibacy as an "indemnity condition" for restoring the sexual purity which existed before the fall. Sex, marriage and the rearing of a family are not for them purely private matters, as they are for modern Liberals. Indeed, in Walsh's opinion, the development of a family-centered ethics such as that found in Unification thought, allows one to avoid the extremes of both Liberal individualism and Marxist statism. He concludes by saying that in seeking to reinstate community into modern urban life, the Unification Church may be considered a postmodern development.

In contrast to Kenneth Ambrose who stresses the disruption of careers and education which frequently occurs when individuals join the Unification Church, Michael Mickler emphasizes the opportunities Unification lifestyle offers unmarried people. He contrasts what he calls "vocational" and "non-vocational" models of being single. A life of vocational singleness is one dedicated to religious service and love of God. Its values have traditionally been affirmed in vows of poverty, chastity and obedience. Although rich in rewards it may be said to be a life of self-sacrifice. The goal of a life of non-vocational singleness, on the other hand, is self-fulfillment. Its primary values are freedom, self-awareness and self-expression. Just as a religious life of self-sacrifice may center on either service to mankind or love of God, a life devoted to self-fulfillment may concentrate on either such goals as travel and adventure or success in one's career. However, Mickler thinks that people who pursue these goals often feel a sense of meaninglessness in their lives. This is not true, he says, of unmarried members of the Unification Church. He claims that "one of the distinctive features of the Unification Church is the manner in which it has incorporated the single life within a symbol-system that integrates 'non-vocational' and 'vocational' singleness." He goes on to show in detail how he thinks the Unification Church has combined the lives of self-sacrifice and self-fulfillment to produce one superior to either alone.

Although Mickler asserts that Unification lifestyle offers the single individual many rewards, he does not advocate singleness as an end in itself. Singleness is considered by Unificationists a time of preparation for marriage. But the satisfactions and rewards of single life, according to Mickler, are retained in Unification marriages. This is true because, just as singleness is looked upon as preparation for marriage, family life is viewed as "an extension of the single state." One can see this, he says, in the frequent separation of marriage partners to pursue Church work. Since Mickler writes as an unmarried member of the Church looking forward to family life, it is understandable that he tends to emphasize anticipated satisfaction rather than problems. However, a balanced assessment of family life as an extension of the single state would obviously have to take into consideration the kinds of problems discussed by Barker and the Spurgins.

Patricia Zulkosky in her paper "Women, Guilt, Spirituality and Family," argues that a pervasive feature of the experience of most women in our society is a sense of guilt. The primary source of this guilt, in her opinion, is Christianity which glorifies self-sacrifice. Women are expected to live for others, especially their husbands and children. They are required to subordinate and hide their own abilities. To take pride in one's talents and to wish to develop them is to be unfeminine and sinful. Women, therefore, feel guilty when they attempt to develop into an independent person. The true sin, however, is not the desire to realize one's self, but the attempt to smother it. Since Christianity is the primary source of this sin, it is doubtful that it can be reformed to deal with it.

One problem in ridding Christianity of its biases against women is that God has usually been conceived in masculine terms in the Christian tradition. Since God is conceived of as androgynous in Unification theology, it would seem to have greater potential for overcoming sexism than traditional Christianity. But Zulkosky points out, although the Unification concept of God is androgynous, the language and imagery of the *Divine Principle* and other

Unification writings are almost exclusively masculine. She therefore asks: "What is the value of a view that holds God is both masculine and feminine, if it is not embodied in the theology, liturgy and devotional practices of the church?" The problem, she says, is not that Unification texts "make blatantly negative remarks about women;" it is that they do not "develop or even mention the role of women in providential history." Woman has a prominent role in the Unification account of the fall, but very little in its doctrine of redemption. This has great influence on Church practice. For example, very few women hold leadership positions.

Could the Unification Church develop a truly non-sexist theology and social praxis? Zulkosky thinks it has the potential but that a number of changes would have to be made. Some of the alternatives she suggests are: eliminating sexist language, describing more thoroughly the role of women in providential history, developing more role models for women by giving them positions of greater authority, and establishing family patterns which will enable women to overcome guilt and develop their potential as human beings.

Since Unificationists hope to transform the world by establishing ideal families in which children free of original sin can be reared, as more and more Church members marry, questions regarding child-rearing will undoubtedly play an increasing role in their thought. Diana Muxworthy Feige's article "Relations-In-Process: Paradigm for Education and the Family" is a first step in this direction. She believes that to understand and direct the development of children we must see their behavior within the context of their social environment. Learning involves social interaction between children and those who mold them. The way a child deals with a disability, for example, depends on both how the child and other people react to it. The most crucial factor in children's development is how adults view their potential. Especially important is what L.S. Vygotsky calls the "zone of proximal development," the difference between actual development and potential development under the guidance of adults and peers. Feige's primary thesis is that not only educational institutions but the family should be viewed as an agency of proximal development. In fact, because the family is the central institution through which God will restore man, it should be seen as the most important agency of proximal development. The goal of education in Unification families, therefore, should be to both develop individual talents and awaken children to their religious duties.

V

Frederick Sontag's article draws a number of parallels between Unificationism and Marxism. For example, both see history as culminating in the establishment of an ideal society with technology and the efforts of a group of dedicated followers playing key roles in bringing it about. The family, Sontag points out, is conceived of in Unification theology in a manner analogous to the way the party is thought of in Marxism. There are, of course, significant differences between Unificationism and Marxism—the primary one being that the former is spiritualistic and theistic, while the latter is materialistic and atheistic.

Sontag defends the Church against the charge that it recruits followers through insincere demonstrations of caring about individuals. "The affection showered on novices," he writes, "is not pure surreptitious 'P.R.' It is an attempt to demonstrate the loving bond which should exist between all members of an ideal family." He believes that the very fact that the Unification movement has grown the way it has "indicates that many have found something satisfying in it which is missing in established religions." The major obstacle in bringing about the ideal society they desire, in his opinion, is that it would require universal acceptance of Unification doctrine. This will not occur because "the history of religions, or of any theory-based enterprise, tells us that it is unlikely that all groups will ever agree on one theory, other than by violent revolution." He concludes, however, that if the Church succeeds in building a truly non-racist, international organization, that would itself be an achievement of great religious significance.

Frank Flinn maintains that Christian theology is a much more essential component of Unificationism than oriental thought.

Indeed, he describes Unificationism as primarily a "Korean indigenization of a specific type of North American Presbyterianism known as federal theology." The distinctive feature of both federal theology and Unificationism is their stress on the communal nature of the fall and restoration. However, Unificationists differ from federalists and most other Christians in viewing the family as the fundamental means by which salvation is to be obtained.

Because Unificationists think marriage was decreed by God, they reject the liberal conception of marriage as a purely private contractual agreement. Flinn believes that in doing this they are restoring marriage to its rightful place from which Liberalism dethroned it. Liberalism, he says, denied man's natural sociability, conceiving of institutions as based on compacts between self-interested individuals. "This contractual understanding of all social arrangements was never far from commercialism. . . . The modern concept of right itself is seen as an agreement between adults on the basis of a perceived 'fair bargain.' " It, therefore, should not be surprising, he thinks, that children, women and minorities who have not had positions of power from which to bargain, have not enjoyed the same rights as white males. The primary defects of a conception of marriage based on Liberal presuppositions, in his opinion, are that it: (1) "gives weight to individuals and their 'rights' as against social beings and their 'obligations'," and (2) destroys the sacramental character of marriage through which we are linked to God.

According to Flinn, Liberals conceive of rights as the result of contracts between self-interested individuals. He thus contrasts rights with obligations. The conception of rights in my article, the final one in the volume, on the other hand, is that talk about rights is merely a way of calling people's attention to their obligations. To claim that one person has a right is to say that some other person (or persons) has a duty. Since one may incur obligations by entering into contracts, some rights are the results of agreements. Other rights, however, are more general and are grounded in respect for persons. I think this is what Locke meant in speaking of certain rights as natural rather than conventional. The primary thesis argued for in my paper is that the kind of obligations we have in a democratic society are different from those owed to family members. This does not mean that in being a member of a family one gives up one's other rights. Since child abuse, for example, is an unfortunate fact of life, it is sometimes necessary to defend the rights of a child against his or her family. This does not imply, as Heinz seems to conclude, that Liberals necessarily think the state more important than the family. Both are equally important. Nor does it prevent one from also thinking of the family in sacramental terms.

Heinz asks at the conclusion of his paper whether the Unification Church, if it had the power, might not attempt to impose its ideals on American society. Both he and Bromley and Shupe in their article imply that the Unification conception of the best form of government is theocracy. However, *Divine Principle* affirms the value of both human rights and democratic government. One way of interpreting the Unification ideal, then, is that Unificationists hope to overcome alienation among the people of the world by bringing about a sense of family and community, while at the same time preserving respect for democracy. I agree with Sontag that even a partial realization of this ideal would be an event of great significance for mankind.

NOTES

1 See *Ten Theologians Respond to the Unification Church*, ed. Herbert Richardson (Barrytown, N.Y.: Unif. Theo. Seminary, distr. Rose of Sharon Press, 1981), pp. 122-23.

2 *Ibid.*, p. 122.

The Archetypal Cult: Conflict and the Social Construction of Deviance

David G. Bromley & Anson D. Shupe, Jr.

In recent years deviance theorists have stressed the centrality of power as a factor in the social construction of deviance. At a structural level conflict theorists have argued that normative definitions of deviance are a product of power differentials and that more powerful groups dominate both the construction of such definitions and the imposition of social control mechanisms. At the social psychological level labeling theorists have asserted that deviance is the product of reaction to an act rather than a quality of the act itself. They have attempted to identify both the process by which deviant labels are applied and the personal, situational and relational characteristics associated with the imposition of various labels.

In this paper we are concerned with an issue related to both of these theoretical perspectives: the conditions under which one out of a group of actors (individuals or groups) comes to be designated as the archetypal offender. In some conflict situations one actor may be selected to symbolize the entire set of "offenders" (i.e., less powerful actors who come to be designated as deviant). Using data on the new religious controversy we shall analyze the selection of the Unification Church as the archetypal "cult." It is our contention that the Unification Church became symbolic of the "cult problem" not because it was the largest, wealthiest, most powerful, most violence prone, most manipulative, or most rapidly growing of the new religions. Rather, we shall argue, the Unification Church became the archetypal cult as a result of two sets of factors: (1) the pattern of conflict engendered with other powerful groups and (2) the organizational requisites of the anti-cult movement.

Background to the Conflict

Early in the 1970s a number of new religious movements appeared in the United States and became the focus of one of the major religious controversies of the twentieth century. The best known of these movements were the Children of God, the People's Temple, the International Society for Krishna Consciousness (the Hare Krishnas), The Way International, Transcendental Meditation, Divine Light Mission, the Church of Scientology, and the Unification Church. These movements differed significantly with respect to their histories, beliefs, and organizational styles (see Bromley and Shupe, 1981). Scientology and the Unification Church actually had been in the United States since the 1950s while the Children of God originated in the late 1960s. The Divine Light Mission and Hare Krishnas grew out of distinct ancient Hindu traditions, while the Children of God and the Unification Church were grounded in Christianity. Some of these groups (e.g., the Hare Krishnas, the Children of God and the Unification Church) were organized communally, while others (e.g., Transcendental Meditation and Scientology) made relatively few lifestyle demands on their followers. Leadership structures also varied enormously. The Reverend Jim Jones apparently dominated the day-to-day lives of his followers, at least toward the end of his leadership; the Divine Light Mission's Guru Maharaj Ji, alternately, served as that group's spiritual master but was relatively inept as an organizer. Prabhupada died some years after transplanting the Hare Krishna movement to the United States and left that fledgling American group with a federated political structure but no single dominant charismatic leader. The new religious movements also ranged in size from the Divine Light Mission and the Children of God, which numbered their American membership in the hundreds by the end of the decade, to Transcendental Meditation and Scientology, each of which could claim as many as several tens of thousands of members.

Despite such obvious differences among the new religious movements, they were viewed by the American public and the media simply as "cults." The term "cults" implied a number of negative characteristics which, it was often assumed, were shared by all of these groups. These alleged attributes included (1) manipulative and psychologically coercive recruitment/socialization tactics, (2) authoritarian leadership, (3) deprivation and exploitation of converts, (4) economic and political adventurism disguised as religion, and (5) deliberate destruction of ties to all outsiders including family members.[1]

This stereotypical conception of the new religious movements was conceived and disseminated by the anti-cult movement, a countermovement which had as its goal the suppression or destruction of the new religions and the "rescue" of individual converts (for a detailed history, see Shupe and Bromley, 1980a). The anti-cult movement consisted of three distinct but mutually supporting groups. The most active and effective wing of the anti-cult movement was the coalition of anti-cult associations, local or regional groups composed primarily of parents and family members of converts to the new religions. These associations sought to arouse public concern, media attention and governmental action against those groups designated as "cults." Closely related to the anti-cult associations was a loose network of deprogrammers, i.e., individuals (professional and amateur) who acted as agents for family members to "rescue" converts to the new religions, often against the latters' will, on the assumption that they had been involuntarily induced to join. The other major wing of the anti-cult movement was made up of fundamentalist and evangelical Christian groups that vigorously denounced the theologies of the new religions since the latters' beliefs either represented sectarian challenges to orthodox Christian teachings or alternative routes to spiritual experience and salvation.

The anti-cult associations and deprogrammers had as their primary goal the extrication of converts to new religious movements. The religious groups opposing "cults" were circumspect on the issue of vigilante style rescue and legalized deprogramming, given the substantial implications for religious liberty. Therefore, it was the former two sets of groups which formed the nucleus of the legal and extra-legal initiatives against the new religions. It was these groups which formulated the brainwashing ideology which provided a basis for legitimating legislation that would grant parents legal custody of their adult offspring and organized informal "rescues" and deprogrammings.

In its simplest form the anti-cult ideology constituted a classic illustration of a conspiracy theory. Conversion to new religions was explained in terms of brainwashing, drugging or spot hypnosis; this explanation effectively reduced "converts" to "victims." The remainder of the anti-cult ideology provided the rationale for such manipulative and abusive practices. Leaders of new religions were portrayed as authoritarians and charlatans who exploited their young followers for power and profit. Thus, these groups were not religious at all but merely self-aggrandisement schemes masquerading as religions to avoid taxation and criminal prosecution. Since conversion was neither voluntary nor to a legitimate religion, even forcible removal hardly represented a serious infringement of constitutional rights or personal freedom.

The foregoing elements of anti-cult ideology have been discussed elsewhere (see Bromley and Shupe, 1981). It is clear that this ideology, however distorted, was extremely functional in mobilizing public opposition to new religion, for it raised the specter of thousands of innocent youth being reduced to automatons in the service of unscrupulous gurus. It has not been as clear why the Unification Church became the symbol of the struggle against cults. We shall examine the pattern of conflict between the Unification Church and other institutions as well as the requisites of the anti-cult movement in order to interpret this outcome.

The Unification Church as the Cult Archetype

There is compelling evidence that the Unification Church quickly became the new religion synonymous with "cult" both in the minds of the public at large and institutional gatekeepers whose support the anti-cult movement sought. For example, the media was filled with stories about glassy-eyed Moonies who had been reduced to automatons by sophisticated mind control techniques. There was a succession of potboiler books by apostates who attested that they had indeed been brainwashed: *Crazy for God* (Edwards, 1979), *Hostage to Heaven* (Underwood and Underwood, 1979), *Moonstruck: A Memoir of My Life in a Cult* (Wood and Vitek, 1979), *Heavenly Deception* (Elkins, 1980), *Moonwebs: Journey Into the Mind of a Cult* (Freed, 1980), *Life Among the Moonies: Three Years in the Unification Church* (Durham, 1981), *Lord of the Second Advent* (Kemperman, 1981) and *Escape from the Moonies* (Swatland and Swatland, 1982). Two of these were made into movies: "Heavenly Deception" and the better known "Ticket to Heaven." In addition there were literally thousands of newspaper and magazine stories of the same genre (for an analysis of a sample of such stories see Bromley, Shupe and Ventimiglia, 1979).

Public officials who began investigating cults as a result of complaints from anti-cult groups frequently focused their inquiries on the Unification Church. For example, at the time she sponsored conservatorship legislation in Connecticut, Senator Regina Smith was quoted in the *Meriden Record-Journal* ("State Senate OKs Smith's Anti-Cult Bill," 8 May 1981) as follows:

> Mrs. Smith said numerous cases of families in her district being "victimized," especially by the Unification Church, prompted her to push the bill, which was the subject of an emotional day-long hearing earlier this year.

Similarly, hearings in the Vermont legislature prior to the introduction of anti-cult legislation focused primarily on the Unification Church. The Senate Committee's final report (Vermont, 1977) stated:

The committee held five days of hearings as authorized
by S.R. 16 and received testimony from approximately
30 different witnesses. . . . Allegations were lodged mainly
against the activities of the Holy Spirit Association for
the Unification of World Christianity, otherwise known
as the "Unification Church . . . "

Sources of Conflict

Family

Since family members of converts to the new religions com-
prised the heart of the anti-cult movement, conflict was most intense with those groups which posed the greatest direct threat to
families. From this perspective the most threatening groups were
those which aggressively recruited young adults and which were
organized communally (thus removing converts from mainstream
middle class domestic and career trajectories). With the exception
of the People's Temple, which recruited both older individuals
and entire families, most of the new religions appealed mainly to
young adults. There was some variation in age range, however, as
groups such as the Hare Krishnas and the Children of God attracted relatively young individuals (i.e., ages 16 to 20), whereas
Transcendental Meditation and Scientology attracted somewhat
older individuals (Wuthnow, 1976: 279-85). There was even greater
variation in the aggressiveness with which new religious movements recruited new members. The Children of God, the Hare
Krishnas and the Unification Church conducted recruitment campaigns on college campuses and in centers of youth subculture.
One major consequence was that converts often were out of immediate contact with their families at the time they were recruited. As
a result, by the time parents learned of their offspring's involvement with one of these groups, major commitments had already
been made. Parents therefore had little opportunity to influence a
decision that they perceived had major, long-term implications,
and their anxiety was heightened by the apparent swiftness of the
change.[2]

Even more disconcerting to parents was the major transformation in lifestyle and direction that accompanied conversion to certain of the new religions. In contrast to groups such as Transcendental Meditation and Scientology, which made few lifestyle demands on members, the Hare Krishnas, the Children of God and the Unification Church all were communally organized. These latter groups portrayed the existing social order as deeply flawed and corrupted and withdrew from it in all but certain public relations and ritualistic modes (i.e., fundraising and recruiting) in order both to preserve their own purity and to set the stage for a transformation of society. Conversion to any one of the three groups involved disposing of most personal possessions, abandonment of former domestic and occupational career plans, separating one's self from former friends and even family, and total commitment and loyalty to the cause. The groups differed somewhat in the specific tactics used to create distance from former relationships, personal transformation and strong loyalties. For example, converts to the Hare Krishnas radically transformed their physical appearances, members of the Children of God assumed new names, and novitiates in the Unification Church recalculated their birthdates to the dates of their conversion. Whatever the specific tactics employed, parents shared a sense that they had lost the capacity to influence and sometimes even to communicate with their sons and daughters.

It is not surprising, then, that the Unification Church, the Children of God and the Hare Krishnas were the new religions that evoked the greatest antagonism among parents. In particular, the Unification Church presented an inviting target to the anti-cultists as a result of its explicit development of a fictive kinship system within the movement. Moon and his wife were designated as "true' parents" clearly differentiated from members' biological parents, and members referred to one another as "brothers" and "sisters." While family imagery is common in communal groups, the Unification Church's explicit development of it made the group particularly useful to the anti-cultists in their campaign to portray the new religions as callous destroyers of family ties.

Church

None of the established religions responded favorably to the appearance of the new religious movements. Most of the converts to the new religions were at one time members of mainline denominations. Although the new religions never attracted enough converts to pose a meaningful threat to the membership base of mainline denominations, their success in attracting young adults was a source of embarassment to these groups. If the Christian tradition in particular was indeed the repository of ultimate spiritual truth, how could the apathy of youth be explained? The success of the new religions forced religious leaders to painful self-examination. As one evangelical Christian writer (Sparks, 1977: 261) put it:

> ...much of what we call the Church has failed—often miserably—in carrying out its role before God, itself and the world. Though it is still loved and even protected by the Lord, it has moved an embarassingly great distance away from its original foundations.

Thus "cults" represented, in Van Baalen's classic words, the "unpaid bills of the church." Further, all of the new religions presented some type of challenge to traditional Christian theology. Some groups, such as the Children of God and the Unification Church, charged that the major denominations had been thoroughly corrupted and fallen away from God; other groups, such as the Divine Light Mission, offered an alternative basis for "true" religious experience that ignored mainline Judeo-Christian tradition.

While all of the new religions drew some opposition from Jewish and Christian groups, those new religions which innovated on the Christian tradition understandably evoked the greatest hostility. They were, after all, most likely to "prey" on "sheep" within the same "fold" or religious tradition. There was little likelihood that the new religions emanating from the Hindu tradition would attract large numbers of American followers or cause many Christians to question their own faith. But new religions in the Christian tradition challenged basic Christian tenets by which many Christians, and particularly fundamentalists, organized their lives. Thus fundamentalists angrily attacked the Unification Church and the Children of God as heretics, considerably more vehemently than other Christians.

Both the Children of God and the Unification Church directly challenged the authority of the established churches. The former's Moses David Berg declared the Christian churches to be totally corrupt while the latter's Sun Myung Moon claimed that God's true will and message could only be understood through *Divine Principle*. From the standpoint of the established churches, if doubts were raised about the truth or completeness of traditional Christian teachings, this would rob them of their meaning, personal sacrifices and commitments made by Christians on the basis of religious beliefs or norms. Berg claimed to be an important prophet; Moon's own biographic characteristics were strikingly close to those he declared would be possessed by the Lord of the Second Advent. If the claims of either man to spiritual leadership were granted legitimacy, then Berg or Moon would command virtually complete authority over all Christians. Of course, Moon's messianic pretensions were particularly offensive to fundamentalists, for Moon would in effect supplant Jesus as *the* Christ, or messiah. Both men predicted an imminent transformation of the world based upon their spiritual revelations. These predictions, if taken seriously, would have required all Christians to mobilize themselves for the imminent last days. Mainline denominations obviously were in no position to make extreme demands on their membership, and their leaders had no interest in pressing for such extreme commitment. Moon clearly posed a greater threat to fundamentalist Christians than Berg. Moon sought to unify (under his own leadership) all Christians, while Berg merely condemned the established churches. Moon developed an elaborate theological system whereas Berg never produced anything resembling a systematic theology. Finally, Moon's thinly veiled messianic utopian claims had much more serious implications for Christians than did Berg's apocalyptic visions.

Government

With a few exceptions the new religious movements have not become deeply involved in controversial political activity. Jim Jones was involved in a variety of local civic projects in San Francisco which initially gave him a rather favorable public image. Although he eventually stirred up considerable controversy, which finally led to an exposé article in *New West* magazine, Jones was named as one of the 100 "most outstanding" clergymen in America by one interfaith group, Humanitarian of the Year in 1976, and recipient of the Martin Luther King, Jr. Humanitarian Award in 1977 (Shupe and Bromley, 1980a: 208-10). Of course, the mass migration he engineered to Guyana and his anticipated move to Cuba or the Soviet Union were sources of considerable embarrassment to the United States Government since Jones, at the time, was openly supporting the cause of worldwide socialism. Scientology openly responded to what it considered to be governmental harassment by infiltrating certain government agencies in order to gather evidence on agency improprieties. On a local level, the Children of God, Hare Krishna and Unification Church all ran afoul of local authorities in the course of fundraising activities. Fundraisers were prosecuted, municipalities were sued, and there was considerable rancor on both sides of the conflict. None of these conflicts, however, involved a challenge to supremacy of the state or to the delicately balanced relationship between church and state.

What distinguished the Unification Church from other new religions was the explicit, theological legitimation of the intrusion of religion into political affairs. According to *Divine Principle* the fall of man was in fact two-fold. The "vertical fall" occurred when Eve was sexually seduced by Satan, who thereby became the spiritual ancestor of humanity. The "horizontal fall" took place when Cain slew Abel, which divided mankind into two warring camps— the forces of Godless communism versus the forces of God-fearing democracies. Each fall had religious/political implications. The consequence of the vertical fall was that mankind became separated from divine purpose. In order to achieve restoration to its divinely intended relationship to God, mankind had to recognize the true source of its problems (through insights contained in *Divine Principle*) and to pay indemnity for the failure to assume its proper responsibility. Once sufficient indemnity had been paid, an opportunity for restoration would be divinely proffered. The implication of this doctrine was that social and political problems could be resolved only through proper *spiritual* knowledge. The church, therefore, clearly assumed supremacy over the state in matters of ultimate policy. Moon's open advocacy of theocracy and the break with traditional American separation of church and state drew opposition from both, for each had a vested interest in maintaining the hard won precedent of non-interference in one another's affairs.

The horizontal fall implied an ongoing struggle between communism and democracy in which, Moon predicted, the latter would win. In depicting this fall and restoration Moon went so far as to specify the roles various nations were to play in this cosmic struggle, including a role for the United States as the "archangel" nation. America was divinely mandated to defend the New Israel (South Korea), the birthplace of the "Lord of the Second Advent" who many converts believed to be Moon himself. On the basis of this doctrine members of the Unification Church actively lobbied for political and military aid to South Korea. Further, Moon defended the Nixon presidency at the height of the Watergate crisis in the winter of 1974, declaring that God had chosen Nixon as president to fulfill a divine providence and only God could remove him. Unification Church officials vigorously denied that Moon had intended support for Nixon personally. They asserted that Moon was advocating a course of forgiveness, love and unity instead of condemnation and rejection, in order to preserve American strength and determination in the struggle against communism. Nevertheless, the link created between the Unification Church and Nixon in the media during 1974-75, coupled with the Koreagate scandal soon after (connecting a number of congresspersons to pay-offs and bribery by South Korean influence peddler Tae Sung-Park) led to high visibility as well as unprecedented journalistic investigation of the Unificationist movement. It was Reverend Moon's announcement of support for the Nixon presidency in 1974, more than any other factor, that triggered negative media coverage of the Unification Church and that prompted a virtual pull-out of Moon's potential sympathizers in Congress.

The various political positions and initiatives by the Unification Church had the further effect of alienating both liberals and conservatives. Liberals were offended by the Church's staunch anti-communism, by its support for what they viewed as an authoritarian and repressive political regime in South Korea, and by the support the Church received from right-wing industrialists and politicians in Japan. In addition, liberals were concerned by protestations from the American Jewish Committee that the Unification Church was anti-semitic (Shupe and Bromley, 1980: 178). In a report to the American Jewish Committee, Rabbis Marc Tanenbaum and James Rudin claimed to have found more than 125 examples of anti-Jewish teachings in the *Divine Principle*. Jews also were extremely sensitive to recruitment of Jewish youth. There were a number of allegations from Jewish spokespersons claiming that anywhere from ten to fifty percent of Unification Church members were Jewish. Despite surveys which refuted these claims, Jewish hostility to the Unification Church remained intense. Other liberal groups which expressed reservations about Unification Church practices and policies included feminist organizations which regarded its theology and organization as sexist, and population control organizations, which worried about the Church's opposition to birth control.

The Church hardly fared any better with conservatives. Its emphasis on collective-communal over private-individual values alienated many conservatives. There also were racial overtones to conservative opposition. The Church actively promoted racial integration both through recruitment and marriage. Church members were encouraged and regularly volunteered for interracial marriages, most often between Caucasians and Orientals. Further, conservatives found it difficult to accept salvation from the East. While a number of Eastern religions had gained popularity in America, most conservative Christians could not accept the prospect of Orientals refashioning Christianity and engaging in reverse missionizing. And there was no possibility that such conservatives would acquiesce to the notion that the messiah could be a South Korean industrialist.

Public Visibility

Given the foregoing potential sources of conflict between new religious movements and the larger society, actual conflict depended partly on the extent to which these movements gained visibility. Several factors influenced public visibility: (1) leaders' activities, (2) the groups' activities and (3) the groups' locations and mobility.

The extent to which leaders of the new religions achieved or sought the limelight varied considerably. For example, Prabhupada, founder of the Hare Krishna movement in the United States, lived the life of an ascetic monk and died a few years after arriving in America, leaving the group without a single dominant leader. He maintained such a low profile that few of even those Americans who had heard of the Krishnas would have been able to name their leader. L. Ron Hubbard has been in seclusion for a number of years discovering stages of enlightenment toward which his followers work. While his name, for a time, became a household word due to his popularity as an author of science fiction and the popularity of Dianetics, Hubbard could today easily pass unnoticed in public. At the other extreme was Jim Jones who became (in)famous as a result of the tragic events at Jonestown; however, this notoriety was the result of desperation rather than design. Jones did seek out public recognition through civic projects and political contacts while the People's Temple was in California, but his efforts yielded a mixture of accolade and notoriety.

Sun Myung Moon stands in sharp contrast to other leaders of new religious movements in the extent to which he sought and attained public recognition. Moon carefully orchestrated five national speaking tours which visited approximately eighty cities between 1972 and 1974 (Bromley and Shupe, 1979b: 150). At each stop there were press conferences and meetings with local or state officials, and local luminaries were invited to the speeches, thus insuring media coverage. In addition, Moon gave speeches at two major public rallies—one at Yankee Stadium and one at Washington Monument. Finally, his public support for Richard Nixon during the Watergate crisis also increased Moon's personal visibility, albeit in a counterproductive fashion. Because Moon had so assiduously sought the public limelight he became a convenient caricature of new religious gurus.

Of all the organizational activities of the new religions, fundraising and recruitment created the greatest public visibility. Several of the new religions achieved a national presence; for example, Transcendental Meditation and Scientology established organizational centers across the country where classes/lectures were offered.[3] However, it was the Children of God, Hare Krishna and the Unification Church which attracted the greatest attention through fundraising and recruitment campaigns. All three groups relied upon public solicitation as a major means of generating financial resources (Bromley and Shupe, 1980 and 1981), and all three organized recruitment teams that sought out young adults.

The Unification Church clearly maintained a higher profile in both recruiting and fundraising than either the Children of God or the Hare Krishnas. Unification theology contained an explicit spiritual rationale for fundraising and made it an integral part of each convert's training. Both because public solicitation provided a major part of the Church's economic resources and because new members were required to fundraise, the Unification Church organized fundraising more systematically and effectively. Even though the Church was organizationally centered on the east and west coasts, it mounted a national fundraising effort by operating a fleet of vans which continuously crisscrossed the country. As a result, the terms Moonie and fundraiser became virtually synonymous. The Unification Church's recruitment tactics gained exceptional visibility for two reasons. First, among the new religions only the Unification Church attempted to develop a national network of campus organizations (much like those of mainline denominations). Efforts to organize chapters of the Collegiate Association for the Research of Principles (CARP) almost always met with resistance and gained considerable local media coverage. Second, the Unification Church was frequently accused of deceptive recruitment practices. Potential converts to either the Hare Krishna or the Children of God hardly could mistake the true identities of these groups. In most parts of the country the same could be said of the Unification Church, since lectures and slide shows for guests contained frequent mention of Moon. However, the west coast branch of the Unification Church, referred to as the Oakland family, taught a more humanistic, less doctrinaire version of *Divine Principle* in an effort to appeal directly to the needs and aspirations of idealistic young adults. Discussions of the Oakland family's connection to the Unification Church and of *Divine Principle* were deferred until potential converts' interest in the group had been stimulated. The Oakland family also made greater use of encounter group style tactics than other branches of the Church. Despite the fact that these recruitment tactics were not characteristic of the Church as a whole, and in fact generated considerable controversy and conflict within the Church, they were seized upon as evidence of manipulative cult tactics. Deceptive and manipulative practices were central to the anti-cultists' allegations of brainwashing and mind control; hence the practices of the Oakland family were generalized to the entire Unification Church and other new religions as well. Once again the Unification Church became a convenient symbol of the "cult menace."

Development of the Anti–Cult Movement

There is little doubt that the Unification Church presented an inviting target to the anti-cultists, given the number and nature of conflicts it engendered with major institutions and its high profile recruiting and fundraising. Still the question remains, "Why didn't the anti-cultists simply combat cults in general?" In part, of course, they did, but the Unification Church clearly was the focus of the attack. There were two major reasons for this decision: (1) the organizational requisites of the anti-cult movement and (2) the developmental timing of the Unification Church and the anti-cult movement.

The anti-cult movement has never numbered more than a few

thousand members, and it has been consistently plagued by membership turnover and organizational fragmentation. Numerous attempts
were made to increase membership size, generate additional revenue
and create a federated or centralized national organization. All of these
efforts met with mixed success at best, particularly in light of the
movement's goals. In order to gain sufficient public and official
support to continue its extra-legal deprogramming campaign or to
gain legal sanctions (in the form of expanded conservatorship/
guardianship provisions), the anti-cultists desperately needed money,
members and visibility. While the movement did gain a great deal
of publicity, mostly as a result of sympathetic hearings given to
distraught parents and wholesale acceptance of atrocity stories re-
counted by apostates (Bromley, Shupe and Ventimiglia, 1979), the
other two crucial resources proved more difficult to mobilize. The
anti-cultists concluded that in order to effectively combat cults in
general, they had to generate solid opposition against one "cult"
and then generalize their attack.

The targeting of the Unification Church was formalized during
the February 18, 1976 "unofficial" public meeting in Washington,
D.C., between a cadre of congressmen and federal bureaucrats
and a group of 352 anti-cult supporters (including parents, other
family members and ex-Unification Church members; see Citizens Engaged in Freeing Minds, 1976a, vol. 1). The meeting was
held, convener Senator Robert Dole claimed, in response to a peti-
tion containing over 14,000 of his constituents' signatures (Dole,
1976). By deliberate consensus of the anti-cultists' representatives,
Sun Myung Moon's Unification Church was chosen as the only
group against which complaints would be brought during the two
hour meeting with Dole and other governmental officials. In a
promotion letter prior to the meeting (Swope, 1976) the logic of
this strategy was clearly stated:

> Because we cannot be effective using the buck-shot approach,
> we must zero in on ONE cult. If our government investigates
> one cult and finds grounds for prosecution, we can move on
> to the other cults. The cult we have chosen is Moon's
> Unification Church.

The anti-cultists faced another major organizational problem: the term "cult" had no empirical referent. The motley assortment of groups categorized as "cults" bore little resemblance to one another in terms of size, growth rates, recruitment tactics, fundraising tactics, socialization techniques, organizational structure, leadership styles, or movement objectives. The only real commonality was that each of these groups offended family members of converts in some fashion by reorienting member's goals and lifestyles away from those espoused by the larger society. The anti-cultists could hardly hope to capture public support or legal sanction for their objectives if all that cults had in common was that parents objected to their offspring's participation in them. Hence, the anti-cultists made a concerted effort throughout the 1970s and early 1980s to portray cults as virtually identical structurally and the consequences of involvment as uniformly pathological (i.e., the "cult syndrome"). In attempting to construct "the cult problem" the anti-cultists obviously needed to make reference to specific groups in order to document their allegations. The Unification Church was the ideal candidate because, as we pointed out in the preceding section of this paper, it had achieved a high, negative profile and it had become embroiled in conflicts with several major institutions. The anti-cultists were able to capitalize on this conflict and visibility, referring to the Unification Church whenever evidence was necessary to bolster their allegations. Of course, a spiraling process ensued; heightened visibility facilitated allegations which served to increase visibility. By the mid-1970s there is little doubt that (with the exception of the People's Temple) the group most likely to be associated with the term "cult" was the Unification Church. Playing upon this association, the anti-cultists simply added references to other groups, with which the public and government officials were less familiar, when seeking allies.

Timing also played a major role in the emergence of the Unification Church as the archetypal cult. The anti-cult movement in fact did not arise in opposition to the Unification Church, but rather as a limited response to the conversion of young adults to the Children of God. In 1971, the twenty-two year old daughter of a California school teacher left home, her fiance and a career as a registered nurse to join the Children of God. When her parents were unable to induce her to leave the north Texas commune in which she was residing, they began a campaign to warn the public of the danger posed by this group. At about the same time, Ted Patrick (later to become the best known of the deprogrammers) discovered the Children of God when his son and nephew were approached by street missionaries and returned home, by his own account (Patrick and Dulack, 1976), noticeably and mysteriously disoriented. The aforementioned parents, supported by Patrick, had gained sufficient press coverage by 1972 that other angry and concerned parents of converts to the Children of God had begun contacting them. Out of informal group meetings among these parents emerged the first anti-cult association, The Parents' Committee to Free Our Sons and Daughters from the Children of God Organization.

Why didn't the Children of God then emerge as the archetypal cult, for as we previously noted the Children of God were similar to the Unification Church in some important dimensions? In fact, by 1973 the anti-cultists had convinced public officials to investigate the Children of God. In that year the Attorney General of New York, with support from the Governor, launched an investigation; although the resulting report was not issued until two years later (New York, 1975). In the meantime, however, the Children of God's prophetic leader, Moses David Berg, had revealed to his followers a vision that the United States was to be destroyed by the hand of God and ordered his followers to Europe. The resulting mass exodus of members left the fledgling anti-cult movement without its chief target.

Parents of converts to other new religious movements had been pressuring this first anti-cult group for assistance, but these pleas were resisted initially for fear that the campaign against the Children of God, a known evil, would be diluted. However, once the Children of God had left the United States in 1972, the number of aggrieved parents and apostates dropped off rapidly. At almost exactly this same time the Unification Church was rapidly growing and gaining visibility. Moon's series of national public speaking tours began in February-March 1972 and ran through December, 1974, with the high point of activity occurring in the spring of 1974. Further, it was in the winter of 1973-74 that Moon mobilized his followers in support of an embattled Nixon presidency, the act that generated journalistic investigation and the beginning of substantial negative media coverage. Finally, it was early in 1972 that mobile witnessing and fundraising teams were formed and began crisscrossing the country in search of members and money. The number of these teams was increased rapidly over the next several years giving the Unification Church a national visibility well out of proportion to its actual membership size. It was therefore a relatively simple matter to redirect anti-cult activities against the Unification Church as concerned parents, apostates and public notoriety which had been associated with the Children of God were now associated with the Unification Church.

There was one point at which another group might have supplanted the Unification Church as the archetypal cult, the period following Jonestown. Virtually all of the anti-cultists' worst fears and allegations seemed to have been confirmed by the mass suicide/murders. The problem, of course, was that in the process of confirming anti-cult allegations the People's Temple had destroyed itself. While the People's Temple could be called up as evidence that the anti-cultists had been right all along, an existing group was needed to personify the continuing danger posed by cults. Somewhat ironically, therefore, the Unification Church was dubbed the "suicide cult," and evidence was gathered from apostates that suicide drills were also practiced in the Unification Church and that another Jonestown might be just around the corner. The Unification Church thus remained the archetypal cult and was shackled with the legacy of Jonestown.

Summary and Conclusions

The social construction of the "cult problem" affords us an interesting case study of the way in which the labeling of deviant groups

proceeds. Labeling and conflict theorists have pointed out that deviant status is a function of the response to an act rather than a quality of the act itself. The success of label application is contingent
upon a power imbalance—an individual or group must lack the
capacity to resist being labeled. Both of these observations are
confirmed in the case of new religious movements. These groups
had numerous antagonists, coordinated by the anti-cultists, and
few allies. The stereotypical image that grew out of the controversy bore little resemblance to reality.

What is particularly interesting about the construction of the
cult problem was the selection of one group to symbolize the "evils"
associated with "cults." As we have shown, the group was selected
as the archetypal cult for a varigated set of reasons. The anti-cult
movement needed a single group to focus upon, partly to maximize
the effect of its limited resources and partly to obscure the fact
that the groups they termed cults had little in common. The Unification Church began to grow precisely at a time when the anti-cult
movement lost its initial target group and needed another. Finally,
the Unification Church had engendered conflicts with several major institutions and achieved high visibility in pursuit of its "world
saving" goals. This conflict and visibility facilitated the process of
gaining consensus that there was indeed a cult problem. This case
study thus illustrates the way that a set of factors (rather unrelated
to relative danger, destructiveness or injury) may converge not
only to produce deviant labels but also selection of one actor
(group or individual) as representative of a whole set of actors
who have been allocated to deviant status.

REFERENCES

Bromley, David G., Bruce C. Busching and Anson D. Shupe, Jr. "The Unification Church and
the American Family: Strain, Conflict and Control." *New Religious Movements: A Perspective
for Understanding Society.* Ed. Eileen Barker. New York: Edwin Mellen, 1982, pp. 302-11.

Bromley, David G. and Anson D. Shupe, Jr. *Strange Gods: The Great American Cult Scare.*
Boston: Beacon, 1981.

—————. "Financing the New Religions." *Journal for the Scientific Study of Religion* 19
(September 1980): 227-38.

—————. "Just a Few Years Seem Like a Lifetime: A Role Theory Approach to Participation in a Religious Movement." In *Research in Social Movements, Conflict and Change*. Ed. Louis Kriesberg. Greenwich, Conn.: JAI Press, 1979a, pp. 159-86.

—————. *"Moonies" in America: Cult, Church and Crusade*. Beverly Hills, Calif.: Sage Publications, 1979b.

—————, and Joseph C. Ventimiglia. "Atrocity Tales, the Unification Church and the Social Construction of Evil." *Journal of Communication* 29 (Summer 1979): 42-53.

Committee Engaged in Freeing Minds. *A Special Report. The Unification Church: Its Activites and Practices*. Vol. 1 and 2. Arlington, Tex.: National Ad Hoc Committee, Committee Engaged in Freeing Minds, 1976.

Citizens Engaged in Reuniting Families. "Memorandum." Scarsdale, N.Y., 30 January 1976.

Coser, Lewis A. *The Functions of Social Conflict*. New York: The Free Press, 1976.

Durham, Deanna. *Life Among the Moonies: Three Years in the Unification Church*. Plainfield, N.J.: Logos International, 1981.

Edwards, Christopher. *Crazy for God*. Englewood Cliffs, N.J.: Prentice-Hall, 1979.

Elkins, Chris. *Heavenly Deception*. Wheaton, Ill.: Tyndayle House, 1980.

Freed, Josh. *Moonwebs: Journey Into the Mind of a Cult*. Toronto: Dorsett Publishing, 1980.

Gutman, Jeremiah. "Extemporaneous Remarks." *The New York University Review of Law and Social Change* 9 (1979-80): 69-71.

Kemperman, Steve. *Lord of the Second Advent*. Ventura, Calif.: Regal Books, 1981.

Nelson, Geoffrey K. "The Spiritualist Movement and the Need for a Redefinition of Cult." *Journal for the Scientific Study of Religion* 8 (Spring 1969): 152-60.

New York, State of. *Final Report on the Activities of the Children of God to Honorable Louis J. Lefkowitz, Attorney General of the State of New York*. Albany, N.Y.: Charity Frauds Bureau, 1975.

Patrick, Ted and Tom Dulack. *Let Our Children Go*. New York: E.P. Dutton, 1976.

Shupe, Anson D., Jr. *Six Perspectives on New Religions: A Case Study Approach*. New York: Edwin Mellen, 1981.

—————, and David G. Bromley. *The New Vigilantes: Deprogrammers, Anti-Cultists and the New Religions*. Beverly Hills, Calif.: Sage Publications, 1980a.

—————. "Reverse Missionizing: Sun Myung Moon's Unification Movement in the United States." *Free Inquiry* 8 (November 1980b): 197-203.

Sparks, Jack. *The Mind Benders*. New York: Thomas Nelson, 1977.

Stark, Rodney and William S. Bainbridge. "Of Churches, Sects, and Cults: Preliminary Concepts for a Theory of Religious Movements." *Journal for the Scientific Study of Religion* 8 (June 1979): 117-33.

"State Senate OKs Smith's Anti-Cult Bill." *Meriden (CT) Record Journal*, 8 May 1981, pp. 1, 4, 6.

Swatland, Susan and Anne Swatland. *Escape from the Moonies*. London: New English Library, 1982.

Swope, George to "Friends" Letter from the National Committee of Citizens Engaged in Reuniting Families, Inc. regarding organization of a Day of Affirmation and Protest, Scarsdale, N.Y., 30 January 1976.

Underwood, Barbara and Betty Underwood. *Hostage to Heaven*. New York: Clarkson N. Potter, 1979.

Van Baalen, J.K. *The Chaos of the Cults*. Grand Rapids, Mich.: Erdmanns, 1938.

Vermont, State of. *Report of the Senate Committee for the Investigation of Alleged Deceptive, Fraudulent and Criminal Practices of Various Organizations in the State*. Montpelier: Senate, January 1977.

Wood, Allen T. with Jack Vitek. *Moonstruck: A Memoir of My Life in a Cult*. New York: William Morrow, 1979.

Wuthnow, Robert. "The New Religions in Social Context." In *The New Religious Consciousness*. Eds. Charles Y. Glock and Robert N. Bellah. Berkeley: Univ. of California Press, 1976, pp. 267-93.

Function of the Family in the Process of Commitment Within the Unification Movement

Kenneth P. Ambrose

The family has been central to the Unification Movement. The ideal world of love is expressed in the family. According to Unification theology "the first man and woman did not fulfill their responsibility, and as a result, they did not perfect themselves, and they left the realm of God's love." (Kwak, 1980). The Fall is used to explain the social problems which confront our society today.

> Confusion throughout society about standards of value and conduct has caused the strong trend toward egoism, and accompanying it, the breakdown of the family and the rapid increases in crime, juvenile deliquency and all kinds of immorality, which are unsettling the foundations of society and causing a loss of hope in the future (Kwak, 1980).

Part of the solution to these problems will be to "create a one-family world society." The family becomes the "basic unit" for the restoring of God's love and the ideal state of being which was lost in the Fall.

> The Principle affirms that only through establishing order in the home can love be planted in the dry heart of modern man,

and only then can a true relationship be established between husband and wife, between parents and children, among brothers and sisters, and among neighbors (Kwak, 1980).

In this paper the author will describe the concept of commitment as related to the family in the Unification Movement using Kanter's model. Next, the author will develop a model demonstrating the progression of the seeking individual, from close personal ties with members of the Unification Movement, to commitment to the group, to acceptance of the ideology of *Divine Principle* and matched marriage arranged by Rev. Moon. The latter then leads to creation of a family and reinforcement of commitment to the group and the *Divine Principle.*

Present statistics show that 89.7 percent of the Unification Church members in the U.S. are between the ages of 18 and 29; which coincides with the average age for marriage in our society. The Unification Church attempts to enhance the stability of the family through the development of commitment to their religious community and God.

The concept of commitment is vital to the Unification Movement. Howard Becker stated that commitment is linked to the concept of "side-bets." The more a person invests of himself into an organization, the more difficult it becomes to leave it, and the more committed he is to it. Underlying all commitments is the system of values to which the individual and the group subscribe.

Rosabeth Kanter further developed the concept of commitment in her book, *Commitment and Community.* While her concern dealt with nineteenth century communes, her theory can also apply to families within the Unification Movement. Kanter defined commitment as:

> A means of the attachment of the self to the requirements of social relations that are seen as self-expressive. Commitment links self-interest to social requirements. When a person is committed, what he wants to do (through internal feeling) is the same as what he has to do (according to external demands) and thus he gives to the group what it needs to maintain itself,

at the same time he gets what he needs to nourish his own sense of self (Kanter, 1972).

The survival of the Unification Movement is dependent upon the ability of the organization to develop commitment within members. This must include not only commitment to the larger organization, but also to the family unit. Within the organization, socialization must produce commitment involving (1) retention of members, (2) group cohesiveness, and (3) social control. An organization may have any of these as paramount to the organization, but has to include all if the organization is to survive.

Kanter develops the concept of commitment and how a "person orients himself to a social system instrumentally, affectively, and morally" (Kanter, p. 68). In defining these various types of commitment Kanter explains instrumental commitment in the following way:

> Commitment to continued participation in a system involves primarily a person's cognitive or instrumental orientations. When profits and costs are considered, participants find that the cost of leaving the system would be greater than the cost of remaining; "profit," in a net psychic sense, compels continued participation. In a more general sense, this kind of commitment can be conceptualized as commitment to a social system role. It may be called instrumental commitment (Kanter, pp. 68-69).

She defines affective commitment as follows:

> Commitment to relationships, to group solidarity, involves primarily a person's cathectic orientations; ties of emotion bind members to each other and to the community they form, and gratifications stem from involvement with all members of the group. Solidarity should be high; infighting and jealousy low. A cohesive group has strong emotional bonds and can withstand threats to its existence; members "stick together." This quality may be called affective commitment (Kanter, p. 69).

Moral commitment is defined as:

Commitment to uphold norms, obey the authority of the group, and support its values, involves primarily a person's evaluation orientations. When demands made by the system are evaluated as right, moral, just, or expressing one's own values, obedience to these demands becomes a normative necessity and sanctioning by the system is regarded as appropriate. This quality is here designated moral commitment (Kanter, p. 69).

The following table by Richardson, Stewart and Simmonds summarizes Kanter's model of commitment.

Basic Elements of Kanter's Model of Commitment

Types	Mechanisms	Effects of Mechanisms
Instrumental Commitment	*Sacrifice*	*Detaching*
	Investment	Attaching
Affective Commitment	*Renunciation*	*Detaching*
	Communion	Attaching
Moral Commitment	*Mortification*	*Detaching*
	Transcendence	Attaching

Published by permission of Transaction, Inc. from *Organized Miracles* by J.T. Richardson, Mary W. Stewart and Robert B. Simmonds, copyright © 1979 by Transaction, Inc.

The idea that one continues to participate in the Unification Movement depends on a person's instrumental orientation. The costs and profits orientation of remaining in the movement or leaving it are related to the person's perception of the benefits he/she could derive if he/she were to remain within the movement vs. the cost of leaving. The sacrifices a person has made and the investment of time, self, and money make it more difficult to leave. If the person has been matched, again the cost can be very great.

Commitment to relationships, to group solidarity, involves primarily a person's cathectic orientations. This is affective commitment. The development of this high solidarity through primary relationships helps in the creation of community. There is a detachment from the "old life style" and communion with the new members.

The moral commitment involves the socialization of the individual to uphold and support the values of the group. The person incorporates these values into his/her life and keeps the norms surrounding these values. In a sense, it is the superego which is operating at this level.

Within the Unification Movement the various types of commitment are visible. The Unification Movement develops instrumental commitment through the sacrifices made by the members. Kanter states that the more it costs a person to do something, the more valuable he will consider it in order to justify the expense. The sacrifices of careers, education, time and in some cases their families of orientation help a person develop a commitment to the Unification Movement. Part of this sacrifice entails relinquishing personal selection of a mate. Within the American society great emphasis is placed on this individual choice; within the Unification Movement the selection may be made by Rev. Moon with the matched couple's approval. The norm is to accept the match and it appears that social pressure from other church members is very great to remain with the person selected by Rev. Moon.

In the matching and marriage, the investment of self and property further links the member with the group and makes leaving costly. To leave at this point would involve not only the loss of a religion, but also one's family. The seemingly irreversibility of investment of self results in the feeling that one has come into the true church and cannot leave it.

Within the Unification Movement the affective commitment involves renunciation and communion. Renunciation of the ways of the world which are in conflict with the Unification Movement can involve being ostracized by one's friends and family of orientation. This renunciation of former support groups makes new converts more dependent on Unification members for emotional support. As satisfaction develops within these emotional attachments, and gratification within the group increases, the feeling of fellowship, group cohesiveness, the "we" feeling and equality are developed.

Moral commitment involves mortification which provides the

person with a new self-image. Fundraising on the street is one form of mortification. The mortification involves the socialization of new members to the *Divine Principle*. The transcendence involves the experience of the power within the community. Rev. Moon's selection of mates for such a large and varied number of members demonstrates this power.

The norm for mate selection in the larger society is very different from that of the Unification Church. Mate selection in the larger society is affected by various factors which Kerckhoff & Davis describe as follows:

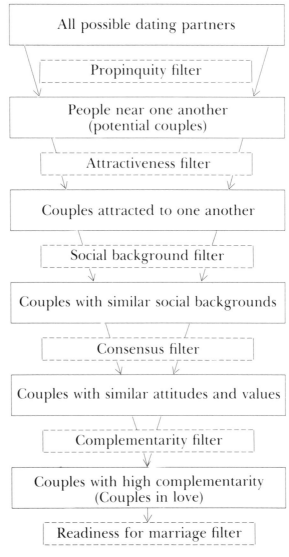

All possible dating partners

Propinquity filter

People near one another
(potential couples)

Attractiveness filter

Couples attracted to one another

Social background filter

Couples with similar social backgrounds

Consensus filter

Couples with similar attitudes and values

Complementarity filter

Couples with high complementarity
(Couples in love)

Readiness for marriage filter

Married couples
A filter theory of mate selection.

This table is an adaptation of data from Alan C. Kerckhoff and Keith E. Davis, "Value
Consensus and Need Complementarity in Mate Selection," *American Sociological Review*,
vol. 27 (1962), and is used by permission of the authors and the publisher.

This model is applicable to the Unification Movement at the consensus filter level. This becomes more important than attractiveness, social background or propinquity. The selection of a mate is a very important decision which has been taken over by the church. The secular society values the individual selection of a mate. The individual's goals, however, are minor in view of the organization's goals which are paramount.

This method of selection has many functional aspects which relieves the individual of the decision of selecting a mate and the peer pressure surrounding dating and engagement activities. Relieved of these pressures a person can devote more of his/her time to church activities.

Part of the Unification emphasis is upon developing a world based upon the family. This emphasis insures all members they will marry, but it also places pressures on those who wish to remain single. The concept of a world family which will bring peace and brotherhood means that members may be matched with a person from another country, another ethnic or racial group. Members make headlines when mixed marriages occur and the couples have not met before. But their commitment to the Unification Movement and to Rev. Moon enables them to accept this match. Part of the success of these marriages may be due to the age of the members. The practice of waiting until members are in their mid-twenties before marriage statistically reduces the risk of divorce.

Marriage is one of the most serious and sacred events in the life of a Unification member.

> Marriage is a serious and holy sacrament for which lengthy preparation is required, and one of the notable aspects is the willingness of the members to have Mr. Moon pick their life partners for them. The concept of "arranged" marriages is alien to young Americans although it has been an accepted pattern for most of humanity during most of history. This is not a compulsory arrangement. Members are urged to express their preferences, but they do have a deep trust in Mr. Moon as the voice of God for them.
>
> One recently engaged man remarked: "You try to have

confidence in your prayer life that God knows what is best for you, that He will work through Reverend Moon to suggest the proper match for you." (Fichter, 1979).

This is counter to the events of engagement in the larger society. The secular society places great importance upon romantic love, individual choice, and sex rather than God and establishing a God-centered family. The following model summarizes the author's thoughts about commitment and the Unification family:

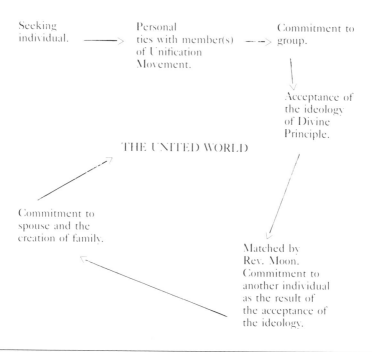

CYCLE OF COMMITMENT TO THE UNIFICATION FAMILY

Seeking individual. ———> Personal ties with member(s) of Unification Movement. ——> Commitment to group.

Acceptance of the ideology of Divine Principle.

THE UNITED WORLD

Commitment to spouse and the creation of family.

Matched by Rev. Moon. Commitment to another individual as the result of the acceptance of the ideology.

The individual is usually converted into the group as the result of friendship with a Unification member, not by accepting the ideology. As the convert sacrifices and invests more of her/himself in the group, the more committed he/she becomes to the group. The convert proceeds through the cycle of attachment to individuals or small groups to the larger group. When the member accepts the ideology of *Divine Principle* she/he has become so committed he/she is willing to accept a stranger as a spouse. This differs dramatically from the rest of society where personal ties are paramount in the selection of a mate. Commitment to marriage among matched couples and creation of family completes the cycle in the seeking individual and reinforces commitment to the group. It is possible that the member could withdraw from the Unification Movement at any point in the cycle.

The Unification Movement has taken positive steps in the building of a strong family unit in a society where changing norms have provided young people little guidance in the purpose and function of the family. Rev. Moon has suggested that the family will be the way to spiritual perfection.

The commitment which the group establishes seems to follow this path of the seeking individual, to the group, to the ideology, commitment to the individual matched by Rev. Moon and to the creation of a family. This strong family commitment reinforces commitment to the total movement.

REFERENCES

Bowman, H.A., and G.B. Spanier. *Modern Marriage.* 8th ed. New York: McGraw-Hill Book Co., 1978.

Bryant, Darrol. *Proceedings of the Virgin Islands' Seminar on Unification Theology.* Barrytown, N.Y.: Unif. Theo. Seminary, distr. Rose of Sharon Press, 1980.

——————, and Susan Hodges. *Exploring Unification Theology.* Barrytown, N.Y.: Unif. Theo. Seminary, distr. Rose of Sharon Press, 1978.

Divine Principle. 5th ed. New York: Holy Spirit Assn. for the Unif. of World Christianity, 1977.

Fichter, Joseph H. "Marriage, Family, and Sun Myung Moon." *America,* 27 October 1979, pp. 226-28.

Kanter, Rosabeth. *Commitment and Community.* Cambridge: Harvard Univ. Press, 1972.

Kerckhoff, A.C., and K.E. Davis. "Value Consensus and Need Complementarity in Mate Selection." *American Sociological Review* 27 (1962): 395-403.

Kwak, Chung Hwan. *Outline of the Principle: Level 4*. New York: Holy Spirit Assn. for the Unif. of World Christianity, 1980.

Lofland, John. "Becoming a World-Saver." *American Behavioral Scientist* 20, no. 6 (July/August 1977): 805-18.

————. *Doomsday Cult*. Englewood Cliffs, N.J.: Prentice-Hall, 1966.

Richardson, James. T., *et al. Organized Miracles: A Study of a Contemporary, Youth, Communal, Fundamentalist Organization*. New Brunswick, N.J.: Transaction Books, 1979.

Sontag, Frederick. *Sun Myung Moon and the Unification Church*. Nashville: Abingdon, 1977.

Stark, Rodney, and W.S. Bainbridge. "Networks of Faith: Interpersonal Bonds and Recruitment to Cults and Sects." *American Journal of Sociology* 85, no. 6 (1980): 1376-95.

Doing Love: Tensions In the Ideal Family

Eileen Barker

Put in its most crude form the problem which this paper attempts to address is: Why is it that the more members of the Unification Church pursue the goal of creating a unified world within which the Ideal Family could flourish, the more they have, at least in the West, become typified as people who cause disunity and division within their own families? To address such a problem demands a sociological critique which, it must be stressed, should not be mistaken for a theological criticism. The paper is at no point concerned with whether Unification theology is true or false in any ontological or metaphysical sense. I write neither as a theologian nor a believer—nor yet do I write·as a disbeliever. I write as a sociologist who has observed those for, and through, whom Unification theology lives.[1]

But although I write as a sociologist I shall not be offering any statistical analyses of questionaires. I have done that elsewhere.[2] Instead I shall try to paint a picture which comes from the vicarious experiences of in-depth interviews, casual conversations and participant observation within the Unification Church and, of course, from my own direct experience of life as a fellow social animal. It is a picture which is complicated and uncertain and one which is in parts as blurred as the social processes it tries to portray; it is a picture of a situation which is, I believe, upheld in some ways by the very tensions which it is its avowed purpose to dissolve, and thus one which can be threatened by its own successes. It is a picture which would seem at times to demand the risk of assuming phenomena describable only in terms the social scientist is rarely well equipped to handle—concepts of love and pain, of gnawing needs and empty longings, of awe-ful rapture and fearful submission, of happy companionship and silent comfort, of joyous relief and niggling doubts, and perhaps above all, of an every-day, taken-for-granted ordinariness which is apparently incomprehensible to the majority of those who take for granted other ordinarinesses lived through other faiths.

From a sociological perspective it is possible that both the greatest strength and the greatest weakness of Unification theology (at least as it has been most frequently taught in America and Europe) is that conversion implies commitment. If you accept the truth of Unification theology as explained in *Divine Principle*,[3] if in particular you accept its "conclusion" that the Lord of the Second Advent is upon the earth, then you are faced with the stark challenge of submission or rejection. Unification theology demands a translation from the transcendent, the cognitive and the spiritual into the mundane, the practical and the daily events of material existence. To believe is to act. To accept is to give oneself to God—and to work with all one's heart, with all one's mind and with all one's fellow Moonies for the restoration of the Kingdom of Heaven on earth.

Most theologies (certainly those within the Christian tradition) lay an especial emphasis upon the value of love. In Unification theology love features not only in those areas in which we have commonly expected its presence—soteriologies, eschatologies and cosmologies—it also has a central role in Unification theodicy. The Fall was due not just to the fact of disobedience toward God's will, but to a disobedience which involved the misuse of love. To have sex is not necessarily to make love. To presume, to preempt a consummation of carnal union without the celebration of union through God is not only to do that which is false and wrong, it is a sacrilege of that which is most true and good.

But of course it is good to love in the right way. The problem is how can we *do* it? Why do we keep going wrong? Fallen nature (original sin) may provide an ultimate "why," but by itself it does little to explain in terms of intermediate, "operational" whys and wherefores. Why might it seem that even a messiah will find he has to reject his own family and do apparently unloving acts? Apart from theological explanations, is it perhaps that there is a paradoxical (possibly concomitant) socio-logic which confounds, or at least confronts, those who would restore the Kingdom of Heaven upon earth? Is there a socio-logic which describes a realm within which more becomes less; within which the single-minded devotion of one's energies towards a single value brings in its wake not only costs in terms of other values, but costs in terms of the very value that is being pursued?

The Ideal Family in Unification Theology

One of the basic tenets of Unification theology is that the fundamental unit of society is the family—neither man nor woman being complete in him or herself until being blessed in a God-centered marriage, sharing a vertical relationship of give-and-take with God and a horizontal one of true love with each other and, to complete what is termed the Four Position Foundation, a further vertical relationship of true, God-centered give-and-take love with their children. Because the only force that is stronger than that of the Principle is the force of love, there is always the possibility that during their period of growth a person might fall through indulging in non-Principled love. The restoration of the world depends upon establishing the Ideal Family in place of the family unit which has existed since the Fall and in which there has been false (Satanically-centered) love. In this process of restoration the role and example of the Messiah is crucial.

Members of the Church who are considered to have reached a sufficiently high level of spiritual maturity are "blessed" in marriage by Reverend Moon. The Blessing is the most important and sacred rite of the Church. It is not merely a wedding ceremony, it incorporates a "rebirth" and a purification sacrament. Although it is not part of the official Unification dogma, almost all the members believe that Rev. Moon is the Lord of the Second Advent. Messiahship is an office in which a sinless man, born of human parents, is in a position to fulfill the purpose of creation—so long as he is accepted and followed. Jesus was unable to fulfill his mission and to get married before he was killed. This was largely the fault of John the Baptist who did not fulfill his role adequately so that the Jews did not realize Jesus' true position. Jesus, through his death, was able to offer the world spiritual, but not physical salvation. It is now the time when the Lord of the Second Advent might be able to complete the salvation or restoration of the world.

> The Messiah must stand before God as the origin of all ideal individuals and must establish the ideal family, which is the Family which fulfills the Purpose of the Creation and is the place where God's love can dwell. He must then also establish the ideal nation and world, thereby realizing the originally intended Kingdom of Heaven on earth, fulfilling the Purpose of Creation. This is the purpose for which the Messiah comes.[4]

A Sociological Perspective on Social Reality

Before proceeding it might be helpful to say a word or two about the sociological perspective. Let it be admitted at once that the sociologist has no special way of assessing the sort of love that exists between a person and God, and, indeed, can have only a limited, external knowledge of the sort of relationships that exist between individual people. The sociologist is mainly interested in social interaction with respect to the social environment which we inhabit. For the sociologist man is *essentially* a social animal—that is to say, man cannot become truly human except through some sort of interaction with others; he is incapable of developing normally the faculties which are associated with the species homo sapiens (language, moral behavior, loving relations) unless he spends time in the company of other members of the species. Few of the small number of feral children who have been discovered have managed to survive their childhood. The human baby develops into a man or woman by "taking in" society through the process known as socialization. This is not to say that man is nothing but a product of society—he is much else beside, nor that society plays an unnegotiably deterministic role. And of course any social reality is as dependent on its members for its existence as they are dependent on the existence of some sort of social reality for their existence.

The concept of social reality is a particularly elusive one to grasp without fading away into nothingness on the one hand, or becoming reified—made into too concrete a "thing"—on the other hand (both of which events can indeed occur to particular aspects of social reality in practice). Social reality is a *reality* in the sense that it exists independent of the volition of any one individual. It is something that faces him whether he likes it or not. He may have more or less success in changing it, but he cannot wish it away. It is a *social* reality in that it consists of the interactions between people and the structures which are formed, insofar as these interactions become institutionalized or patterned through people complying with more or less agreed norms and roles over time. It also consists of the culture, the values, mores and generally held beliefs about the nature of reality and how one ought to act which are shared by, or publicly knowable to, those who participate in that particular social reality. Some aspects of the culture will be known explicitly, perhaps as part of legal, religious or educational knowledge, but other areas are known at an implicit, relatively unconscious level, being taken for granted or considered part of the very nature of things, despite the fact that participants in another social reality might consider such beliefs or practices bizarre or grossly unnatural. Social realities are rarely discrete. They tend, with more or less coincidence according to our social position, to overlap with each other. To some degree each of us faces a slightly different social reality from that which faces our neighbor, and to some degree each of us shares with our neighbor aspects of the one social reality. Social reality is, in short, the environment within which the individual has to enact and to negotiate his interactions with other individuals and which, at the same time, through his interactions, he will preserve or alter in one direction or another.

It is this social environment which members of the Unification Church hope to alter, and which they do indeed alter through their actions. And it is this environment which would appear to present the Church members with a frustrating, "Catch 22" situation.

The Ideal Family and the Social Environment

According to Unification theology we are now living in a time in which the conditions are such that the Ideal Family *could* be established on earth—the potential exists. The members believe that they can be helped to play their role partly through their knowledge and acceptance of *Divine Principle,* partly because of the spiritual significance and rites of the Blessing that Rev. Moon offers each of the couples whom he brings together in matrimony, and partly through the example of the "True Parents," Rev. and Mrs. Moon. The problem is that neither the example nor the actuality of the Ideal Family has yet been fully realizable in practice because of the wider environment within which the Unification Church has to operate. While the Ideal Family is meant to exemplify, to lay the foundation for, and to perpetuate a social environment within which we can all enjoy ideal relationships based on true love, it is the existing social environment which is preventing the Ideal Family from successfully coming into existence. There may well be other responsible factors. I suspect there are. But focusing just on this one double bind we can see that actual interactions between the members and (1) their physical parents, (2) their spouses, and (3) their children, are not without difficulties which seriously threaten the realization of ideal familial relationships.

This has of course been recognized and written about by Unificationists. Rev. Kwak, for example, has frequently discussed the problems of the Ideal Family operating within an external environment which is not ideal—problems for which he offers theological explanations and practical instruction according to the tenets of the Principle. Discussion of the problems is usually couched in terms which imply or explicitly state that the present difficulties are a challenge which need only be of a temporary nature—so long as everyone does what has to be done. The apparently less-than-perfect actions may indeed be seen to constitute a necessary part of the restoration process as those who seem to suffer are in fact being helped towards a more advanced state of growth, or as a firmer foundation is being laid for those who are to come after. The breakthrough out of the vicious circle is, however, expected and hopeful signs are pointed out.

The Ideal Son/Husband/Father Positions in Tension with Society

That the situation to date has been such that ideal family relationships have not been fully realizable is evident when one looks at the family circumstances of Rev. Moon. We are told how he had to cut off relations with his mother, telling her not to visit him in prison if she was going to cry,[5] and how, because of a promise he had made, he took one of his disciples with him to Pusan, leaving his own family behind in North Korea.[6] It is explained that: "He never paid too much attention to his own family." Because the Principle teaches that salvation has to come through restoring the sinner first "Father [Rev. Moon] never really approached his family with the word of salvation but instead poured out his love to the inmates [of the prison] and the members."[7]

Rev. Moon further felt compelled to leave his first wife and two-month old baby son in 1946 when he received a revelation. He left without telling them what had happened and his wife did not know where he was for the next six years.[8] After they were reunited "Father had to choose the lady (his first wife) or the brothers and sisters [followers]. Father was very decisive in choosing the brothers and sisters."[9]

Rev. Moon's present wife and her mother also had to suffer, partly because of the social reality of the situation, but also, it is explained, for theological reasons. It might be worth quoting Rev. Moon at some length in order to indicate the sort of reasons that he puts forward for the suffering and eventual victory of his wife:

> There were many families who believed that the heavenly bride might come out of their own home because of the revelations they had received. Not only one family but many families

believed that. Think what a shocking event it was to those
families to have Mother [Mrs. Moon] chosen. There were also
many spiritual old ladies who were like prophetesses between
God and mankind. I had listened to them as instruments of
heavenly revelation on many occasions, and they had participated in many dispensational roles. Therefore they had a certain pride and authority, and felt that they were the ones who
would decide the bride of heaven. But all of a sudden, without consulting them I chose Mother. . . .

Since their hopes were so great and their expectations so
high, when those hopes and expectations were betrayed their
reaction was equally as deep. Their disappointments and dis-
enchantments were great. . . .

Knowing about this impossible, tense background, as soon
as the holy wedding was conducted in 1960 I asked Mother's
mother to confine herself; she was not to come see her own
daughter too often, or if she did she should come secretly
through the back door. That put Mother's mother in such a
miserable, cast-out position that nobody envied her role. Everyone had thought that becoming Mother's mother would
be glorious, like becoming an empress's mother. But I just
silenced all those expectations and pushed her into a sacrificial
role, not even letting her come to see her daughter freely.

Furthermore, in the first year I treated Mother almost like a
servant instead of my wife. We were bride and bridegroom
but that honeymoon period was nothing but an ordeal on
Mother's part. She started out as a servant because I wanted
her to start out from the very bottom.

The important internal meaning behind my actions in that
period was a test of faith for grandmother and Mother. No
matter what the circumstances, they should not complain or
rebel against me. They had to accept and persevere. That was
the real goal, what I really wanted. And they met that
expectation. . . .

During those years all kinds of things were said, even that
Mother was a failure, and that I was going to hand-pick a new
bride. You can imagine how heartbreaking that kind of rumor
was to Mother. . . .

As the days and years passed, what happened? Since Mother

continually persevered, since she was patient and silent and
upheld her faith in me, eventually the whole environment of
accusation was reversed into respect and admiration. . . .

   At the time we never even discussed these situations. I never
said to Mother, "You must understand this, persevere and win
out because I am doing this on purpose." If I had explained
and comforted her that way, then even though she had won, it
would not have been valuable.

   I have been explaining this in depth, revealing it today [May
3, 1977] to you as I never have even to Mother; this is the first
time in my life I have explained it in such depth. . . .[10]

In the speech from which the above quotations are taken Rev. Moon
explains far more about the theological reasons for his treatment
of Mrs. Moon, but the point that I wish to bring out here is that
he does point to the environment as being an important factor in
explaining his behavior—and it does not seem to have prevented
the young Mrs. Moon from enjoying a close give-and-take relationship with her husband.

   But perhaps, from the point of view of the Principle, the most
poignant familial disruption for Rev. Moon has been the way in
which the existence of the wider environment—his need to minister to the rest of the world—has kept him from giving the kind of
loving attention that the father of an Ideal Family would want to
bestow upon his own children.

   I could not treat my oldest son, Sung Jin, kissing and embracing him, as average parents would. I was very serious in han-
dling my newborn child.

   The mother and father ought to get together in harmony
and kiss the children. Only after my marriage with Mother
was begun in 1960 could I allow Sung Jin to enter my house
and speak briefly to him. It wasn't easy. A child could never
understand, no matter how much blessing he is born with,
why his father would treat him like that. He accumulated much
resentment and he wouldn't understand readily what I said. I
knew that I should do that, but it was not easy. Only after I
made the family foundation strong could I receive my child.[11]

But the children born after Rev. Moon's marriage in 1960 have suffered too. After her own Blessing in June 1981 Ye Jin Nim gave a short, tearful testimony in which she mentioned some of the difficulties which she and her brothers and sisters have encountered through being Rev. Moon's children: "... we felt like we did not have a childhood."[12]

Rev. Kwak in explaining the theological significance of Ye Jin Nim's Blessing talked also about the children's problems and how, because of the social reality within which they found themselves they were deprived of "normal" childhood relationships with (1) their parents, (2) other members of the Church, and (3) the wider society.

> When they go to school, because they bear Rev. Moon's name, no one can accept them as just ordinary people; everybody has a certain viewpoint of them. Furthermore, in our church everybody expects perfection of them. Also, they cannot freely bring friends over to visit them. Our members and leaders, because they expect too much from them, cannot be close to them, and even their parents have little time to spend with them. . . . True Parents' life style does not allow them to spend the time that a father and mother should spend with their children. Many times, children need to discuss something with their father and mother, but True Children have no opportunity.
>
> Why does Father do this? One of the main traditions Father has had to establish is to love Cain; therefore, he has given us, as Cain, more love than he has given his own children. Hopefully, from now on, he will have more time to take care of his children; but actually, he recently went to Europe to begin a new phase of public pioneering life.[13]

Tensions in Church Member's Family Relationships

The rift that has developed between many members and their physical (non-Unificationist) families is a familiar enough story. While much of the press reporting on "The Church That Breaks Up Families"[14] is sensationalizing rubbish, there is no doubt that many parents have suffered considerable anguish on learning that their (adult) child has become a Moonie. It is also true that many a Moonie has suffered considerable anguish from his parents' inability to understand his point of view—to see social reality as he has learned to see it.

That such divisions occur will not come as a surprise to the sociologist or historian of new religious movements. It is almost a sociological law that those who hold strongly to a belief system which radically challenges a generally accepted status quo will have to isolate themselves from those with whom they disagree, at least in the early stages of a movement's development, and this will frequently lead to familial estrangement. The Gautama Buddha abandoned his wife and son so that he could escape from a social environment which was too all-encompassing for him to be able to see what he believed was to be seen beyond its limits. Jesus of Nazareth declared

> For I come to set a man at variance against his father, and the daughter against her mother, and the daughter-in-law against her mother-in-law.
> And a man's foes shall be they of his own household.[15]

And, even more relentlessly,

> If any man come to me, and hate not his father, and mother, and wife, and children, and brethren, and sisters, yea, and his own life also, he cannot be my disciple.[16]

The fairly obvious point is that if an individual wants to follow a set of beliefs and a way of life which is at variance with the rest of society then, as a social animal, he will, except in a few, rare cases, need some sort of support from other individuals. It is not just the kind of psychological comfort we all get from being among like-minded people that he will need, but the deeper support of a social context within which the new language, concepts and vision of reality can be "lived" through everyday interactions. The group, if it is to "work through" its "social policy" needs an environment that can both reinforce and keep alive its way of looking at the world, and protect it from the continual questioning and disbelief of those who still hold to the picture of reality from which the convert has defected. And of course, if those who wish to question the new beliefs are the very people who socialized the individual into his original beliefs then the separation may (sociologically speaking) have to be all that more complete.

There is a somewhat ironic twist to this situation that might be mentioned here, namely, that those who join the Unification Church are more likely to do so because of, rather than in spite of, their parents' values and attitudes. I have discussed this at some length in "Identity within an Unorthodox Orthodoxy" and "Who'd be a Moonie?"[17] but perhaps I should repeat here that Moonies tend to share with their parents a certain amount of idealism and strong-mindedness and to place a particular value on the concepts of duty and service to others.

It is these values of duty and service to others which can give rise to some heart-searching internal conflicts once the Church member himself contemplates his role as a parent. To sacrifice oneself can provide a wonderful opportunity to be of service. To sacrifice one's parents might be an unfortunate necessity in some cases; but parents are probably old enough to look after themselves, or at least to accept some responsibility for their own future. And it is towards the future that the Unificationist must look. But what happens if it seems to be necessary to sacrifice that very future? While it may be one's duty to sacrifice oneself, is it not also one's duty *not* to sacrifice, but to accept the responsibility of parenthood? Does not that responsibility mean that the child should be brought up in an ideal environment of parental care?

Questions of financial security and health insurance which rarely, if ever, bother the minds of the young Church members, start to nag at the minds of Blessed or matched members. But even more fundamentally, many of the young parents can find themselves torn by the fear that they will be unable to develop the sort of intimate, loving relationship with their children of which they had dreamed. If the Ideal Family is the basic unit of society, should the basic unit be split up; should the husband's mission be in one state or one country while his wife is fundraising elsewhere? Is it right for parents to have to harden themselves against becoming too emotionally involved in their children's lives? While those who work at the nursery to which Moonie parents send their children may be well-trained, responsible and loving fellow Unificationists, and while the Little Angels' School in Seoul to which it is expected many of the children will go, undoubtedly has facilities which are superior to those of many a local school in the West, what about the Ideal Family unit?

The tensions arising here are the familiar ones associated with what the economists call opportunity cost. In a situation in which not everything can be done because of a finite supply of scarce resources (such as time, money and personnel), the pursuit of one goal or value has to be done at the expense of another goal or value. If one "does love" for one's immediate family, it can be at the cost of "doing love" for the rest of the world. If one loves Mankind, the price can be that one has no time or energy to love men and women.

While the either/or does not have to be absolute, the Unification Church, like many a millennial movement before it, has to work out a calculus of costs and profits in terms of means and ends. Priorities have to be allocated and losses and sacrifices risked. For Rev. Moon the order of priorities is clear: "God wants an individual to sacrifice himself for his country more than for his family, and to sacrifice himself more for the world than for the country."[18] Or: "Even though somehow you become worthy parents, the next step means sacrificing them for the sake of the whole. The wife you love so much must go out and the children you love so much must also sacrifice...."[19] It is not that Rev. Moon discounts the importance of the family unit. It is a central part of the Principle and he makes many statements about the crucial role that parents have to play in passing on the correct traditions to their children. But as the Ideal Family cannot operate in a social environment which is *not* ideal, the immediate family has to be sacrificed (though obviously with as little cost as possible) for the sake of the larger whole.

Tensions in the Triad

There is much more that could be said about the relation between the whole and the parts and about long-term and short-
term goals,[20] but I would like to turn now to consider a totally
different aspect of the Ideal Family—that of its being God-
centered— and to suggest that this can, in a perhaps not altogether
expected fashion, be the source of certain tensions of a curiously
sociological nature. Here it is necessary to reiterate what has already been stated—that this is a paper written from a sociological
perspective, in no way claiming to touch upon theological verities.[21]

It is a central and absolutely necessary aspect of the relationship
between a husband and wife in the Unification Church that their
relationship should be God-centered. This is more than saying that
it should not be Lucifer-centered. It should, in a positive and active
sense, have God as the main focus, the *raison d'etre,* of the union.
The primary duty of each member of the partnership is to try to
see things—and indeed his or her spouse—from God's point of
view. God is loved above all, and from and through the individual's
vertical love for God will flow his or her horizontal love. The
theological, and indeed, the practical advantages of such an attitude within marriage are fairly obvious.[22] It is perfectly possible
that for the Ideal Family in the ideal environment there is nothing
but advantage to a God-centered marriage, but in actual marriages
in which the partners are attempting (rather than completely
realizing) a God-centered union, there can be tensions resulting
from the relationship being that of a triad (association of three)
rather than a dyad (association of two).

> The sociological structure of the dyad is characterized by two
> phenomena that are absent from it. One is the intensification
> of relation by a third element, or by a social framework that
> transcends both members of the dyad. The other is any distur-
> bance and distraction of pure and immediate reciprocity. In
> some cases the dyadic relationship is more intensive and
> strong. . . . Likewise, they carefully avoid many disturbances

and dangers into which confidence in a third party and in the triad itself might lead the two.[23]

Sociologically speaking the dyad has different properties—that is, different potentialities and different constraints—from the triad. These potentialities and constraints mean that the relationship can be both helped and hindered in the search for true love in the sense of mutual understanding. By looking for those features that God would value in one's partner one is given a positive rather than a negative approach, but this can also lead to a denial, or a lack of facing up to the very real problems that can exist between two people and regarding which the mutual negotiation may be necessary for the resolution of the problems. While on the one hand the "intervention" of God can be a valuable assistance, on the other hand relying on his intervention or mediation can result in a loss of *direct* contact, of direct understanding, of the feelings of empathy that direct reciprocity can stimulate. Even when one is dealing with the most anthropomorphically conceived God, the capacity of human beings, even those who have received the Blessing, to know for certain that they are really seeing through God's eyes, or, even more to the point, that they are being seen by their partner through God's eyes, can be severely limited. As one frustrated young man put it "I just don't recognize myself in the picture she says God has given her of what I'm really like. I wish she'd come off it and try to be a bit more approachable and understanding."

Allied to such grounds for suspicion and frustration there can develop more serious problems of communication and, subsequently, of power. While God himself can certainly not be accused of a policy of "divide and rule" there is a sense in which belief in his omniscient presence within the marriage contract can lead to "alliances" which exclude, almost as easily as they include, the other partner. This may be experienced as a subjective or as an objective social reality. It can take the somewhat self-righteous form of "Well, I have God on my side" or "You are making things difficult, but with God's help I shall cope." Or it can take the more

petulant form of "You're always with God these days—what about
giving me a bit of time for a change?" In either case the "eternal
triangle" effect can be as destructive as the arrival of an importu-
nate lover or mistress.

It will of course be legitimately argued that God himself would
not be the cause of anything but an enhanced relationship between
two people. I hope it will be realized that nothing I have said would
deny this. The point that I have been trying to make is that, while
honestly trying to "do" love through God, human beings can, in
certain circumstances, be observed to get further from, rather than
nearer to, their goal, and that to some extent some of this failure
can be understood in terms of the tensions that can arise between
two people when they have to take a third into account. This is not
to say that centering on the third cannot function to promote mutual reciprocity—it can, with profit. It is merely to point out that
there is a socio-logic which makes the properties of a triad different from those of a dyad and these can, in certain circumstances,
include costs.

Concluding Remarks

In this paper I have tried to document a few of the sociological
difficulties encountered by those who are attempting to create the
Ideal Family. It has not been argued that the Ideal Family cannot
exist, and it has certainly not been argued that the families of
Unification Church members are any less successful than those in
the wider society. On the contrary, what evidence there is suggests
that by several criteria (such as the divorce rate) they could if anything be more successful.

But the Ideal Family does not yet exist, and one reason is that the
family does not live in isolation from the rest of the social
environment, and so long as other members of the society have
other interests or other ideals (or, believing in the same ideals,
believe that these should be implemented by different means) there
is likely to be strife between members and non-members in proportion to the extent that the members wish to change the social real-

ity of the dissenting non-members. Of course Unificationists could opt for creating their own, enclosed community (such as the Hutterites or some Anabaptist groups have done—though they have not succeeded in overcoming all difficulties),[24] but this is not the Unificationist goal.

Whether or not the Catch 22 situation of the relationship between the environment and the establishment of the Ideal Family can in fact be overcome, I cannot know. As a sociologist all I have tried to do is to indicate some of the tensions and costs inherent in attempts to establish the Ideal Family under present circumstances. It is plain that good will and the Blessing are not in themselves sufficient foundations for the Ideal Family. Whether the spiral is one that can be broken out of remains to be seen. That there are difficulties is indisputable. Perhaps the last word should be left to Rev. Moon:

> The Bible says that your own family is your worst enemy. Even now in the 20th century this is a paradox, and people try to interpret it in their own way. If I am asked if I and my family have achieved this standard, I can confidently say yes. If you have not crossed over that threshold, then you have nothing to do with that. This is the Principle. It is not that I enjoy doing this, but it cannot be by-passed. If you are conducting laboratory experiments, you must do so in accord with natural law. Otherwise your experiments will fail. We cannot add and subtract at our will from Principle. I cannot do that and God cannot do so either. You have to tread on the path of Principle. How wonderful it would be if we could override it. As intelligent as I am, there is no other choice. I want to say OK and let you pass, but I cannot.[25]

NOTES

1 I would like to express my thanks to the Social Science Research Council of Great Britain which has funded my research into the Unification Church.

2 Inter alia "Who'd Be a Moonie?" in Bryan Wilson, ed., The Social Impact of New Religious Movements (Barrytown, N.Y.: Unif. Theo. Seminary, distr. Rose of Sharon Press, 1981).

3 Divine Principle (Washington, D.C.: Holy Spirit Assn. for the Unif. of World Christianity, 1973).

4 *Outline of the Principle: Level 4* (New York: Holy Spirit Assn. for the Unif. of World Christianity, 1980), p. 57.

5 Won Pil Kim, *Father's Course and Our Life of Faith* (London: Holy Spirit Assn. for the Unif. of World Christianity, 1982), p. 81.

6 *Ibid.*, p. 91.

7 *Principle Life*, November 1979, p. 9.

8 Kim, pp. 145-46.

9 *Ibid.*, p. 147.

10 *Blessing Quarterly* 1, no. 2: 23-24.

11 *Blessing Quarterly* 3, no. 2: 7.

12 *Today's World* (August 1981): 7.

13 *Ibid.*, p. 17.

14 This was a headline used by the *Daily Mail,* against which the British Unification Church lost a libel action in 1981.

15 Matthew 10:35-36.

16 Luke 14:26.

17 "Identity within an Unorthodox Orthodoxy," in *Identification and the Revival of Orthodoxy,* eds. William Shaffir and Louis Greenspan, (Waterloo, Ont.: Wilfrid Laurier Univ. Press, 1982.

18 *Tomorrow's World* (August 1981), p. 4.

19 *Blessing Quarterly* 3, no. 2: 8.

20 Some of the issues are discussed from a different perspective in Karl Popper, *The Open Society and its Enemies* (London: Routledge and Kegan Paul, 1945).

21 See my "The Limits of Displacement: Two Disciplines Face Each Other" in *Sociology and Theology: Alliance and Conflict,* eds. D. Martin, J. Orme-Mills and W.S.F. Pickering, (Brighton, Eng.: Harvester Press, 1980).

22 I have discussed some of these in "Living the Divine Principle," *Archives de Sciences Sociales des Religions* 45, no. 1 (1978).

23 Kurt Wolff, *The Sociology of Georg Simmel* (New York: Free Press, 1950), p. 136.

24 See for example W.S.F. Pickering, "Hutterites and Problems of Persistence and Social Control in Religious Communities," *Archives de Sciences Sociales des Religions* 44, no. 1 (1977).

25 *Blessing Quarterly* 3, no. 2: 8.

Families Within a Family: Spiritual Values of Hutterites and Unificationists

Timothy Miller

Intentional community has been a persistent theme in human history for millennia. We know, for example, that separatist communal groups such as the Essenes were operating in ancient Israel before the time of Jesus, and similar movements existed in other ancient cultures as well. In Christian history the intentional community has played a prominent role in shaping basic ethical patterns of life; especially after Benedict (d. 543 C.E.) outlined a structure through which communities of men and women could foster the spiritual development of their members, community came to be seen in both Eastern and Western churches as the highest form of Christian living. Although the Protestant Reformation had the effect of deemphasizing communal life in favor of nuclear families, the communal urge has persisted there as well; the Episcopal and some of the Lutheran churches, to name only two traditions, continue to foster the communal ideal in traditional form to some degree. Meanwhile, in relatively recent times the old ideal has burst forth in renewed forms; particularly in the nineteenth century, America witnessed the founding of hundreds of utopian communities in which the classic desire for belonging to a limited group was enshrined. And again with the rise of the hippies in the late 1960s we found that old desire cropping up in the formation of thousands of intentional communities, some of them surviving for only a period of weeks or months, but others surviving for over a decade and today looking very much as if they will be with us for some time.

The typical communal structure has been such that the community itself has been the "family" of the participants. In a relatively few cases, however, an unusual two-tiered system of families has emerged, a system in which the larger family, or community as a whole, remains the focus for communal identity, but in which the traditional biological family has also been retained as an important unit within the larger structure. As it happens, some of these communities which have developed what I am here calling the "families within a family" system have turned out to be among the most enduring and productive of all communities.

This paper will examine the dual family structure of two of these communal movements which survive today, the Hutterites and the Unificationists. Before I proceed to an analysis of these two groups and their family structures, however, I would like to note that several other important groups have adopted a similar system. One major example of that today is the Society of Brothers, or Bruderhof, which operates colonies in New York, Pennsylvania, and Connecticut. In the definitive study of the Society of Brothers, Benjamin Zablocki writes:

> The Bruderhof has been called a monastery of families, and in some ways this description is apt. The family is the most important unit in the community life. Unlike the kibbutzim, which have social policies aimed at weakening family structure, the Bruderhof, following the Hutterian model, does everything possible to strengthen it. Each family lives together in its own apartment. Special times are set aside just for families to be together. Birth control is abhorred: large families are considered natural and wholesome; and each new baby is welcomed by the whole community with joy.[1]

But, Zablocki notes, the emphasis on nuclear families occurs strictly within the confines of the Bruderhof as a whole: "The Bruderhof marriage ceremony emphasizes the fact that *eros* must be subordinated to *agape,* that the sexual and emotional relationship of the couple must be based on the spiritual brotherhood of the entire group."[2]

Other more recent groups also recognize the role a traditional family can play in fostering the larger goals of an intentional community. The Farm, for example, which is often cited as the most successful of the "new age" communes which have arisen since the hippie era, has kept the basic family structure intact even though its rural homestead in Tennessee has grown into the thousands of members. As Stephen Gaskin, the spiritual leader of the Farm, has written,

> On the Farm our marriages are till death do you part, for better or for worse, blood test, the county clerk, and the works. When we got to Tennessee, almost none of my students were married to each other because I hadn't been able to marry anybody and they didn't know anybody they wanted to marry them, so they were just being together. And when we got there and we said, "What does it take to be a preacher in Tennessee?" And they said it takes a preacher and a congregation and you're a church. So I didn't have to do anything as such, I'd just send a couple down to get a blood test and go to the county clerk's and get a marriage license, and they come back to the Farm, get married on Sunday morning, I sign it as a minister who marries them, and they go back in and they're legally married. And they're morally married too, because we get married after the meditation in the morning, when everybody's really stoned and everybody's in a truth-telling place, and you say those vows, you know, that you'll stay with somebody and that you really mean it, and there's four hundred folks digging it and paying attention and pretty stoned and pretty telepathic with you. It's a heavy ceremony—we get stoned on weddings when we have them. Sometimes folks are so heavy at weddings—people say their vows so heavy and so pure it just stones everybody.[3]

And the Farm also is serious about child-raising, which is done both by the biological parents and by the Farm family as a whole:

> We believe in staying in contact with our kids . . . You stay in contact with them, and they're part of your family and they be with you. They don't grow up and run away and grow their hair long when they get sixteen or something, or in our case cut it. They'll stay home and grow their hair long, and help you out with the thing. We tell our kids where it's at. I think the idea of letting kids go crazy until they're six years old and then putting them in public schools where they have to snap right now, you know, is a funny way to treat a kid. You ought to try to keep them sane and together . . . It ain't just a question of how you do it, it's a question of understanding what you're trying to do. What you're trying to do is to *don't teach a kid to be a rip-off.*[4]

There are several other groups which could also be cited as examples of the families-within-a-family model. In this paper, however, we will focus on two groups which have used the concept to great communal advantage; we will attempt to understand how the concept has advanced the spiritual and social values of the Hutterites and Unificationists.

The Hutterites are, of course, by far the older of the two groups. Their roots, now somewhat obscured by the passage of time, are in the Anabaptist movement which was influential in parts of Europe prior to the Protestant Reformation. The Hutterites are the most militantly communal of all of the surviving Anabaptist groups; whereas other surviving Anabaptists tend to emphasize community through a system in which families enjoy the fellowship, support, and help of other families (as in the classic case of a Mennonite barn-raising), the Hutterites have given up private property altogether. All land and buildings and equipment are owned by the community as a whole; one's personal possessions are limited to the most intimate and necessary things, such as clothing and toilet items. Families live in apartments which belong to the colony; they work together at the collective farming effort under community guidance; and they share equally in the production of the enterprise. Something must be working in the Hutterite system, because the movement is today, after existing for hundreds of years, stronger than ever before. Indeed, the territorial expansion of the Hutterites (new colonies are started frequently to handle the increase in Hutterite population) has become a volatile social and political issue in several of the states and provinces in which they live.

Marriage and family are as basic as any values in the Hutterite system. A demographic study covering the period from 1874 to 1950 showed that only 1.9% of the men and 5.4% of the women over the age of 30 had never married. Since 1875 there had been only one divorce among Hutterites, and the average completed family had 10.4 children.[5]

Marriage is very much a part of the faith for Hutterites. Marriage usually occurs shortly after baptism, typically when the participants are in their early twenties. For much of Hutterite history, until about 150 years ago, before their migration to the United States and Canada, marriage partners were matched by colony leaders. But, as Victor Peters notes, "This practice was not popular, especially among the young people. When a young girl appealed to [Johann] Cornies, a Mennonite administrator in charge of the supervision of 'foreign' colonies, the latter advised the Hutterians to discontinue the practice. It was dropped and has not been revived."[6] John Hostetler tells how it used to be:

> Those wishing to marry informed the servant of the word and at the appointed time in spring and fall were called to one of the principal Bruderhofs. Here the matching followed the religious service. Many of the prospective couples had never met each other. Men and women lined up on opposite sides of the room. A man would choose one of three women. The woman could refuse, but if she did she could not marry until the next matching.[7]

Today individual Hutterites choose their own spouses, but the choice is still heavily influenced by parents and peer groups, and most marry their own kinfolk. Boys and girls usually meet on intercolony visits, when a group from one colony journeys to another colony to help with a work project. Courtship, which can last for several years, is carried out entirely within a group context; parental consent remains a standard requirement for matrimony. When a couple decide to marry, the prospective groom journeys to the colony of his intended bride and seeks the permission of her parents and colony. When the parents have agreed to the marriage, colony members are summoned to the church building and a short engagement ceremony is held. There are community festivities for two days, then the groom takes the bride, her family, and her personal belongings to his own colony where, after further festivity, a marriage ceremony is performed following the Sunday worship service. Then there are further social celebrations before the newlyweds take up residence in their new apartment on the groom's colony. Weddings are a major highlight of Hutterite life, and usually take place when farm work is at a low ebb—that is, not during planting or harvest seasons. Because of the time and expense involved in weddings, multiple weddings are encouraged, with as many as five couples being united at the same time.

Although Hutterites do value the nuclear family, the welfare of the colony as a whole is always paramount. Each couple is given an apartment in one of the communal dwellings, buildings which have been built according to the same design since the sixteenth century. There is little privacy; it is a Hutterite tradition, for example, that visitors do not knock before entering an apartment. An apartment is just a place to sleep and store things; one's meals, baths, and most other parts of life are taken elsewhere.

Children are valued highly, and in the absence of birth control tend to come fairly rapidly. Children are understood to belong to the whole colony, not only to the parents. Their religious training begins when they first take solid food, at the age of about one month; the mother folds the baby's hands into hers as she offers thanks for the food. Discipline also starts early, since socialization is crucial to the communal enterprise. As John Hostetler and Gertrude Huntington have observed, "A child is believed to be completely innocent until he is observed to hit back or to pick up a comb and try to comb his hair. When he hits back, or knows what a comb is for, his level of comprehension is believed to be sufficiently high that he can be disciplined. He shows both self-will and understanding."[8] The basic rationale for strict discipline is contained in a 1652 Hutterite book, *Ein Sendbrief*:

> Just as iron tends to rust and as the soil will nourish weeds, unless it is kept clean by continuous care, so have children of men a strong inclination towards injustices, desires, and lusts; especially when children are together with the children of the world and daily hear and see their bad examples. In consequence they desire nothing but dancing, playing and all sorts of frivolities, till they have such longing for it, that you cannot stop them any more from growing up in it.... Now it has been revealed that many parents are by nature too soft with their children and have not the strength to keep them away from evil. So we have a thousand good reasons why we should live separated from the world in a Christian community. How much misery is prevented in this way. For do we not hear it often said: How honest and respectable are these people,: but look what godless children they have brought up.... Sometimes father and mother have died long ago and nothing is left of their earthly remains, but their bad reputation still lives among the people who complain that they once neglected to discipline their children and brought them up disgracefully.[9]

By the time they reach school age, children have a very low status in the colony. During their school years they are taught unquestioning obedience to authority. But the families are filled with love, and most Hutterite children grow up to become faithful members of the community. Their status grows as they grow older, because age is regarded as an indication of wisdom.

In short, the nuclear family is important; family ties are strong until the child reaches full adulthood, indicated, usually, by baptism and marriage, and the ties persist after that (for example, there is a continuing interest in the welfare of relatives now living at other colonies). Attachments remain even when a family member commits the overpowering sin of leaving the colony for the secular world. A woman's mother comes to help her when she has a new baby, and relatives elsewhere are visited whenever possible. At the same time, however, the principal "family" is the colony itself. As Hostetler has concluded, "The Hutterite colony functions in many ways like an extended family. Because Hutterite society has institutionalized a continuing relationship between parents and children,.the family is emotionally less demanding and less exclusive than is the rule with middle-class Americans."[10]

There are many pronounced differences between Hutterites and Unificationists. The Unification Church is not from the Anabaptist tradition; its members do not live in permanent colonies and do not, for the most part, till the soil. But the concept of families within a larger family is very much alive there.

It would appear that Unificationists are predisposed to affirm the importance of family life when they enter the movement. Eileen Barker, in her study of British Moonies, found that

> By almost any criteria, the majority of Moonies came from what they, and others, would consider to be "good homes.". . . Mothers were unlikely to have worked while their children were at school, and were very unlikely to have done so before they went to school. . . .Over four-fifths of British Moonies saw themselves as having enjoyed average or (for nearly a half of them) above average material well-being (with respect to housing, food, and other material comforts); and roughly three-quarters said their spiritual well-being was about (one third), or above, average.[11]

Thus it might be reasonable to conjecture that the Unification emphasis on family might be appealing to prospective members who understand the importance of that social institution. That emphasis is pervasive—I have seen it repeatedly in *Divine Principle,* in Unificationist theological writings, and in conversations with Unification Church members.

The family becomes an important topic early in *Divine Principle.* Barely a dozen pages into the work the four position foundation, which is the theological underpinning of the family structure, is introduced. The standing of the four position foundation in *Divine Principle* is lofty indeed: "The four position foundation is the base for the fulfillment of God's goodness and is the ultimate goal of His creation. This is the base through which God's power is channeled to flow into all of His creation in order for the creation to exist. Therefore, the formation of the four position foundation is ultimately God's eternal purpose of creation."[12] Somewhat later, *Divine Principle* talks at length of various foundations designed to receive the Messiah—and all are embodied in families.[13]

Young Oon Kim, the premier Unification theologian, explains the importance of the family in Unificationism at greater length in her book *Unification Theology*. She writes,

In the twentieth century, Protestant doctrines of man have stressed human relatedness amd responsibility. An individual becomes a mature person through his connections with others. No one can really exist by himself or for himself. Men are social creatures. They are born into a society and are molded by their group. Process theology and liberation theology stress this social dimension of man. Both oppose a purely individualistic interpretation of human nature. Who we are and what we do depend upon our involvment in group life and activities.

Unification theology takes into account man's relatedness and responsibility by using the family as a model. For *Divine Principle* the God-centered family represents the best example of how God works in history. God creates men and women to seek togetherness. Their union leads to biological regeneration, personal fulfillment and social progress. As a base of four positions, to use the Unification theology term, the family ties which bind together God, husband, wife and children prove the fundamental pattern for all worthwhile forms of human relations. An ideal society can be erected once a truly God-centered family comes into being.

God originates the family structure, making it an instrument for the realization of His parental love and authority. But nearly as important are the responses we make to our fathers, mothers, brothers, sisters and children. Only if these kinship relationships are positive and creative is it possible to manifest the full give and take of love with God and our fellowmen.

The family is also the chief place for learning our social responsibilities. We come to accept our duty to God in most cases as a result of our respect for our parents and obedience to their commands. We also learn how to relate to society by our experience in relating to every member of our family circle. Except in rare cases, men's natural sense of responsibility develops and flowers or is stunted by their family environment in the first half dozen years of life. For this reason, the God-centered family provides the most important base of four positions for personal regeneration and social reconstruction.[14]

Kim further explains the importance of the nuclear family in other writings, especially *Unification Theology and Christian Thought*.[15] Clearly in her understanding of Unificationism, the family does, as she says, "serve as the foothold for God's sovereignty in the physical world and a fountainhead of love for each member of the family."[16] Other Unification theological works, such as the anonymously authored *Unification Thought*, similarly support family centrality.[17] Non-unificationists writing about the movement have also described the family as central to the teachings.[18]

So far we have been discussing the nuclear family, but for Unificationists as for the Hutterites it is not the only family. The family model in fact extends to the movement as a whole. Unificationists frequently portray themselves as members of a worldwide happy family, and "the family" is their familiar appellation for the movement.

Little, if anything, seems to have been written on the theological importance of this larger "family," but its functional importance in the movement seems clear enough. For example, I once asked a Unificationist in my town just how it was that attractive young men and women could live in close communal settings without just occasionally lapsing into sexual encounters. His answer was that you could do it just as you could live with your sister (or brother, as the case might be) without being strongly led to commit incest. Apparently this sense of brotherhood-sisterhood operates as a sexual brake; it is a strong motif in daily life right up to the point at which one receives the second blessing and marries one of one's brothers or sisters.

This larger sense of family may also contribute to such internal unity as exists in the movement, especially when it is confronted with outside threats, such as deprogramming or government harrassment. In contemporary America many of our social institutions are fragile and undependable, and even though the family in its typical form is hardly immune to deterioration, it stands symbolically, at least, as a haven. When one is criticized by hostile members of the public, it is reassuring to be able to retreat to the safe womb of a loving family, and it is this sort of womb that Unificationism seems to provide for its members. Thus family terminology pervades Unificationism; members are brothers and sisters, and Mr. and Mrs. Moon are father and mother, the true parents.

Before concluding I need to allude to one charge against Unificationism frequently made by opponents of the movement. This is the allegation that, as Joseph Fichter has summarized it, "membership is disruptive of family life. The new convert leaves home and family, brothers and sisters, to dedicate himself entirely to the religious calling."[19]

Certainly there is much truth in that allegation. When one leaves one's old family for the new one, there is often a good dose of bitterness from those who feel rejected. However, Unificationism itself is only incidental to the situation. The unfortunate fact is that many persons today experience, upon reaching young adulthood, alienation from their biological families, and that alienation can be intensified when the person opts to participate in a group which seems deviant to his or her parents or siblings. Thus some parents react with horror when a new allegiance on the part of their son or daughter becomes apparent, just as they often do when a son or daughter announces that he or she plans to marry someone the parents consider unfit. Many parents, of course, do not exhibit such a reaction, and in those cases the old family ties remain intact; but when that hostility does occur, the parents often fail to realize that what is happening is actually an affirmation of family values, not a rejection of them. The real problem lies in the overall deterioration of traditional family structures, not in the workings of a group with a strong family identity.

But we digress from our central point. Several hundred years ago the Hutterites proclaimed a dual family loyalty, one which affirmed the standard biological family within a context of a larger, loving community. In our own century another new religious movement has said essentially the same thing, that life should be centered in families within a family. The more some things change, the more they remian the same. Let us conclude with these words of Young Oon Kim:

> He who does not love and cannot love is dead. Such individuals are really the most selfish and most miserable. Where can they learn how to love except in the family which is the most natural nursery? As a child we receive affection and care from our parents. This love is largely passive or receptive. As one grows and enters in marriage he or she understands the importance of mutual love. When one becomes a parent, love is expressed unconditionally without expecting to be rewarded. . . . Thus a good family, particularly a God-centered family, provides an ideal environment for one to learn the three basic forms of love in a natural way. Hence *Divine Principle* highlights the centrality of the family: namely, the restoration of love which would fulfill God's purpose of creation. Such teaching appears to be rather novel these days.[20]

NOTES

1 Benjamin Zablocki, *The Joyful Community* (Baltimore: Penguin, 1971), pp. 116-17.

2 *Ibid.*, p.118.

3 Stephen Gaskin, "Householder Yogis," in *Hey Beatnik! This Is the Farm Book* (Summertown, Tenn.: The Book Publishing Co., 1974), unpaginated.

4 *Ibid.*, section on "Kids."

5 Joseph W. Eaton and Albert J. Mayer, *Man's Capacity to Reproduce: The Demography of a*

Unique Population (Glencoe, Ill.: Free Press, 1954), pp. 16, 18, 20; cited in John A. Hostetler, *Hutterite Society* (Baltimore: John Hopkins Univ. Press, 1974), p. 203.

6 Victor Peters, *All Things Common: The Hutterian Way of Life* (New York: Harper & Row, 1965), pp. 92-93.

7 Hostetler, *Hutterite Society*, p. 237.

8 John A. Hostetler and Gertrude Enders Huntington, *The Hutterites in North America* (New York: Holt, Rinehart and Winston, 1967), pp. 60-61.

9 Peters, p. 98.

10 Hostetler, *Hutterite Society*, p. 204.

11 Eileen Barker, "Who'd Be a Moonie? A Comparative Study Of Those Who Join the Unification Church in Britain," in *The Social Impact of New Religious Movements*, ed. Bryan Wilson (Barrytown, N.Y.: Unif. Theol. Seminary, distr. Rose of Sharon Press, 1981), p. 67.

12 *Divine Principle* (New York: Holy Spirit Assn. for the Unif. of World Christianity, 1973), p. 32.

13 *Ibid.*, pp. 239ff.

14 Young Oon Kim, *Unification Theology* (New York: Holy Spirit Assn. for the Unif. of World Christianity, 1980), p. 32.

15 See Young Oon Kim, *Unification Theology and Christian Thought* (New York: Golden Gate, 1975), pp. 13-14, 21, 185ff.

16 *Ibid.*, p. 21.

17 *Unification Thought* (New York: Unification Thought Institute, 1973), pp. 228ff.

18 See, for example, Frederick Sontag, *Sun Myung Moon and the Unification Church* (Nashville: Abingdon, 1977), pp. 108ff.

19 Joseph H. Fichter, "Marriage, Family and Sun Myung Moon," *America* (27 October 1979).

20 Kim, *Unification Theology*, p. 80.

The Family:
The New Christian
Right's Symbol for
a Lost Past,
The Unification
Movement's Hope for a
Second Advent

Donald Heinz

A pro-family movement began to emerge in the United States in the middle 1970s. Participants in the movement hope to make the family a dominant theme in the politics of the 1980s. The passing of the Equal Rights Amendment by Congress in 1972, the Supreme Court decision on abortion in 1973, and new federal regulation of private religious schools mobilized diverse interest groups which eventually came together in a pro-family coalition. Strongly associated with these issues, the New Christian Right came to public attention in 1979 and played an active role in the politics of the 1980 election year.

During the same period in which pro-family coalitions were emerging in the United States and the New Christian Right was embracing the family as a major issue, a new religious movement, the Unification Church, which had risen in the Orient, began to receive significant attention in the United States. Particularly well focused in its evangelistic endeavors, in its theological message, and in its distinctive behavioral patterns was a new vision of the family.

This article is primarily an examination of the role and function of the family in the political and social programs of the New Christian Right. A briefer, second section of the article examines the role of the family in Unification theology and practice. Some comparisons are tentatively offered in the conclusion.

The Family: The New Christian Right's Symbol for a Lost Past

The New Christian Right has embraced the family as one of its dominant issues. There may be several reasons for this. The health and welfare of the family, in a time of significant social change and stress, preoccupied so many Americans that the family presented itself as the kind of issue on which a new social movement could ride to visibility and political power, just as the New Left came to political power over Vietnam. It is also possible that leaders of the New Right seized on this moral and social issue of the New Christian Right for their own purposes. The family looked more promising for the mobilization of an active constituency than traditional, conservative economic policies. The New Christian Right was scarcely unaware that Biblical religion and American civil religion also resonated strongly with sentiments concerning the family. The family can also serve as a code word for a return to patriarchy, a recovery of male dominance, a containment of the women's movement, a restriction on female sexual freedom.

While there is signifcant power of explanation in the above hypotheses, I want to develop in this paper an alternative interpretation of the role the family plays in the rhetoric and programs of the New Christian Right. It is the thesis of this paper that the family presents itself to the New Christian Right (and to segments of the American public) as a means for recovering a lost past and putting America right again. In such an agenda the symbol of the family functions both expressively as a vehicle through which a lost past can once again be experienced and recovered by the participants in the movement and instrumentally as an ideological weapon by which a system which ignores or threatens family values can be subjected to coercive reform.

Arguments for the first half of this thesis, the family as vehicle for experiencing and recovering a lost past, are developed upon the theory of German sociologist Arnold Gehlen's study of the fate of such institutions as the family in the modern age and upon the subsequent proposals by Peter Berger and Richard Neuhaus regarding mediating structures. Arguments for the second half of this thesis, the family as ideological weapon for coercive reform movements, build on anthropologist Mary Douglas's analysis of purity, ritual, and symbol and their meaning for individual, society, and cosmos.

Expressing and Recovering a Lost World

Arnold Gehlen contends that two results of modernity are institutional differentiation and bureaucratic augmentation. From this has come a structural bifurcation of human life into public and private spheres. Amidst social, geographical, and worldview mobility, there has been a steady process of de-institutionalization. According to Gehlen's theory, however, institutions are as necessary to humans as are instincts to animals. Institutions are the human constructions through which humans find their way and make their meaning in the world. The dilemma of modernity is that men and women find themselves acting in a foreground of growing, multiplying choices against a background of increasingly destabilizing institutions. The public sphere, to be sure, remains heavily institutionalized, but in ways that are abstract, impersonal, bureaucratic, and rationalized. But as humans in modern societies turn elsewhere for meaning and identity, they face a de-institutionalized private sphere. Thus they discover themselves to be homeless in society and in the cosmos. In reaction, they often express themselves in de-modernizing impulses.[1]

The underlying aspiration of de-modernization, then, is the quest for ways of being at home again in society and modern life. Responding to this dilemma of modernity, to the feeling of homelessness, to the de-institutionalization of the private sphere, Peter Berger and Richard Neuhaus (1977) have proposed the concept of mediating structures, which they define as those institutions standing between the individual's private life and the large institutions of public life. Four such mediating structures are neighborhood, family, church, and voluntary association. Because of its roots in the Enlightenment, American liberalism has been blind to the political functions of mediating structures and has focused its reformism on the individual and on a just public order. If anything, the rights of the individual are defended against mediating structures, e.g., the child against the family, sexual license against neighborhood values. Berger and Neuhaus argue that mediating structures are essential for a vital democratic society, that public policy should protect and foster them, and that, wherever possible, public policy should utilize them for the realization of social purposes. If there is merit in these proposals, then the cultivation of the family need not be written off as a naive and impossible, if understandable, attempt to go home again.

Berger and Hansfried Kellner (1977) have argued in particular that marriage and family may be seen as social arrangements which create meaning and lend order to individual existence. The plausibility of one's world depends upon the strength and continuity of significant relationships with others. Marriage and family function pre-eminently to provide this.

Against the background of Gehlen's theory and the Berger-Neuhaus public policy recommendations, the New Christian Right's enchantment and obsession with the family may be examined. It may be assumed that participants in the New Christian Right, and many others who are somewhat attracted to this movement, are suffering the dilemmas of modernity described above. One often hears a longing for another time, a time when Gemeinschaft (community) was not lost to impersonal Gesellschaft (society).

But what distinguishes the New Christian Right from others in the United States who have not moved in this direction? Religious conservatives have never embraced modernity in the same way American liberalism, religious and secular, has. Participants in the New Christian Right are likely to feel the values which they hold to have been rejected and displaced by status elites in government, higher education, and the media. With populism (and many on the left!) they share the aspiration to return control to the neighborhood level and away from centralized bureaucracies. Their grounding in a particular Christian worldview, one convinced of the continuing normative authority and contemporary relevance of the Bible, leads them to accept the family as a God-given institution and to define it in traditional ways.

There is an attempt to recover an ideal, if not an ideal time. Much has been made by demographers and contemporary social critics that the "traditional family" is no longer a dominant empirical reality in modern America. It is therefore suggested that the New Christian Right is naive or totalitarian in holding up that model as normative. Unrecognized in this critique, however, is the appropriate role of ideals, even "impossible ideals," as Christian ethicist Reinhold Niebuhr (1935) has argued. To hold up an image, or a Biblical archetype drawn from the Genesis creation accounts, is to engage in an act of meaning-making and meaning recovery. Embracing ideals and holding them up to public view can function as expressive social action, that is, action which has meaning in and of itself, apart from any instrumental political goals sought or accomplished. To lift up an image of a God-ordained structure is to attempt to re-set society's sights, to recover a divine order of things. The image promises order and norm amidst the chaotic choice of modernity. The image uncovers the roots of a lost past. However the political programs of the New Christian Right turn out, the resonance with the family and the attempt to experience and live in that ideal reality may enable participants to live in what Berger (1969) calls the "plausibility structure" within which the worldview they are affirming is confirmed.

Thus, according to Gehlen's theory, the longing for community and the cultivation of meaning at a level other than that of mega-structures makes sense against the backdrop of modernity. The choice of the family is also appropriate, given the worldview of conservative Christianity. Even if not worked out theoretically, even if defended only in the satisfying rhetorical language of morality, the focus on the family would seem consistent with the Berger-Neuhaus proposals and with the right's own declared goal of getting centralized government off one's back and returning identity and control to the common person. Indeed, the recent White House Conference on the Family argued again and again in its recommendations that the first step to the health of the family was to terminate all the public policies which are inimical to the family. Then the family could begin to become all it could be..

The Berger-Neuhaus proposals are much more carefully nuanced than I am detailing here, and the Christian Right may not be willing to embrace the pluralism built into these proposals. The argument here is only that the return to the family, the focusing of political action around that institution, need not be seen only as a crass act of political expediency or a poorly masked return to patriarchy. It could also be an effective response to the current problems of modern American society.

Re-Ordering and Re-Imposing a Lost World

Mary Douglas has developed an elaborate theory of ritual, purity, symbol, and social group which may help interpret the normative role of the family in the ideology and political program of the New Christian Right, especially, if its leaders are understood as attempting coercive reform of American society. A key element in Douglas's analysis is her treatment of purity. To understand purity rules is to understand much about a society. Pollution rituals impose order on experience, support classification and clarification of forms, and reduce dissonance. Such rules are typically social-ized at the level of the individual's body. Thus attitudes about the body may arise from society's larger image of itself. The human body becomes a universal symbol system. A certain understanding of the body accompanies certain social structures. Bodily control correlates with social control. Douglas's study of food taboos in Leviticus leads her to conclude that the confounding of a classification system with respect to food threatens to confound the general scheme of the world. Food rules connect to maintaining boundaries and extend not only to society but to the cosmos. Douglas has tried to develop a model which can correlate rules of body purity with social organization and with cosmological structures. Because humans inhabit numerous bodies simultaneously—physical bodies, social bodies, and bodies of thought—they naturally seek maximum consonance of experience. Experience has a vertical dimension which cuts across all these levels of structure.

Rituals signify a heightened awareness of these levels of structure and a great sensitivity to the symbolic action which expresses their consonance. As these symbols become institutionalized at various levels of reality, ritual attention to them functions to sustain a general order of existence. According to Clifford Geertz (1935), it is in ritual that "the world as lived and the world as imagined, fused under the agency of a single set of symbolic forms, turn out to be the same world." Ritual expresses and reinforces (socially constructed or divinely ordained) reality.[2]

It is my hypothesis that one role the family plays for the New Christian Right can best be understood in view of Douglas's theory. I am assuming that the family, including the important attempts to define and structure it normatively, functions for the Christian Right analogously to the body in Douglas's theory. Thus the family correlates with social system and cosmology or worldview.

In his "Ninety-Five Theses for the 1980s" Jerry Falwell, founder of the Moral Majority, includes twenty-four theses concerning the family. Falwell states that God himself has instituted marriage and that the definition of ideal marriage is the joining of one man to one woman for one lifetime, with the husband as the divinely appointed head of this institution. Children are a normal expectation of this union, and they belong to the family not to the state. Condemned as anti-family are the following: government interference in child-rearing, communal living, abortion, homosexuality, polygamy, child abuse, wife abuse, substance abuse, premarital sex, incest, adultery, pornography, no-fault divorce laws, the Equal Rights Amendment, and certain Internal Revenue laws. Falwell asserts that no other institution in human history has proven so successful or satisfactory to humans and that any nation which has ever allowed the family unit to deteriorate has always automatically been marked for destruction.

I am arguing that the New Christian Right sees in the family an image of a lost or neglected universal order. The reason peoples and nations become ripe for destruction when they ignore the family is that they are ignoring the very order of reality, without which no one can continue meaningfully to live. To define the family, to tend its boundaries, to live in its reality is to live the meaning of society and the meaning of life in the cosmos. Such an attempt, such ritual homage to the symbol of the family, cuts vertically across family, society, and cosmos.

It was not theory, however, which turned the attention of the New Christian Right to the family. It was their perception of federal interference in family life and, more important, their view that federal power has been used to delegitimize the normative place of the traditional family and legitimize, support, and even establish alternative lifestyles. Thus, not only modern society but federal power has contributed to the blurring of a fundamental order of reality. The pluralism of modern life has itself also relativized the traditional family and confounded the general scheme of the world. Thus the Christian Right responds to governmental redefinitions and the pressures of modernity.

But there is more involved than saving the family. Perhaps alert boundary tending and coercively imposed traditional definitions can restore divine order to a society moving toward chaos. Thus the family becomes a key element, perhaps the key element, in a political program of coercive reform by a social movement which understands its values to have been abandoned by status elites in government, higher education, and the media. The movement, engaged in a politics of lifestyle, would not, in this analysis, simply be contending over alternative ways of living but over which value system is congruent with universal order. To say this in religious language, fighting for the family is fighting for God, who instituted the family. To go further, fighting for the family is fighting against all those elements in modern society which threaten to hasten the eclipse of God and lead us further toward chaos.

The Chaos of Sexuality

A reordered cosmos needs to be erected in face of the chaos of sexuality. The purity of family life can bring order to this chaos, legitimizing and bounding sexual drives. Attending to issues of sexual purity can be a way of attending to issues of social structure and to meaningful closure in worldview. Apart from the question of the life of the unborn, abortion threatens to abolish sexual taboos, and release sexuality from family structures. Such a deregulated sexuality could destabilize life in community and edge humanity toward chaos.

It was to be expected that the New Christian Right might fasten onto sexual issues. Conservative Christians have always specialized, as it were, in issues of personal morality. An apparent obsession with sexuality may stem partly, as is often charged, from a peculiarly Christian denigration of the body (but both cross-cultural historical studies and the work of Douglas may call this judgment, in its one-sidedness, into question) or from a moralistic attempt to deal with one's own sexuality. I am here arguing, however, that if traditional moral concerns led them to sexuality as an issue worthy of attention, there are deeper, structural reasons for such a choice as well.

The strictures against homosexuality and against the Equal Rights Amendment, however much homophobia and sexism there may be mixed into them, function, in this analysis, as a protest against any blurring of the classification system through which humans bring order to their personal and public lives—and through which humans are thought to mirror a divine order. To argue as Falwell does that homosexuality is anti-family may be to argue that homosexuality floods us with dissonance and muddies society's image of itself. Pledging allegiance to family life and enacting in our own lives the ideal family are rituals by which we sustain, throughout the social system, a general order of existence and fuse the ideal world with the lived world.

There may also be an underlying feeling that an abortion culture may break a chain of meaning in which pregnancy can or must come from sexual activity and that such pregnancy is to be ordered within the bounds of the family. Pregnancy arrives almost as a punishment—or publicly visible social anomaly—for those who engage in impure sexual activity, i.e., sexual activity outside the boundaries of family or outside a chain of meaningful causality. An abortion culture encourages us to assume there is no danger in disturbing such boundaries, in acting against such order. We are lured into thinking that chaos does not threaten, that there are no effects at the level of the social system or of the cosmos.

The Chaos of a God-less World

At best God's connection to the modern world is tenuous. No doubt people who respond to the New Christian Right feel this as acutely as others. The family is a primary order through which God is thought to govern the world. To lose the family is to lose the ordering presence of God in the midst of an otherwise chaotic social world. Tending the boundaries and welfare of the family is a ritual through which we restore (and impose) divine order on society and vertically reconnect God to all three levels of human experience: individual, society, and cosmos or worldview.

An abortion culture threatens to disconnect God as the author of human life from sexual activity and procreation. A break in divine causality is introduced by a technological procedure and by individuals whose body/family life no longer mirrors the divine ordering. In the view of the New Christian Right the rituals of sexual activity within family bounds are being denounced. Motherhood and the holy occupation of raising children (socializing them into the truth about the divine ordering of human life) are also denigrated. Abortion, then, becomes a ritual of secularism, which has often been defined as the process through which more and more dimensions of human life are withdrawn from under the interpretive power of religious symbol systems.

The Family: The Unification Movement's Hope for a Second Advent

I have argued above that the New Christian Right's preoccupation with the family may be viewed as a means for recovering a lost past and putting America right again. Embracing the family promises the participants of the New Christian Right an expressive social action which experiences and recovers a lost past and an instrumental political action which attempts to subject to coercive reform a social system which ignores or threatens family values. These efforts occur in a setting in which religious values are being eclipsed by secularism, significant human needs for community go unanswered by a technological, bureaucratic society, and the entire system seems to stand in need of revitalization and new forms of legitimation.

It is beyond the scope of this analysis to examine the Korean roots of Unification theology for possible similarities to the American setting in which the New Christian Right's interest in the family emerged. Because the Unification movement is still alien to American social and political realities and because considerable anti-cultist hysteria has been fanned against the Moonies, there has as yet arisen no resonance between Unification theology and practice and those dimensions of American life to which the New Christian Right has been responding. Nor does it seem likely that any resonance will occur. The salience of the Unification movement's religious and cultural agenda has been experienced only at the individual level, in the lives of those who became devotees of Rev. Moon. This would lead one to expect that the American Moonies will forge their concerns for the family into a unique social ethic, different from that available to the New Christian Right. Of course, there are religious reasons for that as well, which count as heavily as the markedly different access to the American imagination available to the two movements. Although the Unification movement apparently wishes to call itself Christian and has as its significant root a conservative Protestant missionary context, the religious significance of the family for Unification theology is drastically different from its significance for the theology of the New Christian Right, although there may be some deeper similarities that are not immediately obvious. I turn first, then, to the political and social ethical significance of the family for the Unification movement, then to its religious significance.

Political and Social Ethical Significance of the Family

At no time in the foreseeable future will the Unification movement be in a position, as the New Christian Right may be, to engage in attempts at coercive reform. For the New Christian Right, that is the attempt to reimpose a system of values upon status elites which have long since abandoned them, to bring its own order to social chaos. Moonies in the United States have not successfully claimed Christian symbols as their own, and, because of the Korean origins of their movement cannot claim the earlier American past as a birthright denied them by the modern forces of secular humanism.

If instrumental political action around the issue of the family is closed to the Moonies, expressive social action is likely to continue as the dominant posture. In any open society, groups even on the fringe of the social system are always able to speak and behave publicly in ways which express their solidarity with a symbol system which seems true to them. The payoff of expressive social action is the resonance with a larger system of meaning coming back to the individual participants, the strengthening of faith through communal action, the solidifying of identity and boundary within the movement, the ethical satisfaction of affirming publicly one's ideals. Through public celebrations and enactments of the ideal family, Moonies create private and public meaning for themselves and lend order to their personal existence, while giving a witness to a public ideal they hope society may some day emulate.

There is an element of coercive reform in such expressive social action, but the coercion is all directed inward. The demands which the Moonie ideal family makes upon the devotees of the movement are enormous: long period of separation even after marriage, strict sexual abstinence before marriage, the arrangement of both partner and time of marriage by Rev. Moon, the theological pressure of living up to being agents of a new creation in one's family life. All impulses to control, all urges to reshape a system, all totalitarian drives must be directed inward, while a soft face is turned toward American society. The internal pressure which builds up inside the devotee must be great, even given the significant satisfaction and self-realization which the movement seems to offer.

In a different and earlier age, the sixteenth century Anabaptists attempted to exert great self-discipline in creating a holy community and also suffered significant external persecution. Out of this came a powerfully meaningful communal and religious life and occasional outbursts of craziness and grandiose efforts at totalitarian new creation. No such outbursts have surfaced among the Moonies, although there may be some personal pathologies among devotees which can be traced to the great pressures for internal control associated with their family ethic. It may be noted that in small communities where the Moonie presence is more apparent, society sometimes projects onto the Moonies totalitarian intents.

Congruent with a self-expressive rather than an instrumental political action, the family ideology of the Unification movement seems to reflect an intentionalist social ethic. Edward Long (1970) discusses intentionalism as one of three ways of implementing ethical decisions, along with institutionalism and operationalism. Central to the intentionalist motif is the attempt to infuse new spiritual zeal and moral earnestness by first developing a high spiritual devotion in a core group. "Intentionalists generally seek a heroic ethic, a demanding morality, and the satisfaction attending the performance of special duties" (Long, 1970, p. 252).[3] The intentionalist cherishes the dedicated group, intense zeal, and unique moral visibility. Such sharply focused vision and action are the best hope for bringing about social change and revitalization, but they are hallowed whether or not they prove instrumental, simply as one's call to holy community by God.

Unification theology emphasizes the God-centered family as the best example of how God works in history. It provides "the four position foundation" (God, husband, wife, child) for the coming Kingdom of God and an ideal society. It is the base for personal regeneration and for social reconstruction. There is an assumed parallel of orders of reality: parents/family/society/nation/world/ Kingdom of God. Out of this ethos of the ideal family is to flow an ever widening social ethic. Indeed, it seems the devotees address the perennial issue of moving from personal to social ethics by imaging the future society as a kind of extended family.

Religious Signifcance of the Family

For the New Christian Right the family is God's way of ordering creation and the fundamental community into which and within which God calls people and relates to them. These ideas would no doubt be accepted by Unification theology, but there are additional and very significant distinctives. For the Moonies, the family seems to function as an achievement of righteousness necessary for the arrival of the Kingdom of God. The family is also a "plausibility structure" within which Unification doctrines are experienced as persuasive and believable. The family becomes a model demonstration of the reality into which devotees seek to evangelize and socialize prospective converts.

According to Unification theology Jesus' mission failed because the public rejection of his mission, the unrighteous society into which he came, kept him from marrying and inaugurating a perfect family through which the Kingdom of God could arrive. The stringent sexual and family ethic practiced among Moonies seems an attempt to recover that failed momentum and recreate a righteous society in which a new advent of God's presence could arrive.

An interesting analogue may be the first century Essene community at Qumran, about which the Dead Sea Scrolls are so informative. Especially noteworthy is the "Manual of Discipline" of this sectarian, Jewish, messianic movement. Turning aside from mainstream Judaism they committed themselves with holy zeal and eschatological vision to a separatist communal life of intense piety and ethical achievement, hoping thereby to produce a righteous community of a new covenant which would warrant the coming of the Messiah.

The Unification family ethos is a heroic one in which every dimension of sexuality, courtship, marriage, and family life is clothed with the sacred. It is not just that Rev. and Mrs. Moon function as ideal parents who will produce an ideal family which will be the instrument for the arrival of the Kingdom of God (hence the appearance of Rev. Moon is associated with the "second advent"). *All* devotees are called to participate in the restructuring of family life so that a modeling of God's will can occasion the arrival of the Kingdom. Family life becomes a gift, a task, a special kind of achievement which carries great promise.

For devotees the Unification families are a promise to be fulfilled, a model of a realized theology, and extended for those not yet married, a present gift of community. In these several dimensions the family functions as a powerful plausibility structure (Berger 1969), a social-structural base for religion's reality-constructing and -maintaining tasks. The Moonie family is a basic structure within which Moonie theology is believable, even compelling. Given the family, the theology makes sense. Indeed, theological tenets come to resonate with the experiences the devotees are having in community.

The family not only makes especially plausible the tenets and behavior of the movement. It exerts a powerful pressure for continuing in the movement. To relinquish the theology is to leave behind the most nourishing and meaningful community many of the devotees have ever known. One's world, one's symbolic universe may become implausible outside the family. Apostasy from the theology would be divorce from the family, and vice versa. If one thinks in anthropologist Clifford Geertz's terms of religion as a cultural system, then Moonie theology expressed in Moonie family may be seen, in the words of Geertz's famous definition of religion, as "a system of symbols which act to establish powerful, pervasive, and long-lasting moods and motivations by formulating conceptions of a general order of existence and clothing these conceptions with such an aura of factuality that the moods and motivations seem uniquely realistic." To abandon the theology requires abandoning a deeply meaningful and resonant religious-cultural system, in which the family serves as the foundation stone.

Finally, the Unification family functions as a paradigm for Moonie reality, a "model home" for inquirers to inspect, a demonstration project for where the movement is going. The potential convert is invited to find in the family empirical verification for the movement's theological beliefs, affirmations, and behavior. A devotee can see and experience as well as believe. "The proof is in the pudding." "What you see is what you get." The family is the base and the behavioral extension of the belief system.

Of course, the movement takes a great risk in opening itself up so obviously for empirical disconfirmation. What if Rev. Moon's children turn out to be less than ideal? What if divorce or delinquency strike the movement's family life? For the time being, it seems that Unification families confirm the faith of most participants, although significant stumbling blocks occasionally arise.

Conclusion

There have been many hypotheses to account for the New Christian Right's fixation on the family as a central issue in its platform. Without minimizing the roles of sexism, political expediency, and conservative morality, I have argued in this paper for an alternative interpretation of the role the family plays in the rhetoric and political action of the New Christian Right. The family functions for expressing, recovering, and imposing a lost past. This hypothesis has built upon the theoretical work of Arnold Gehlen and Peter Berger in their analysis of modernity and of Mary Douglas in her analysis of rituals of purity, natural symbols, and their correlation with social structure and cosmology. It is also related to the public policy proposals regarding such mediating institutions as the family that have recently been made by Peter Berger and Richard Neuhaus.

Modern men and women find themselves homeless in the cosmos, alienated by excessive choices and an overly rationalized public sphere and a de-institutionalized private sphere. Amidst this loss of meaning, identity, and order, the family offers itself as a means through which a lost world can once again be expressed and recovered. But there is more. By ritually attending to the symbol of the family, by tending its boundaries and keeping it pure, we can produce a consonance with all three levels of human experience: individual, society, cosmos or worldview. Thus we not only do not lose the family as a primary institution through which we discover and express meaning. We gain the family as an instrument through which order can be reimposed on a secular society moving ever closer to chaos.

Unification theology arose in an entirely different context from that of the New Christian Right. The focus on the family in the Unification movement is inextricably related to a grand theological trajectory which would seem to have little in common with the visions of the New Christian Right. The Unification family, guided by perfect spiritual parents, will be the instrument through which the Kingdom of God will arrive and the failure of Jesus' ultimate mission will be set right. The family is an achievement of righteousness, a paradigm for God's will in the world, a plausibility structure within which Unification beliefs and practices become especially credible, a demonstration project which offers the proof of the pudding to potential converts.

Because the Unification movement is not indigenous to the United States, has no large following, and produces little resonance with most Americans, the political style available to the Moonies, around the issue of the family, is very different from that available to the New Christian Right. Moonie behavior patterns associated with the family constitute an expressive social action (rather than an instrumental political action), which, however, is very powerful for the devotees themselves. The Unification family ethos seems a good example of an intentionalist ethic, in which the ethical strategy is concentrated on a holy community and on the zealousness of the devotees. Whatever coercive element the family ethos may have is turned inward in stringent demands for moral heroism, not outward in attempts to impose a reordering of society.

The Unification movement's preoccupation with the family may, however, display greater similarities to that of the New Christian Right than are immediately apparent. For both movements the family is a basic paradigm for how God orders reality, makes the divine presence known, and relates to people. For both movements the family is the basic social and theological unit (for the fundamentalists of the New Christian Right a much more basic unit than the Church). For both there is a grand symmetry of family/ society/nation/God.

Perhaps the Unification construction of a righteous family as antidote to the sinfulness which keeps the Kingdom from arriving is parallel to the hope of the New Christian Right that the Christian family will be the means through which God's promise for the American experiment will once again have the chance of coming true. It may be a function of the upward mobility and new access to power of the New Christian Right that it has moved from its intentionalist-evangelistic position earlier in this century to more direct confrontation with the social system. The New Christian Right has moved from a position of social quietism and pessimism which channeled all energies into a special community and an idiosyncratic call from God to a political strategy of recovering and perhaps enforcing an ideal family/society long since abandoned by contemporary status elites. If this operationalist mode (Long, 1967) of mobilizing power to balance power is not altogether successful, there is also a committment to an institutionalist strategy through which currently neglected religious values will be gradually knit back into the fabric of our public life. If the Unification movement had sufficient political power and access to the American tradition and symbol system, would it attempt to mobilize its theological idealism into social reality through political action rather than ethical modeling?

NOTES

1 An excellent, brief introduction to Gehlen's theory is that of James Davison Hunter, "The New Religions: Demodernization and the Protest Against Modernity," in *The Social Impact of New Religious Movements*, ed. Bryan Wilson, (Barrytown, N.Y.: Unif. Theo. Seminary, distr. Rose of Sharon Press, 1981).

2 An extremely useful review of Douglas's theory is that of Sheldon Isenberg and Dennis Owen, "Bodies, Natural and Contrived: The Work of Mary Douglas," *Religious Studies Review* 3, no.1 (January 1977). In these two paragraphs I am leaning heavily on their summary.

REFERENCES

Berger, Peter L. *The Sacred Canopy.* Garden City, N.Y.: Doubleday, 1969.

——————, Brigitte Berger, and Hansfried Kellner. *The Homeless Mind.* New York: Random House, 1973.

——————, and Hansfried Kellner. "Marriage and the Construction of Reality." In *Facing Up To Modernity.* New York: Basic Books, 1977.

——————, and Richard John Neuhaus. *To Empower People: The Role of Mediating Structures in Public Policy.* Washington, D.C.: American Enterprise Institute, 1977.

Douglas, Mary. *Purity and Danger: An Analysis of Concepts of Pollution and Taboo.* London: Routledge and Kegan Paul, 1966.

——————. *Natural Symbols: Explorations in Cosmology.* London: Barrie and Jenkins, 1970.

Falwell, Jerry. *Ninety-Five Theses For the 1980s.* Moral Majority mailing.

Geertz, Clifford. *The Interpretation of Culture.* New York: Basic Books, 1973.

Hunter, James Davison. "The New Religions: Demodernization and the Protest Against Modernity." In *The Social Impact of New Religious Movements.* Ed. Bryan Wilson. Barrytown, N.Y.: Unif. Theo. Seminary, distr. Rose of Sharon Press, 1981.

Isenberg, Sheldon and Dennis Owen. "Bodies, Natural and Contrived: The Work of Mary Douglas," *Religious Studies Review* 3, no. 1, January 1977.

Niebuhr, Reinhold. *An Interpretation of Christian Ethics.* New York: Harper and Brothers, 1935.

Long, Edward LeRoy. *A Survey of Christian Ethics.* New York: Oxford Univ. Press, 1967.

The Restitution of Family as Natural Order

Na'im Akbar

Introduction

The traditional family in the Western world has been under siege most intensively over the past twenty-five years. The Western social scientist's fetish with objectivity and his allegedly value-free faith in the infinite flexibility of the human condition have done much to undermine the value of the family. The family has traditionally gained much of its strength from the fundamental assumption of the inalterability of the essential family structure. Advances in medical science, biological science, and most importantly, speculations of the social scientists have fostered a basic doubt about the form, components, or even the necessity for family.

Unfortunately, inadequate attention has been given to the correlative occurrence of massive and degenerative social and human problems as tacit and ethical support has been given to the decline of traditional family life in the Western world. In 1973, the Senate Subcommittee on Children and Youth held hearings entitled: "American Families: Trends and Pressures." Senator Walter Mondale chaired these hearings and indicated:

> The more our work focused on what might be called the
> categorical problems of childhood—abuse, inadequate child

care, sudden infant death, and all the rest—the more we became convinced that we were dealing with symptoms, not causes. The more I looked at the problems affecting children and the kind of help they needed, the more I became convinced that we should be focusing on the condition of the families and on their ability to discharge their fundamental child-rearing responsibilities.[1]

It would not be farfetched to trace many other human problems such as crime increase, sexual violence, divorce rates and much depression to the deterioration of the traditional family. Only woefully few social scientists believe as does renowned developmental psychologist Urie Brofenbrenner that:

It is no accident that in a million years of evolution, we have emerged with a particular form for the raising of children . . . and it is the human family.[2]

Such tidbits from the voluminous accumulated data clearly suggest that family life is under siege and its deterioration is having profound impact on the development of our children.

We must avoid the temptation to become faddish in our attack on contemporary social conditions and the attribution of difficulties to family deterioration. As Sally Helgesen recently observed in an article in *Harper's:* "pro family has become as faddish as autonomous individualism was in the 60s."[3] Such faddish banner-carrying ultimately begs the question of the real genesis of our social problems and it invites an oversimplification of analysis which ultimately drags us into greater difficulty. The yearning for return to the days when tradition reigned supreme carries with it an overgeneralized yearning for the ethnocentrism, racism, sexism and rugged militarism which paralleled those times. Advocates of pro-family stances must be careful that they do not ally themselves with persons of dubious political intent camoflaged under a banner of "return to moral basics."

The hypothesis of this discussion is that one of the difficulties confronting the contemporary family is the self-fulfilling quality of scientific or social theories about human and social functioning.

One such fundamental hypothesis has emerged from the brilliantly inspired, but humanly inimical theories of Sigmund Freud. His assumption that family life is inevitably an erotic and tragic drama of animal instinct has functioned as a most destructive self-fulfilling prophecy. "Aggression forms the basis of every relation of affection and love among people," says Dr. Freud.[4] Freud's preoccupation with sexuality creates a limiting conception of family which breeds inevitable conflict.

A theoretical perspective coming from the psychologists which is equally as destructive as the Freudian hypothesis is that of the Behaviorist. The Behaviorist views family functioning and child development as no more than a series of techniques. Child-rearing is viewed as a process of stimulus manipulations rather than as the complex interactive intimacy of dynamic family processes. So unlike the Freudians, who tend to overattribute hidden motives and dispositions, the Behaviorist operates as if they are not there or views them as irrelevant. Family interactions and the rearing of children are viewed as no more than a series of arrangements of rewards and punishments, and their value might be more adequately accomplished by machines. In fact, some radical behaviorists have advocated the superiority of machines in rearing children. Unlike earlier notions of the importance of parental affection and parent/child interactions, the current focus is that effective child-rearing is a result of good "parenting skills" rather than a result of being good, caring human beings. The very reduction of familyhood to certain technical skills is indicative of the destructive mentality which is accepted as good science and good humanity in contemporary society.

Both the pessimism about the human condition implicit in the Freudian theory and the mechanomorphic theory of the Behaviorists have resulted in disasters for the contemporary family. The large numbers of experts and therapists growing out of the Freudian and neo-Freudian tradition have all but created family discord by advocating the inevitability of such conflict. One is encouraged to reduce the inevitable neurosis by minimizing restrictions on the free expression of sexual interest and aggressive feelings within the family. Many Freudian-influenced families tolerate previously unheard-of miscon-

duct from their children in the name of avoiding neurosis by un-
bridled permissiveness. Three generations raised within such a cultural
motif no longer consider peace within the family an expected norm.
Along with the medical discoveries which currently boast of their
capacities to produce surrogate mothers by artificial insemination,
extra-uterine fertilization, and an abundance of similar techniques
and promises of even more daring experiments, the mechanical image
of family renders it even less a necessity. The "single parent" has
become an increasingly sought family structure in light of the concept that family life is no more than a technique rather than a process.
With numerous popular conceptions of open marriages, child adop-
tion by homosexual couples, and absentee parenting, the family has
been placed in the category of the dispensable social organization.

The Natural Family

The argument of this discussion is that the family is a naturally
prescribed organization whose function is to foster the development
of undeveloped life. Family structure and processes must be evaluated only in the light of their adequacy in fulfilling this fundamental
function. The concept of family being a "prescribed" organization
speaks to the inadvisability of its alteration. The suggestion that this
prescription has a "natural" genesis carries an implication of inalterability as well. Despite such implications of inalterability, we are
fully aware of the broad flexibility in the human make-up. We do
not advocate a maladaptive rigidity. Natural developmental processes
are dictated in lower animal forms by instinct, hormones and other
biochemical processes which demand that certain things occur or
death becomes imminent. The human being, on the other hand, is
permitted to respond to urges with an undictated nature or respond
to suggestions emanating from the natural world and its rhythms.
The rhythms, cycles and processes of the natural world urge an imitation on the part of the human, but the processes cannot coerce
imitation. Through the ability to record and retain events, attend to
history, culture and even receive revelation (the acquisition of previously unexperienced information from non-sensory processes), men

are invited to follow certain courses for their proper development. The courses to which they are invited are not arbitrary possibilities but represent processes which have stood the test of time and space (or geography). The idea of "natural prescriptions" has more enduring validity than the relativistic and arbitrary concepts of Western social scientists, who have proven themselves woefully inadequate in identifying remedies for escalating human and social problems. The validation of natural principles guiding human conduct is found in the consistent success of nature in preserving and expanding herself. Validation is also present in the ancient scripts from the Divine and the contemporary rediscovery of those principles by those who have given their lives in pursuit of Truth.

Another implication of our definition of "family" is that all human life is incomplete and is in the process of developing or unfolding. Consequently, family life is necessary for human beings at all stages of their lives and not just at the period of physical helplessness. The usual social science definition views the family as "an organization for the raising of the biologically immature until it reaches biological and social maturity." This rather narrow definition of family accounts, in large part, for many of the social problems which have been developed in modern society.

Our conceptualization is that the family should be viewed as a multi-dimensional process. It has concrete and specific characteristic manifestations which expand to become increasingly abstract and general. It is actually a process of concentric dimensions of manifestation. There are certain generalizable principles which can be observed at the lower and more specific layers which serve as inferences for the higher and less observable levels or dimensions of family life. (See Figure 1.)

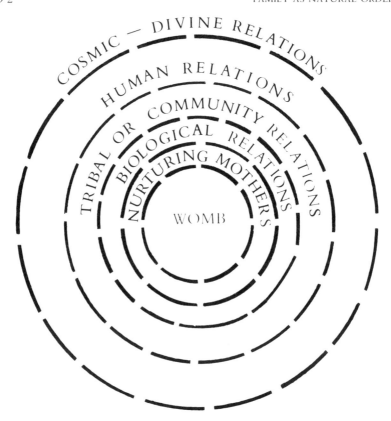

Figure 1: The ascending spheres of the multi-dimensional concept of the "Natural Family."

The most basic and observable level of family is actually the biological womb of the mother. There is a prototype of family process which can be understood from the functioning of the womb. The womb's primary functions are *nurturance, protection, sacrifice, immunization* and the overall processes for the facilitation of developing life. These fundamental processes characterize effective family functioning at each dimension of family life. A more extensive description of this model would be necessary to fully describe the application of these principles to each dimension of family as illustrated in Figure 1. Unfortunately, neither time nor space will permit such an extensive explanation in this context.

Before moving our discussion to some consideration of actual contemporary models which utilize this conceptual model in attempting to rebuild family life, it is necessary to say a couple of words about the functions of family life. The functions of protection, nurturance, sacrifice, etc. have a particular goal. This goal is the preservation of "constructive life development." The constructive life of the human being is one of physical survival, emotional stability, rational and moral advancement. Anything that interferes with these processes is an anti-life force which the "family" is obligated to attack or offer secure shelter against. Therefore, the "tribal" dimension of family is responsible for education because a part of its protective function is to protect against forces of ignorance or superstition which may retard effective rational development and community progress. The "tribal" dimension of family is responsible for providing a reservoir of self-knowledge in order to nourish the developing life into proper recognition of who it is; this is food for the rational development. Family or community has a responsibility to monitor the agencies in the society to insure that they are cultivating constructive moral and rational life.

In the same way that infection of the umbilical passage or leakage of the aminotic sac suggests destruction of the developing fetus, comparable disruption in the protective function of family portends the destruction of human rational and social life. The family (biological kin or tribal relations) represents the prototypical womb over developing life, whose function is to insulate, buffer and immunize that life to insure its development and expansion. Therefore, a functioning family must move defensively when it observes anti-life forces at work.

Certainly, this becomes a frightening commentary on contemporary society when we observe the state of the family. These nurturant and protective functions which we have described have been seriously handicapped by the deterioration both structurally and functionally of what is currently conceived as family. The natural family sees itself as responsible for the developing life of all its members and all of its members are viewed as developing life.

Models of Natural Family Restitution

The idea of the family in Unification theology is strikingly similar to the concept of the natural family which we have discussed above. In "The Principles of Creation," it is stated:

> The basic unit of the Kingdom of Heaven is the true family, the basic Four Position Foundation. The true family is the basic foundation for God's vertical and horizontal love and the perfect object of God's Heart. With this true family as a base, a true society, true nation, and true world would have been realized.[5]

This concept that the family is fundamental for the establishment of wider relationships is quite consistent with the foregoing discussion. One dimension added by the concept of the "natural family" is the identification of "God's blessing" in an even more basic manifestation, i.e., the womb, where we can observe the processes of family at work and available for study and application. The man/woman relationship and the human relationship to God are viewed as basic, but one has a recourse only to "Divine instruction" in order to understand s-3process of those relationships. By observation of the fundamental expression of family which we have described as the womb, we can observe concrete examples of how family should work and what should occur in the relationship. Obedience to God becomes parallel to respecting and observing natural law. What is described in *Divine Principle* as man's relationship to God, is viewed as man's understanding, and relationship to natural processes as being critical to establishing the "ideal family."

Certainly the concept of the "natural family" may be viewed as somewhat reductionistic when compared with the rather elaborate theological system centering around the concept of family in Unification theology. The thesis of this discussion is that societies fulfill their fundamental assumption about the nature of their relationships. "As a man thinketh in his heart, so is he," we are told in the Bible. Therefore faith in the concept that family is a basic blessing from God and that it has been given by God as fundamental for man's development, creates a view of family life as

inalterable, potentially harmonious and guided by certain universal principles. It is this ontological difference in the view of family
which makes family life functional and minimally problematic for
Unification believers, but creates gross difficulty for the Freudian,
Behaviorist or others who operate from a set of assumptions which
do not view family life as axiomatic for human development.

Despite the somewhat non-Western way that marriages are arranged within the Unification movement, there is considerably
greater success in establishing functional families than one finds
outside of that movement. Marriage partner selections are made
by the religious leader, Rev. Moon, and the duration of the courtship and the ultimate blessing of the marriage is given by Rev.
Moon. The freedom to choose one's marriage partner without interference is viewed as a fundamental freedom by the criterion of
most Western thought. This freedom is rather strongly defended
because of the Western assumption that marriage and family life
are "individual" matters or matters between "individuals." The
Unification believer understands that marriage and family life are
matters between man and God and one who is most knowledgable
of God's way is probably best qualified to make such selections.

One assumption that apparently operates within the Unification
concept of family is that intermarriage between ethnic and racial
groups will facilitate the development of the "one world family."
Marriage between Occidental and Oriental, Black and White is
viewed as a step toward resolution of world hostilities between
such alienated groups. The concept of the natural family presupposes the establishment of one's nurturance within his "tribal"
group as a prerequisite for "human relations." In other words, the
person can be adequately nurtured in the higher group only if he/she
has been adequately nurtured in the lower community. If one has a
negative concept of self or an ignorance of self as a result of inadequate nurturance from the mother or biological relations, then it is
difficult to undertake tribal relations. However, there is a presumed
"automatic" readiness for good human relations if one has been
able to establish good "tribal" relations. So, unlike the Unification
procedure, world brotherhood grows naturally from good, mutu-

ally accepting tribal brotherhoods. However, the process of restitution may require some extreme grafting procedures in order to reestablish natural family life.

The African-American family has been particularly ravaged by contemporary deterioration as well as the historical disasters of slavery and oppression. The various Christian denominations have not consciously focused on family life and, therefore, have not been particularly successful in fostering strong family values among African-Americans. Many of the positive moral values fostered by most Christian churches have done much indirectly to strengthen the African-American family. The one religious group which has explicitly directed its efforts towards restitution for the African-American family has been the Islamic religious community in North America. Particularly, has this been the case for the Nation of Islam, led for forty years by the late Elijah Muhammad and subsequently under the leadership of his son, Waarith Deen Muhummad in its present structure as the American Muslim Mission.

Certainly the accomplishments of the Nation of Islam in this regard are probably most widely known. In Elijah Muhammad's rather basic language, he suggested:

> Until we learn to love and protect our woman, we will never be a fit and recognized people on the Earth. . . . My beloved brothers in America, you have lost the respect of your woman and therefore you have lost the respect for yourself. You won't protect her; therefore you can't protect yourself. Your first lesson comes from your mother. If you don't protect your mother, how do you think you look in the eyes of other human beings?[26]

Elijah Muhammad rather directly equated respect for womanhood with the positive development of family life. His analysis concluded that slavery and oppression in America had damaged the family by undermining respect for the black woman as well as resulting in the black woman's loss of respect for herself. Restitution of family life could be accomplished by the restoration of respect for the woman. He encouraged the black woman to respect herself and avoid self-negating identification with white women. Mr. Muhammad instructed his followers to:

> Stop women from trying to look like them. By bleaching, powdering, ironing and coloring their hair; painting their lips, cheeks and eyebrows; wearing shorts; going half-nude in public places; going swimming with them and lying on beaches with men. . . . Stop them from going into bars and taverns and sitting and drinking with men and strangers. Stop them from using unclean language in public (and at home), from smoking and drug addiction habits. Nothing but Islam will make you a respectable people.[7]

These prohibitions, directly adressed to women in this context were similarly enforced for men.

Elijah Muhummad established classes for women (The Muslim Girl's Training and General Civilization Class) and for men (The Fruit of Islam Class). These classes instructed men and women in proper conduct and respect for each other.

Family life was identified as the only proper Islamic life. Premarital and extramarital relations were strictly prohibited. Violation of this restriction was punishable by public exposure and temporary suspension from the Muslim community life. The community served as the primary source of enforcement for the strict marital code of the Nation of Islam. These prohibitions are not unlike those expounded by the Unification Church. The Church community serves as the vehicle for enforcement, much as the Islamic community did. The consequences of violation are not quite explicit in the literature of the Unification Church. Both groups see marriage and family life as a fundamental religious responsibility. Men and women are encouraged to observe these restrictions out of a direct obligation to God (Allah).

There is an additional element in the teachings of the Nation of Islam which stands in stark contrast to the position of the Unification Church. This relates to the issue of racial intermarriage. One objective of the Nation of Islam was not only the restitution of family life but the restitution of racial pride which had also been systematically destroyed during slavery and subsequent oppression of African-Americans. Elijah Muhammad, no doubt felt that self-love was fundamental. He observed:

> One of the gravest handicaps among the so-called Negroes is that there is no love for self, nor love for his or her own kind. This not having love for self is the root cause of hate (dislike), disunity, disagreement, quarrelling, betraying, stool pigeons and fighting and killing one another. How can you be loved, if you have not love for self? . . . Love yourself and your kind.[8]

As a result, his interpretation of intermarriage was as a device of self-rejection. Mr. Muhammad insistently suggested that:

> The white man does not want us to destroy their race by inter-marrying with them. They will even kill you to protect their women. Can you blame them? No, blame your foolish self for not having enough respect for your own self and your own nation to do likewise.[9]

Not unlike many staunch caucasian segregationists, Elijah Muham-mad equated integration with intermarriage:

> You educators, you Christian ministers should stop preaching integration. The most foolish thing an educator can do is to preach interracial marriage. It shows the white man you want to be white. . . . What are we going to integrate for? What do you want to marry a white woman for, when we are Black men? That is going to ruin our family. We will spot up our family. What does she want a black man for? Or what does the black man want the white one for?[10]

Mr. Muhammad clearly equated family destruction or destruction of the black man/woman relationship with destruction of the race. He said:

> Today, the white race, the black man's worst enemies, has planned to make a last try to destroy the black man by pretend-ing to be their friends and allow intermarriage. Many Ameri-cans (especially the Southerners) don't like the idea, but will finally be persuaded by their more learned men when they see no other way of making a final stroke at the black man.[11]

This concern about destruction of the race is also reflected in his admonitions regarding birth control. It is interesting to note that while Elijah Muhammad acknowledged the religious motive for the admonition, racial preservation was of foremost consideration. He observed that:

> Using the birth control law against production of human beings is a sin that Allah (God) is against and for which he will punish the guilty on the day of Judgment. Both the Bible and Holy Qur'an's teachings are against birth control . . . The motive behind these schemes is not designed to promote the welfare of black families, but to eliminate these families in the future.[12]

The selection of marriage partners is another area of contrast between the Nation of Islam and the Unification Church. Both groups clearly acknowledge that God (Allah) through his representative(s) is best qualified to make a wise choice of a marriage partner. Whereas this privilege is reserved for Rev. Moon himself (with occasional input from local officials) by the Unificationists, a more decentralized posture was taken by the followers of Elijah Muhammad. In the Nation of Islam, selection of marriage partners was strictly regulated by the local leader of the women's organization of the Temple (Mosque) who was referred to as M.G.T. (Muslim Girl's Training, etc.) Captain, and by the men's F.O.I. (Fruit of Islam) Captain in consultation with the Temple's minister. The selection was usually an individual choice, though approval by these officials was necessary in order for the marriage to occur. Occasionally, certain members were matched or encouraged to "talk" with each other by Temple officials. Marriage without such approval was prohibited by the community.

It is important to keep in mind that most of the procedures regulating marriage and the establishment of family life were altered with the death of Elijah Muhammad, the ascendancy of his son Waarith Deen Muhammad and the subsequent revamping of the Nation of Islam to the American Muslim Mission. As of 1975, all of the above procedures were rather radically modified with no diminution of the importance of family nor the Divinely prescribed basis for family life. Waarith Deen Muhammad, the son of Elijah Muhammad and current leader of the American Muslim Mission, has taken the homespun philosophy of his father's and placed it into a sound Islamic theology framework. W.D. Muhammad says:

> We say that God created male and female from a single being, and from the male and female spread many countless children. Human society starts when a man and a female come together, accept to live with each other, and decide to become one family to multiply themselves. According to the teachings of Islam, when two people come together to form a union, they come to each other as two halves, not as two wholes. The Holy Qur'an teaches us that the creation of the species began with a single being. That single being was made into two beings (male and female) to form the human family as we know it.[13]

This fundamental concept that family is established by Allah (God) and that the relationship between man and woman is an inalterable and axiomatic relationship serves as the foundation for the Islamic conception of family. The view of man and woman as separate halves (a reality validated by biology) is critical in understanding the correct match between male and female and the foundation of their relationship as being the growth of society and the human family as a whole.

The writer has been greatly influenced by Islamic ideas, the writings and lectures of Waarith Deen Muhammad. The fundamental hypothesis of this paper is rooted in basic Islamic thought. As W.D. Muhammad observes:

> Islam is a religion that is in accord with the natural life of the people. Simplicity is highlighted throughout the religion. When you understand the simple rules of nature, you see that Islam is not complicated.[14]

In fact Islam is referred to as the *din ul fitr* or the faith which is based on the order of nature.

Our point is that this fundamental alteration in how family life is viewed has had probably the most profound impact on improv-

ing the family life of its predominantly African-American membership. Muslim families in large urban centers where the pressures on family dissolution are maximal have thrived in much greater
proportions than comparable families. Again, as with Unification
followers, we attribute this to the view of family life contained in
the theology or worldview of the Muslim. As with Unification
theology, family life is viewed as Divinely inspired, inalterably
natural, potentially harmonious and the pathway for social and
personal development. The family unit is viewed as essential for
religious growth as well as for the flourishing of the Islamic
community. It is essentially this idea which ties together the
Unificationist, the members of the Nation of Islam and the members of the American Muslim Mission. Both Rev. Moon and Imam
W.D. Muhammad emphasize the religious foundation of family
more than did the Honorable Elijah Muhammad who acknowledged the religious function but clearly emphasized the tribal (or
racial) function of family. Certainly, the social situation and the
needs of African-Americans as well as other people have changed
considerably since the mid 1930s when Elijah Muhammad began
his teachings. Perhaps, it is because of Mr. Muhammad's emphasis
on racial pride for forty years that Rev. Moon and Imam Muhammad can present a meaningful raceless concept in the 1980s.

Waarith Deen Muhammad strongly objects to the ethnicizing of
the Islamic religion and takes exception to the tremendous racial
emphasis of his father. Instead he suggests that the principles and
practice of Al-Islam and strict adherence to Quranic injunction are
adequate for the establishment of strong family life while maintaining the early emphasis of his father that family life is the basis for a
good Islamic life.

An irony is that despite Elijah Muhammad's anti-establishment,
anti-Christian and pro-black conception of marriage and family
life, the vast majority of marriages were performed by sympathetic Christian ministers, justices of the peace or other public
officials, once the match had been approved by Temple officials.
Since the leadership of Imam W.D. Muhammad, the marriages
have been performed by Muslim Imams (ministers) who are li-

censed as official clergy in the areas where they live. Many couples married under the administration of Elijah Muhammad through the old procedures had remarriage ceremonies during the early years of W.D. Muhammad's administration. A similar detail of interest is that these ceremonies were originally performed only by W.D. Muhammad, and it was some time before people accepted the authority of other Imams to perform their marriages. As the Unification movement continues to grow, "The Blessing" which is currently reserved for Rev. Moon may be assigned to others, although this will initially generate some degree of distrust of the new procedure as occurred when W.D. Muhammad discontinued the practice and dispensed the responsibility of the local ministers (Imams).

Unlike the practice of the Unification movement, marriage partners are personally selected, but the selections are highly regulated by religious and social considerations. Muslims are highly encouraged to marry those who believe like themselves or those most closely related in belief (Christians). Again W.D. Muhammad observes:

> Both the male and female come from a family, so each of them has blood ties with the family that is very close to them. The Holy Qur'an says that these family ties, which are very dear and very precious in one's life, are to be respected and revered.[15]

Similar to the Unification concept of family, the shared focus on Allah (God) is the fundamental principle for family development.

> The Holy Qur'an tells us that "He that obeys God and His Apostle has already attained the highest achievement." Of all the saving powers that we have in our marriage, the best one is obedience to Allah and obedience to the instruction that we receive from the Holy Prophet.[16]

But as we observed above, the principles for the functioning of the marriage are found in Divine Instruction and in the laws of nature.

Conclusion

Family life is rapidly deteriorating in modern technologically developed, basically Western society. The consequence of this deterioration is far-reaching in terms of its impact on overall social organization and good human relationships. The argument has been put forth that one of the reasons for the difficulties faced by the modern family is the self-fulfilling prophecy of the -1imistic concepts of family life which are primarily coming out of social science theories. The concept of family as an alterable structure and the recent upsurge in efforts to identify alternatives to traditional family life have grown out of these misguided academic perspectives. Medical science's developments in discovering alternative methods for reproduction outside of the family structure and revisions in the societal ethical standards which legitimize such alternatives have created additional support for the need to modify the concept of family.

Such ambiguity about the nature and process of the family has created the atmosphere which feeds family dissolution. The hypothesis has been put forth that the family is a natural structure which is inalterable and unique in its function. It is described as fundamental for the development of the person, for the society as a whole and for human relations in general. The principles guiding family functioning are fairly clearly inferred from the functioning of the womb itself which is described as the prototype of family.

Efforts to restore the family have met with only sporadic success in the modern societal context. Two relatively successful examples are the work of the Unification movement and the American Muslim Mission. The elements held in common by these models are not dissimilar to the Islamically inspired model of the Natural Family developed in this discussion.

NOTES

1 W. Mondale, "Government policy, stress and the family," *Journal of Home Economics* (Nov. 1976), p. 12.

2 *Ibid.*, p. 12.

3 S. Helgsen, "Theoretical Families: Honor thy Children." *Harper's,* (Jan. 1982), p. 16.

4 S. Freud, "Civilization and Its Discontents," in *The Standard Edition*, vol. 21. (London: Hogarth Press, 1955), p. 113.

5 C.H. Kwak, *Outline of the Principle: Level 4* (New York: Holy Spirit Assn. for the Unif. of World Christianity, 1980), p. 24.

6 Elijah Muhammad, *Message to the Blackman* (Chicago: Muhammad Mosque of Islam No. 2, 1965), pp. 58-59.

7 *Ibid.*, p. 60.

8 *Ibid.*, pp. 32-33.

9 *Ibid.*, p. 60.

10 *Ibid.*, p. 319.

11 *Ibid.*, p. 107.

12 *Ibid.*, pp. 64-65.

13 Wallace D. Muhammad, *The Man and the Woman in Islam* (Chicago: Hon. Elijah Muhammad Mosque No. 2, 1976), p. 17.

14 *Ibid.*, p. 17.

15 *Ibid.*, p. 20.

16 *Ibid.*, p. 23.

REFERENCES

Akbar, Naim "Sanity for the African-American family." The Seventh Annual National Conference on the Black Family In America, Louisville, Kentucky, March 1980.

Freud, Sigmund. "Civilization and Its Discontents." In *The Standard Edition*. Vol. 21. London: Hogarth Press, 1955.

Helgsen, S. "Theoretical Families: Honor thy Children." *Harper's*, 264, no. 1580 (Jan. 1982).

Kwak, C.H., *Outline of the Principle: Level 4*. New York: Holy Spirit Assn. for the Unif. of World Christianity, 1980.

Mbiti, J. *African Religions and Philosophy*. New York: Anchor Books, 1970.

Mischel, W. *Introduction to Personality*. 3rd ed. New York: Holt, Rinehart & Winston, 1981.

Mondale, Walter. "Government Policy, Stress and the Family," *Journal of Home Economics*, Nov. 1976.

Muhammad, Elijah. *Message to the Blackman in America*. Chicago: Muhammad Mosque of Islam No. 2, 1965.

Muhammad, Wallace D. *The Man and the Woman in Islam*. Chicago: Hon. Elijah Muhammad Mosque No. 2, 1976.

Nobles, W. "Africanity: Its Role in Black Families." *The Black Scholar* 5, no. 9 (1974).

Three Models of Family: Marriage Encounter, Parenting for Peace and Justice, Blessed Family

Jane Zeni Flinn

The late twentieth century has been described as an era of unprecedented family breakdown. Observers have cited the rising rates of divorce, illegitimacy, and extramarital sex—a pattern that has been dubbed serial monogamy. Traditional roles of men and women have been challenged, and new, positive roles have been slow to replace them. Church attendance has fallen, along with the religious sanctions for traditional family values. The inevitable backlash has come in the form of the Moral Majority and the media evangelists appealing for a return to conservative Christianity and the nuclear family. Unfortunately, such prophets have offered a mishmash of platitudes rather than a coherent model for family life.

Christians face a real dilemma when it comes to the family. The Moral Majority notwithstanding, Christian theology has never granted a central role to the family. Roman Catholics may idealize the Holy Family, but a virgin mother, celibate foster father, and sinless son do not make a very helpful model for real family relationships. Protestants minimize the roles of Mary and the saints, but the result is an even weaker image of family—the exclusively male lineage of Jesus and God the Father.

Christians who are seriously committed to marriage and the family are searching for new models—practical, spiritual, human, supportive of women as well as men. Platitudes or distant ideals are not enough. To be of real use, a model must suggest a way of life for the family, articulated in some depth and detail. Such models do exist. Worldwide Marriage Encounter, the Parenting for Peace and Justice Network, and the Blessed Family in the Unification Church provide three different blueprints for family spirituality. All three are dedicated to human love within the home, family prayer, and social action in the world outside. It is not hard to see why these movements are attractive to families who have been looking for meaning and direction.

Marriage Encounter

Worldwide Marriage Encounter has reached more than a million couples in less than fifteen years. Introduced to the U.S. in 1967, and popularized by the writings of Fr. Chuck Gallagher (1975), ME's roots include the Spanish Cursillos and the Catholic Charismatic Renewal. ME appeals, however, to a much broader spectrum of Catholics than its origins would suggest. It has also produced offspring in other denominations—Episcopal (1971), United Church of Christ (1974), as well as Baptist, Methodist, Lutheran, and Seventh Day Adventist Encounters.

The ME message is spread during intensive weekends for couples held at retreat houses or motels. A donation of $100 or $200 per couple is typical, but the fees are voluntary; many ME couples donate child care for the weekend and double their contribution so that another couple can afford to attend. At a recent weekend in suburban St. Louis, most participants were twenty-five or thirty-five years old, ranging up to about sixty. There were factory workers, sales executives, homemakers, and doctors, along with a few academics and a few celibate clergy. Except for the clergy, everyone came in couples. Most people were active in their home parishes and often in the Pro-life and Charismatic movements as well.

ME sessions are led by a team of three encountered couples and a priest. Each team presentation is followed by a time for the couple to apply what they have learned through "dialoguing": husband and wife share their feelings in letters, which they then exchange, read, and discuss in private. Couples leave behind their televisions, telephones, watches, and the usual daily distractions. Yet time is highly structured—ten minutes to write, then a bell, ten minutes to dialogue, another bell, then back to the conference room for another session. The entire focus is on the couple; group sessions involve no public sharing except by the presenting team. Even socializing around the snack table and walks around the neighborhood are frowned upon, so a husband and wife have no alternative but to spend the better part of the weekend encountering each other.

The presenting teams model good communication, showing the new couples how to express feelings honestly and openly. They read aloud samples from their own dialogue letters on such themes as fear, work, God, trust, sex, children, death. They provide slogans ("Feelings are neither right nor wrong"; "Love is a decision") and guidelines for effective dialogue ("If you can substitute 'I think' for 'I feel,' it's not a feeling, it's a judgment"). They indirectly challenge traditional sex roles by asking, "When are you a 'married single'?" and telling how they became less isolated by sharing more of their work and play with their partners. Couples at an ME weekend learn by doing. They struggle to communicate, only to come up against their own masks and defenses. The theme of one session is "The Impossible Dream" from the Man of La Mancha; couples are urged to keep on trying, to believe in the dream of a marriage based on love and intimacy.

The stress is on sharing. One problem is that ME tends to ignore the complementary need for privacy, autonomy, the dignity of being allowed to cope with one's own problems. Along the same lines, Mary Vander Goot (1982) speaks of the need for "immersion" in a relationship, followed by "emergence" into a stage where independence is as treasured as intimacy. ME might do well to consider the process of emergence, and ways married people can help one another at this stage. On the other hand, each couple enjoys a great deal of privacy on the weekend. They need not discard their own value system or conform to anyone else's ideals in order to benefit from the ME tools of communication.

One of these tools is prayer. God is Love working in human relationships. So if a man and woman share their deepest selves, they will share their experiences of God. Couples are encouraged to pray together, and to dialogue on passages from scripture ("God's love letter to us") or on such questions as "How do I feel when I know you are God's gift to me?" The image of God in ME is traditionally Catholic. Yet the stress is on a very personal spirituality, a willingness to trust and share with God as with one's marriage partner. Several metaphors are used to express the ME ideal. Couples are told that the Sacrament of Matrimony is their special source of grace, their calling to become the Body of Christ: "Love one another as I have loved you." An encountered couple is compared to the Trinity— husband and wife united in the Spirit. The family itself is called the "Little Church"—one, holy, catholic, and apostolic—sharing love in the home, in prayer, in the church, and in the world community.

ME looks at social action indirectly, as a natural result of the sharing that starts in the family. Each ME weekend, following a prescribed format, starts with a session called "encounter with self." Then come sessions on "encounter with spouse," "openness to God's plan," "the sacrament of marriage," "matrimonial spirituality," and finally "sharing couple power." Thus the program creates a widening circle of relationships. A couple's love, acceptance, and faith provide the atmosphere that fosters healthy children. ME suggests that this same atmosphere can transform the church and the civil community. Wouldn't it be wonderful, the leaders suggest, if the whole world could be encountered? The ME theme song, "New World Somewhere," reflects this vision that links the person, the couple, the family, and the wider society through God's love.

The vision is just that—no attempt is made to spell out the economic and social changes that would be needed, or to look at the power of institutions to control or prevent change. The strength of ME is not in social action, but in the intensive training in communication. Yet it is not unreasonable to claim that children raised in an ME environment will gain the self-esteem and communication skills to cope effectively in the world outside the family.

ME is much more than a weekend experience. The key to a deeper, more intimate marriage is the practice of "daily dialogue." Couples are urged to set aside twenty minutes of "prime time" each day—ten minutes to write, ten minutes to share feelings. (Couples leave the weekend with a calendar and lists of dialogue questions in case they run out of topics.) In many parishes, ME "communities" meet bi-weekly for dialogue and support. If couples continue with the program, they tend to make changes in lifestyle. They may, for example, move beyond rigid husband-wife roles, beyond the separate worlds of the "married singles," by sharing household tasks and outside interests. They may work on their childraising practices. Older children may be included in "family dialogue" on house rules, love and prayer. The ME journal, *Worldwide Spirit,* devoted the September 1981 issue to conflict resolution, the use of dialogue to deal more openly and constructively with family problems. Encountered couples are urged to become active in parish and community work related to family values; to share the faith of their "Little Church;" to recruit new ME participants. For many, a marriage encounter weekend is both an emotional peak experience and the start of a new way of life.

Parenting for Peace and Justice

The Institute for Peace and Justice in St. Louis was founded in 1970 by James and Kathleen McGinnis. In 1980, the Institute developed a National Parenting for Peace and Justice Network to provide resources and workshops for families trying to "integrate social ministry and family ministry" (McGinnis, 1981: 3). NPPJN is now an ecumenical movement led by parent teams in more than twenty cities.

PPJ programs attract religious educators, social workers, academics, homemakers, and church leaders—both couples and singles. At a recent St. Louis workshop, most participants were in their thirties and forties, a few younger. The group was more homogeneous than ME, consisting largely of college educated people who had been active in the peace and civil rights movements of the sixties. They now wanted to build on these values in raising their own families.

A PPJ workshop may fill two and a half days of a single weekend, or seven evenings spread over as many weeks. Cost is about $35 per person, but fees are adjusted according to ability to pay. The group generally meets at a retreat house under the leadership of a couple trained in previous PPJ programs. Most sessions follow a lecture-discussion format, making the atmosphere more casual, less intense, than an ME weekend. Films, individual worksheets, and small group sharing help people analyze such problems as racism, sexism, violence, and poverty in the context of their own families and communities. The whole group then brainstorms more constructive approaches, which the team leaders record. For the evening meal, everyone is invited to the homes of host families, and out-of-towners may be overnight guests.

In contrast to Marriage Encounter's stress on the couple, the focus in a PPJ weekend is on the entire family. Parents are taught some of the skills of group leadership. They discuss ways to reduce conflict, listen to feelings, create an affirming atmosphere, and raise more responsible, caring children. The key to democratic process in the home is the family meeting where feelings can be aired and group decisions made. Participants role play a problem-solving session. They talk about how to prepare a meeting agenda, and when to let children take turns chairing.

PPJ helps parents analyze the hidden curriculum, the values and beliefs that underlie the ones they think they are teaching their children. The first theme is stewardship. How does our lifestyle confirm the materialism of the wider society? How can we challenge it? Participants share ideas for simplifying the family diet, budget, recreation, holidays, and energy use. They examine the influences of TV and advertising, and suggest ways they have taught their children to be critical viewers and consumers.

Next the group considers how non-violence can be taught through daily experience in the home. Fighting children, gun play, media violence, spanking, and the use of parental power—when families deal with these issues they are also dramatizing and teaching about the issues of war and peace. The emphasis is on helping children solve their own conflicts.

Finally, parents explore the possibility of a multicultural and nonsexist family life. They probe their own unstated stereotypes: Who does the laundry? Who pays the bills? Who stays home from work when a child is sick? And they look at the role models their children see: What color is the pediatrician? The teacher? The babysitter? What messages about race and sex do children pick up from their books, movies, and family recreation? Parents are challenged to change—gradually, one step at a time.

Prayer is stressed as the source of strength and unity in the PPJ family. "The divorce of spirituality from social action, or of faith from good works, has in the recent past produced both some burned-out activists and some navel-gazing contemplatives" (McGinnis, 1981: 113). Instead, children can experience the call from Jesus to work for peace and justice. Spontaneous family prayer is suggested at meals, at bedtime, at home liturgies, on camping trips. Here, the open democratic style of the family meeting spills over into family worship. God is described as beyond race and sex, yet close enough for a personal relationship with a child, working in history for peace, justice, and love. As in ME, the family is called the Body of Christ, a key metaphor suggesting that each member brings about the life and harmony of the whole.

PPJ spells out more directly than ME the roles of parents and children in the Body of Christ writ large, the global family. The leaders explain that even young children will care about social action provided the issues are made real to them: they need personal contact with victims of injustice, and a concrete role suited to their level of maturity. Members share experiences with volunteering at the Catholic Worker House, sponsoring children abroad, supporting self-help crafts centers, writing letters to government officials, boycotting products of certain companies.

Most of the suggestions are not new. In fact, they are much like the projects many PPJ adults worked on fifteen years ago as student activists. What is new about the program is that it translates social values into real family situations. Refusing a Nestle candy bar does more to raise a child's consciousness than to promote change in the company's marketing practices. The strength of PPJ—like ME—lies in its view of the family as an educational center for learning positive human values. The theme is expressed in the song, "Let there be peace on earth, and let it begin with me."

PPJ is too new to evaluate the long-term impact of the workshops. Participants take home a stock of ideas in the form of two books plus their own worksheets and notes. A quarterly newsletter alerts them to such issues as violence and sexism in toys, or Christmas without conspicuous consumption. Families are encouraged to promote the network by requesting speakers, films, and tapes for parish and school groups. In St. Louis the Institute for Peace and Justice is available for followup meetings; in other cities support groups and team leaders keep members in touch. But the structure most basic to PPJ seems to be the family meeting, where conflict resolution, prayer, and social action meet in the home.

Blessed Family

The Unification Church, led by Korean evangelist Sun Myung Moon, has gained members in every nation in the non-communist world. Rev. Moon's system is based on the Old and New Testaments, and spelled out in *Divine Principle* (1959—English edition, 1973). Unlike most Jews and Christians, Unificationists place marriage and the family at the very center of God's plan for the world. Marriages are arranged by Rev. Moon, and children that are born to these "blessed couples" have a special status in the church. The first 36 couples were married in 1961; today there are almost 3600 Blessed Families, some with children already old enough for marriage.

Becoming a Blessed Family is a good deal more complicated than getting into Marriage Encounter or Parenting for Peace and Justice. The Blessing, or wedding, takes place two or three years after a couple is matched (engaged). And to be eligible for matching, one must have been a member of the Unification Church in good standing for about three years, leading a disciplined life of celibacy, church service, and evangelism. The church recruits and trains converts through a variety of weekend, one week, and three week workshops. There is no cost for the training itself, but during the period of apprenticeship most American members must work full time for the movement, taking only a subsistence income. A 1976 survey revealed that most UC members come from middle-class families and had at least some college background. In their teens many experienced a loss of religious meaning, and a subsequent disillusionment with the counterculture and the peace and civil rights movements. Today they find in their church a new call to change the world (Judah, 1981: 1, 4-5).

The UC does not provide workshops specifically to prepare couples for the Blessing. There is, however, a pattern of implicit training. Each convert is guided by a "spiritual parent," and all church work is performed by teams led by designated "mother" and "father" figures. The system is intended to teach family roles as well as group cooperation. The growing "home church" movement exposes single members to couples who are actively living their church ministry and serving their community. Religious education materials such as the *Outline of the Principle* (1980) help to clarify the marriage relationships, spiritual life, and social action expected of Blessed Families.

Male and female are seen as complementary opposites, like the Oriental yin/yang or the anima/animus of C.G. Jung. Thus a husband and wife need one another for wholeness, to develop "heart." Parenting a Blessed Family is the highest goal of individual human life, the model for all other relationships. The system suggests the possibility of equal and flexible roles for men and women. In practice, however, the Blessed Family tends to have rather traditional sex roles, a reflection, perhaps, of the male-dominated Biblical and Oriental societies. There is also a tendency to reinforce the stereotypes of male (active, dominant, intellectual) and female (passive, receptive, physical), an issue debated both in the church and outside (Getz, 1982).

Far less traditional are the racial attitudes fostered in the Blessed Family. Rev. Moon deliberately brings together couples from diverse nations, races, religions, and social backgrounds. A multicultural family is prized as a microcosm of the world community of the future. Unfortunately, at present there is no formal preparation for the challenges of a multi-cultural lifestyle. Oriental and American Unificationists, for example, may assume very different norms for the behavior of "mothers," "fathers," and "children." Blessed couples have struggled to define these roles in a way that makes communication possible.

Childraising in the BF is a mission. Children are to be the forerunners of a new age, commited to justice, love, racial equality, church service, discipline, sexual morality, economic stewardship, and anti-communism. How these values are to be taught is rather vague. As the BF age and their children increase, it seems crucial that they map out their own patterns for socializing the next generation. They might, for example, adopt the ME dialogue to deepen communication within the couple, or the PPJ family meeting to translate social issues into everyday life experiences. They might look to successful multicultural families outside the church to raise their own consciousness of stereotypes and of ways to counter them. Parents can, for example, show their children how to cope with prejudice, ignore stares, answer questions simply, and accept themselves with a bit of humor (Flinn, 1981).

Most children are raised in nuclear families, but community child care is common since one or both parents may be called away for periods of missionary work lasting months or even years. These long separations contradict the stated ideal of Unificationist marriage. Although most BF accept such sacrifice as part of their calling, they may experience major tensions (see Barker, this volume).

Blessed couples see their role as establishing "God-centered families." Rev. and Mrs. Moon are described as the True Parents, the model for other Unificationists. A Blessed Family gathers each morning for prayer and a pledge of commitment. Spontaneous family prayer is encouraged as a way of relating to God with "heart" as well as with intellect. To the BF, God is not only heart and mind, but also male and female, the image of the ultimate parent. The key metaphor is the "Four Position Foundation"—God/Mother/Father/Children—which identifies the family with the very principle of creation. *Divine Principle* says, for example, that the BF recreates the Garden of Eden. Children are taught that God weeps over the sin and suffering in the world, and longs for them to build his Kingdom on earth.

Building the Kingdom of God requires concrete action. Witnessing, fundraising, recruiting church members, and religious education involve children as well as parents. Like PPJ—and more directly than ME—Blessed Families organize to promote change in the larger society. For example, church teams have been assigned to large scale missions witnessing on college campuses. Blessed Families have expressed their political views in rallies against communism or in favor of military defense. (It is interesting to note that God's will is linked to the political "right" in the BF and to the political "left" in the PPJ, although neither group can be neatly pigeonholed.)

The BF has less community support in the U.S. than in Japan or Korea, where the UC is stronger. Through a system of God-coupling, three families may be matched as a "trinity" which meets to pray, share experiences, and support one another. The Trinities are still more of an ideal than a reality in the U.S., and since prejudice against the UC can make other social life difficult, some Blessed Families experience a sense of isolation. The UC maintains a family life office with responsibilities ranging from religious education to marriage counselling. Former director Nora Spurgin, a social worker, also edits the *Blessing Quarterly,* a periodical with a circulation of about 1000. Blessed couples submit articles to the *Quarterly* sharing the challenges of missionary work, the pain of marital separations, and insights on childraising and family spirituality. In addition, the UC sponsors a wide range of ecumenical conferences, a few of them dealing with the family. In May 1981, five Unificationist couples spent a weekend with six couples from other faiths discussing marriage, children, religious education, and the theology of the family. Publications of such conferences give the Blessed Families a growing body of literature and contact with a wider community sharing similar goals.

Three Models

Marriage Encounter, Parenting for Peace and Justice, and the Blessed Family suggest new directions for the nuclear family. They show that the nuclear family need not be patriarchal, authoritarian, ingrown, materialistic, a mere reflection of the values of its society. In fact, they suggest that the family can be an effective source of change. The family can offer a critique of current values by providing a place where children can learn more peaceful, more loving, more spiritual, more socially committed ways of living.

All three models give practical help to people who want to change. They deal with problems of sex roles, prejudice, love, conflict, and communication in the home. They are based on a broader spiritual sense of family, and encourage parents and children to pray together. They see the family as the image of God and of God's work in the world, drawing members beyond their nuclear relationships to a sense of mission and social action. The term "global family" can be a gross oversimplification. But, its use can teach children that what they do at home is relevant to the problems they will face in the wider world. As Virginia Satir says,

> Troubled families make troubled people and thus contribute to crime, mental illness, alcoholism, drug abuse, poverty, alienated youth, political extremism, and many other social problems. . . .Everyone who holds a position of power or influence in the world was once an infant. How he uses his power or influence depends a good deal on what he learned in the family as he was growing up. If only we can help troubled families become nurturing—and nurturing ones even more nurturing—the impact of their increased humanity will filter out into government, education, business, religion, all the fields that determine the quality of our lives. (Satir, 1974: 18-19).

ME, PPJ, and BF bring quite different answers to the dilemma of the modern family. When viewed as educational structures, however, they show striking similarities. All three use the human resources model: a core group is trained, then immediately sent out to recruit and train new members. Unlike hierarchical churches and social institutions, these groups need not develop a class of highly trained leaders with a mass of weakly-committed followers. Modes of behavior are learned by doing—books and lectures may support but not replace the direct experience.

The human resources model is not new. It was used by St. Paul and other early missionaries to spread Christianity throughout the known world in less than a generation (Donovan, 1978). Today it is the model for a score of self-help programs beginning with Alcoholics Anonymous, and for such effective staff development programs as the National Writing Project. The human resources model makes possible rapid growth along with strong individual commitment. It is a style of education well suited to send God-centered families into a world community.

Today's couples cannot return to the models of the fifties, the thirties, or some imagined golden age. But they can learn ways to transform the nuclear family. They can look to the contemporary models of Marriage Encounter, Parenting for Peace and Justice, and the Blessed Family—and perhaps move on to create new forms.

	MARRIAGE ENCOUNTER	PARENTING FOR PEACE & JUSTICE	BLESSED FAMILY
ORIGIN	Spain: Cursillos U.S.: Charismatic movement Worldwide ME—1967 Roman Catholic, later groups in other churches	U.S.: peace/civil rights movements Institute for Peace & Justice (St. Louis, 1970) National PPJ Network—1981 Christian ecumenical	Korea: Rev. Sun Myung Moon Old & New Testaments plus *Divine Principle* (1959) 36 Blessed Couples—1960 Unification Church, members from many religious backgrounds
TRAINING	Intensive weekends—overnight Leaders = encountered couples + priest Cost = $100-$200 per couple Training focus = couple Process = husband & wife dialogue	Weekends (daytime) or series of evenings Leaders = PPJ trained couples Cost = $35 per person Training focus = family Process = lecture + small group discussion	3-5 years church activity Leaders = mother & father figures Matching by Father Moon No $ cost/fulltime church work Training focus = family Process = apprenticeship
MARRIAGE: **COUPLE**	Communication & intimacy	Communication & group leadership	Wholeness & recreation of True Parents
	Accept feelings Dialogue: possessions, sex, God, death, etc.	Accept feelings Develop awareness	Accept feelings Develop "heart" Multicultural couples
SEX ROLES	Flexible—shared activities	Consciously nonsexist	Male + female = complementary flexible/traditional
CHILDREN	Atmosphere of love, faith, openness, conflict resolution Family dialogue with teens Teach children by example + sharing	Values of stewardship, faith, love, multicultural/nonsexist living, conflict resolution Family meetings Teach children by example + group experience + discussion	Values of love, service, faith, sexual morality, stewardship, racial equality Shared mission Teach children by example + direct instruction

	MARRIAGE ENCOUNTER	PARENTING FOR PEACE & JUSTICE	BLESSED FAMILY
SPIRITUALITY:			
GOD	Traditional Catholic + personal God = love working in relationships	Christian + personal God = beyond race & sex God calls to peace, justice, love	Judaeo-Christian & *D. Principle* + personal God = Parent God = heart/mind, male/female God calls to create family & Kingdom
PRAYER	To live Sacrament of Matrimony Scripture = God's love letter Family prays together & with ME Community	To share Jesus's life Family prays together, plans home liturgies	To comfort God's heart Family prays together, makes morning pledge
METAPHOR	Family = Little Church = Body of Christ Trinity: husband/wife/God	Family = Body of Christ	Family = Garden of Eden Four Position Foundation: God/husband/wife/children
SOCIAL ACTION:			
FORMS	Parish family life programs Faith sharing Pro life movement Recreation, work, anything shared as a couple Stress = indirect	Church social action programs Pacifist & anti-nuclear movements Opposing racism & sexism Supporting victims of poverty & political oppression Social action shared as family Stress = direct	Evangelism Fundraising for church Opposing racism & communism Supporting military defense Mission shared as family Stress = direct
POLITICS	Open	Left	Right
METAPHOR	Big Church/New World Somewhere	Global Family	Kingdom of God
SUPPORT:	ME Communities *Worldwide Spirit* + local newsletters	Some local support group in NPPJN *PPJ Newsletter*	Some "trinities" of families *Blessing Quarterly* Ecumenical conferences & pubs.
RECRUITMENT:	Human resources model	Human resources model	Human resources model

Jane Zeni Flinn
University of Missouri—St. Louis
1982

REFERENCES

Barker, Eileen. "Doing Love: Tensions in the Ideal Family." In this volume.
  Divine Principle. New York: Holy Spirit Assn. for the Unif. of World Christianity, 1973.

Donovan, Vincent. *Christianity Rediscovered: An Epistle from the Masai.* Notre Dame, Ind.:
  Fides/Claretian, 1978.
  Flinn, Jane Zeni. "Many Cultures, One Family." *America,* Oct. 31, 1981, pp. 261-63.
  Gallagher, Fr. Chuck. *The Marriage Encounter: As I Have Loved You.* Garden City, N.Y.:
  Doubleday, 1975.

Getz, Lorine. "Hermeneutics of the Future: A Feminist Critique." In *Hermeneutics and
  Horizons: The Shape of the Future.* Ed. Frank K. Flinn. Barrytown, N.Y.: Unif. Theo. Seminary, distr. Rose of Sharon Press, 1982.

Judah, Stillson. "From Political Activism to Religious Participation: A Study of Conversion in Some American Youth Cults." *New ERA Newsletter,* 1, no. 3 (1981), 1, 4-5.

McGinnis, Joseph and Kathleen. *Parenting for Peace and Justice.* New York: Orbis Books,
  1981.

Outline of the Principle: Level 4. New York: Holy Spirit Assn. for the Unif. of World
  Christianity, 1980.

Satir, Virginia. *Peoplemaking.* Palo Alto, Calif.: Science and Behavior Books, 1974.

Spurgin, Hugh and Nora. "Blessed Marriage in the Unification Church." In this volume.

Vander Goot, Mary. *A Life Planning Guide for Women.* New York: Edwin Mellen, 1982.

FOR FURTHER INFORMATION

The Blessing Quarterly. c/o Holy Spirit Association for the Unification of World Christianity.
  4 West 43rd St., New York, NY 10036.

National Parenting for Peace and Justice Network Newsletter. c/o Institute for Peace and Justice.
  4144 Lindell #400, St. Louis, MO 63108.

Worldwide Family Spirit. 1097 Jefferson Ave., Akron, OH 44313.
  Worldwide Marriage Encounter Headquarters. 3711 Long Beach Blvd., Long Beach, CA
  90807.

Blessed Marriage in the Unification Church: Sacramental Ideals and Their Application to Daily Marital Life

Hugh and Nora Spurgin

Families today are in crisis, in part because for many marriage has become merely a secular contractual arrangement which can be terminated at will. In contrast, the Unification Church seeks to revive such traditional values as premarital chastity, fidelity, and parental heart, while simultaneously introducing some novel religious concepts and practices. Unification though affirms a moral code and belief system which stress both nuclear and extended families as a channel through which the spirit of God can work. The Movement highlights the spiritual depths of love, marriage, and parenthood. For Church members, God is experienced as a full and essential Partner in the give-and-take inherent within familial relationships.

The Blessing

What does it mean?

The doctrines of marriage and the family are fundamental to

Unification thought and lifestyle, and cannot be understood apart from their religious context. They are the central focus which unites the Church's ideal with everyday experience. In the Unification Church the most sacred rituals are the engagement and wedding ceremonies, referred to as "the Blessing." For the faithful, the Blessing connotes far more than a ceremony. It is one of the few Unification sacramental liturgies and includes practices similar in form to communion, baptism, penance, matrimony, and other traditional Christian sacraments. It is a moment of encounter with God, of rebirth. Ideally the Blessing provides us with moral assurance and spiritual benefits.

One does not automatically become spiritually mature. The ideal needs to be actualized experientially. Thus, the Blessing is said to be "conditional" (i.e., dependent upon human fulfillment). Blessed couples are those who have received the Blessing, including the responsibilities, commitments, opportunities, and promises implied. Blessed couples perceive themselves as in the process of becoming the "true" or ideal people that God desires. "Blessed" marriage is a special holy marriage through which one attains a new position before God. We will explain more about the theological meaning of this, but first let us mention our own introduction to the Unification Church.

Personal Experiences

In this paper we will give some personal experiences as a "Blessed" couple, as well as a general understanding of marriage in the Unification Church. We were married in 1970 in the wedding of 777 couples performed in Seoul, Korea, by Rev. Sun Myung Moon. We had joined the church independently of one another, almost four years earlier for Nora, and two years earlier for Hugh, and had both lived in the National Headquarters center in Washington, D.C., in the late 1960s.

Nora joined the Church while working on a master's degree in social work at New York University. Her interest in studying the extent to which religious systems change people's basic values (for a master's thesis) led her to two young women who were teaching the Divine Principle (Rev. Moon's teachings) which she studied and eventually decided to adopt. Upon graduation Nora moved to D.C. in order to work and train in the headquarters center and continued to work professionally as a therapist.

In 1968 Hugh obtained a master's degree in public administration from Syracuse University and went to Washington to work as a management analyst with the Department of Navy. One month after arriving in D.C. he met the Church. Agnostic and interested in politics, he was attracted to the answers the Divine Principle provided to his questions and the social breadth of the church's world view. (Nora taught him part of the Church's teachings.) Hugh continued to work for the U.S. government. Over the next two years both studied, taught, worked, witnessed, prayed and worshipped together.

In America the movement at that time was small and the feeling was somewhat like that of the early disciples of Jesus. There was a strong sense of purpose, of being "chosen" to help bring the kingdom of Heaven on earth. Our lifestyle was very simple. We worked at jobs to support ourselves and our spiritual efforts.

Later on we will share our personal experience of our matching, Blessing, and subsequent marriage. However, let us explain some of the ideological underpinnings of the faith, attitudes and practices which are so much a part of our lives.

The Theology of the Blessing

The Blessing is at the ethical and theological center of Unification lifestyle and thought. Ethically it is essential because the daily life, practices, and attitudes of Unification members, single as well as married, revolve around it. Single members look forward to the moment when they will receive the Blessing, thereby entering a new stage in their spiritual growth. They are eager for the arrival of the day when they will be wed, hopefully, to their ideal complement, an eternal spouse. From a Moonie perspective, although a single member works, fundraises, witnesses, studies, and preaches, those tasks are secondary to what is happening internally to prepare him or her for the Blessing. Presumably Blessed members are even more aware of both the benefits and the struggles inherent within the concept and experience of being Blessed, since the Blessing forms an integral part of their lives. To be a sacrificial, exemplary couple is neither easy nor trite.

Theologically the Blessing is central because marriage and the family are among the most basic of concepts within Unification thought and tradition. This statement is supported by an understanding of the following basic doctrines of the Unification Church: (a) God exists and is the origin and pattern for all human life, values, emotions, and institutions; (b) the internal and external traits of humans reflect the characteristics of God their creator; (c) God is the origin of the two genders, male and female. Though a man has elements of femininity, essentially he is a male; though a woman has elements of masculinity, essentially she is a female; (d) God's ideal since the beginning of time was for love, families, spouses, parents, children, and people in general to be "true people (according to their original nature),"[1] but because of the fall of man, such ideals have yet to be realized; (e) ultimately every person who is living, has ever lived, or will ever live, will eventually be able to become a true person able to love others and the creation with the same quality of love as God; (f) the central and most fundamental social institution is the family centered on God; God did not make the individual completely, emotionally self-sufficient; people need people; everyone needs someone to fully love and with whom to share; (g) though capable of reaching individual maturity alone, and thus able to achieve a certain degree of fulfillment, each person is designed to form a larger unit with his complement. To fully reflect God's nature (which is both masculine and feminine), and fulfill one's own emotional needs to a higher degree, there is a need to experience being a spouse and raising children; and (h) only with Christ's second coming and the beginning of a new age, can the eschatological hopes and goals discussed here be fully achieved.

Like all aspects of life, marriage and children are gifts from God. They are blessings that are possible only because God created and continues to sustain the world. According to the Biblical account in Genesis, marriage and progeny are God's second great blessing to Adam and Eve. In total there were three blessings given to them by God. The first blessing, to be fruitful, meant that each individual was to be responsible for perfecting his or her character by developing a relationship with God. The second blessing, to multiply and fill the earth, meant to achieve perfection on a social level, to create an ideal family and community. The third blessing, to have dominion over creation, indicated that all people should (on the foundation of the first two blessings) exercise a dominion of love over the natural world. The first blessing concerns individual maturity; the second, social development; and the third, ascendancy over creation. As part of the second blessing, the family occupies a central position between the other two blessings. It is a connecting link between the individual and the world.

Chosen Families

Adam and Eve—the Original Family

God did not intend Adam and Eve to marry, according to Rev. Moon, until they had become mature, until they could stand as true husband and wife. Otherwise they could never be true parents to their children. Adam and Eve were allowed the opportunity, and given the responsibility, to participate in creation of their own characters. They were to keep God's commandments, especially the commandment not to eat the fruit (interpreted by Rev. Moon to mean not to live a married life without an indication from God that they had reached the appropriate level of spiritual maturity). By remaining obedient, they would have become co-creators with God. If they had developed their own spirits, God would have taken it as a condition for their participating in the creation of the entire world. This would have then entitled them to dominion over the natural world.

Unfortunately, Adam and Eve had a premature, unprincipled sexual relationship. They failed to obtain God's approval. Their marriage was never blessed.[2] History has been, Unification thought teaches, a continual attempt by the Creator to find couples who meet spiritual requirements to be blessed. God's desire has always been to have an ideal couple on earth. He wants a couple who can show others the appropriate pattern of God-centered love and marriage needed to create an ideal family. Unfortunately most relationships are self-centered and less than loving. God's plan, then, would be for a Blessed couple and family, to serve as a nucleus, and to extend that paradigm to all those willing and able to meet the qualifications for a blessed marriage and family. Thus a new dispensational family would be established, centered upon the highest of spiritual ideals.

The Restored Family and its Messianic Role

As Unificationists, we believe that nearly 2,000 years ago, Jesus came as the Messiah to establish on earth an ideal family, community, nation, and world, which he called the kingdom of Heaven on earth. He was able to achieve complete perfection only on an individual level before being crucified. Humanity was not yet ready to accept the perfect love and truth which he brought. He achieved spiritual, but not physical, salvation. He was unable, at that time, to substantialize in the social order God's ideal for humanity. Such a realization awaits the second coming of Christ. Jesus was always single; he had no natural family which could serve as an example to others; he had no progeny; hence he could provide no example for husband-wife/parent-child relationships.[3]

After J-2, God continued preparing the world for that messianic family to which other families could be spiritually "grafted" and thus restored to God's original intention. For us, that time is now—and Rev. and Mrs. Moon are the central family through whom we as followers can find new meaning for marriage and family life.

Extending the Restored Family

As Unificationists we skip the current practice of romantic courtship, trusting choice of a spouse to our spiritual leader, Rev. Moon. We can say that a Unification Blessed marriage begins with the matching, and members consider it a privilege to be matched and subsequently Blessed, even though arranged marriages are foreign to much of contemporary culture.

Built into the faith of a member is a sincere trust in Rev. Moon as a vessel through whom Divine guidance is given. There is a great deal of idealism and high expectation among single members. Thus, we have confidence in the method and in the specific choice of the matching process. Nevertheless, emotions are very real and (regardless of the ideal) there is the reality of facing a real person complete with liabilities as well as assets, weaknesses in addition to strengths. This is the person one must decide whether to accept "for better or for worse," not only "until death do us part," but for eternity! Existentially it is a moment laden with great emotion. For some the path is simple and clear: acceptance is absolute. God's decision, as revealed through the founder of the Church, is their choice. They have no other personal preference. For others, there is great caution and consideration before the couple makes a decision to accept or reject the suggestion of Rev. Moon.

It is through a matching process in which Rev. Moon selects spouses that the marriages of most Unification couples are arranged. Occasionally there are recommendations by a major Church leader. Such was the case for us. In 1970, when we were matched, Rev. Moon was not in America, making our engagement somewhat different. The Korean missionaries working in America discussed potential candidates with Rev. Moon, then returned to America to talk with each individual about the matches they had discussed with Rev. Moon. Because the person Rev. Moon had suggested for Nora had left the Church, Nora was asked by Dr. Young Oon Kim if there was someone she would like Rev. Moon to consider. After prayerful consideration, she said Hugh. Recalling her reasoning, Nora declared, "I knew we were very different and he was younger than I, but I always felt good being around him and things always went well when we worked together. However, I had no idea how he felt about me as a wife rather than a co-worker. I was worried he would think I was too old for him." (Nora is six and a half years older than Hugh.)

Hugh recalls, "I was surprised when Dr. Kim asked me who I

would like to marry. Although I had often felt drawn toward Nora, I tried hard to focus on doing the work and will of God and not to have romantic feelings for her. However, because Dr. Kim asked my preference I told her Nora. Though we had never talked about it, I thought it was a great match. I called her to let her know I also had talked with Dr. Kim, and was baffled when she hesitated about getting married. When I told her I'd always cared about her even though I had never revealed it, she immediately changed and became excited about going to Korea for the wedding." Nora later said she was worried Dr. Kim would pressure Hugh and wanted to know what he really felt. Our pictures were sent to Rev. Moon who then approved the match. In more recent engagements, Rev. Moon has been personally present, choosing men and women who then consulted privately with each other, returning to give their acceptance or rejection of the match. But in those early days, he only came to America for brief visits.

The Ceremonies

After the matching, a holy wine ceremony is conducted to formalize the engagement. Externally, it may resemble a eucharistic service, but it has a different meaning. During that ceremony, we believe, new life is given by God through Rev. and Mrs. Moon to each couple. At that point the commitment is binding and eternal. Through the taking of the wine and participation in the ceremony, sins are forgiven and rebirth occurs. The couple is then offered to God as newly recreated beings, pure and free of past sins. In the same position, theoretically, as the newly created Adam and Eve (i.e., undefiled by original sin), they become a replacement before God for their "fallen" ancestors. Part of a new spiritual lineage, they have the potential to become parents of offspring freed from sins of the past. The taking of the wine is a symbol of new life flowing into the body. Externally the couple is recognized as a married couple, internally they are viewed as new citizens of the kingdom of God.

For the wine ceremony to be efficacious, several elements are needed: a mediator, holy wine, and an eligible couple. As mediators, between God and man, Rev. and Mrs. Moon are believed to bring the blessing of forgiveness to fallen people and lift them up in the sight of God so that they can be accepted as new citizens in the kingdom. One might liken it to receiving citizenship in a nation which is not one's native land. The holy wine is a symbol of new life. The newly engaged couple stand in the position to restore God's lost children; from their descendants a new order of heavenly children will populate the world.

The final step in transmission of the Blessing is the public wedding. Though externally resembling other services, there are elements which are different. A distinguishing feature is its size; usually a large number of couples are married simultaneously. Although some individuals have been wed in small, private ceremonies, most Unificationists were married *en masse*. Since their paradigmatic marriage in 1960, Rev. and Mrs. Moon have officiated at many weddings, including eight mass weddings: 36 couples in 1961, 72 couples in 1961, 124 in 1963, 430 in 1968, 777 in 1970, 1800 in 1975, and 2075 and 5,837 in 1982. (In addition, there were small, private weddings, including Blessings in America of 35 couples in 1976 and of 74 in 1977.)

With the Blessing ceremony, Unification couples are married, ready to begin the responsibilities of married life and parenthood. However, there is one more specific requirement before family life begins. To make a spiritual foundation for the family, a 40-day period of sexual abstinence is observed before consummating the marriage. This is a period of prayer and preparation. Since the wedding is a mass wedding (not individualized according to personal situations) depending on each couple's situation there may be even longer periods of separation before the couple is ready to begin the marriage. For instance, couples may be asked to complete a certain mission or meet some spiritual requirement before starting a family.

The Making of a Unification Marriage

Attitudes toward Marriage

As Blessed couples we believe that a perfect marriage is made, rather than found; a perfect spouse grows, rather than appears. As single people, we are taught that it is one's spiritual responsibility to "perfect oneself" while on earth, where opportunity is provided for the working out of kinks, irregularities, and "less than desirable traits" in one's personality. Perfection is viewed as the maturing and fulfilling of one's potential, and should not be confused with robot-like sameness. Single members with idiosyncrasies and personality difficulties are often advised to work out their problems prior to marriage, since problems may intensify in the intimacy and constancy of the marital relationship. In fact, group and communal-style living is believed helpful in polishing off rough edges and in expanding one's ability to love, thus preparing the single person for potentially successful marriage.

Beyond the sacramental value of the Blessing, married life is considered a further opportunity to perfect oneself. Whereas a solitary person can keep greater distance between himself and others (able to hide his real self and problems), a spouse and parent is constantly challenged to grow and change. To many Church members this is a challenge sought and valued. Marriage is approached and nourished in the Unification Church in the above context, thus making it a part of a couple's spiritual responsibility in life to work out a good relationship, coming before God together as a new creation which transcends the sum total of the two individuals.

One may ask what makes Unification marriages different, apart from the arrangement and the scale of the wedding. We would be foolish to imply that there are no problems—Unification couples are real people. Coming from all sorts of backgrounds and experiences, our common faith is a great source of strength, yet we also go through crises and tests of faith, and couples sometimes feel they have irreconcilable differences. Practically speaking, we have the same struggles other couples have—personality conflicts, financial problems, child-rearing problems, etc.

A New Value System

Although our day-to-day married life may look very similar to that of others, from our training in the Divine Principle we have gained several valuable elements.

One attitude learned is the value of fidelity. Spiritual meaning is given to the maintenance of faithfulness; therefore, a trusting relationship usually can exist. A blessed wife of eleven years, Anne Edwards, gives this advice: "Be faithful. Be determined to be committed to God, the True Parents, and your mate forever. He or she will feel this and reward you with gratitude and a similar fidelity. Once you make this commitment with mind and heart, you are free. With the secure center of commitment and fidelity, we can go anywhere in the garden of marriage without fear of loss."[4] This fidelity is essential for the spiritual and emotional growth of the children as well.

Secondly, our common faith gives strength and meaning to everything the Unification family is and does. Parents and children have a framework around which to judge right from wrong, and into which fit the pieces of life into a larger perspective. We develop our own Sunday School curriculum and give our children religious training which we hope will help them to understand the beauty and mystery of the spiritual side of life, as well as give them a well-rounded sense of who they are, and a practical guide for living a life of goodness and success. Our experience has been that children are very naturally religious and understand theological concepts far better than one would anticipate. We were surprised to overhear our four and five year old children discussing whether God is inside or outside the world and asking whether God had a Mommy and a Daddy.

Thirdly, as Unificationists, we have been taught not to fear struggle. The difficulties in life are there to be overcome—not avoided. Problems in marriage are viewed as presenting a challenge for growth. Rev. Moon often stresses learning to embrace an ever-widening circle of people. To be able to love ever more deeply is considered one of the greatest goals in life. It is with this attitude that many couples enter into interracial, intercultural marriages.

Rev. Moon once said that a black mother looking into her child's blue eyes cannot help lose feelings of racial resentment.

Fourthly, there is the support of others who share the same belief system. In the Church we have a tradition of trinities of couples. Although not yet well developed in America, the ideal is that three couples care for each other in such a way that they will be willing to live as an extended family—taking responsibility to help one another in time of need, praying together, and raising children in the enriched atmosphere of a large number of role-models. Korean couples who have employed this system tell of the moral, financial, and emotional support they have received from other families of their trinity at such a time as the death of a spouse. Japanese couples explain how they share apartment buildings and work out cooperative baby-sitting arrangements. In all situations, the three couples serve each other so that all can make some contribution to the larger mission.

Until recently, many of the couples in America have continued to be part of the center life, living communually and often serving in a capacity of house-parents to single members. However, with the recent Blessing of many more couples, many are moving into homes and apartments and becoming vital parts of the community. This new providential era of home church[5] will probably change the structure and methods of the church, as well as its image. In one sense, the church will be far less visible. Rev. Moon has often said that his desire is not to build big churches—or even a new church at all—but to bring truth and rebirth to humanity—no matter what the external structure.

The Demands of a Family

The lifestyle of Unification members in America has been primarily a communal, celibate style seemingly more appropriate for young, single members. With the introduction of a small number of Blessed marriages (only twenty couples in the U.S. until 1975) to the Church commmunity, couples often served as leaders or parent figures to the "Family" of single members congregated in a local center—a role which recognized and allowed for the nuclear family to exist and grow within the core lifestyle of the Church. The role had dignity and provided a means of support for the family in the midst of the larger extended Family. However, as new, larger groups of couples joined the ranks and began to have children, the Church had also begun broadening and differentiating, and this earlier role could not easily be applied. For instance, a larger number of couples in a center must have the opportunity to grow and expand their nuclear families; they can no longer fit the style of the single members.

The increase in the number of couples and in the size of their families, compounded by the growth of Church business enter-prises and other activities, is in the process of changing the lifestyle. For some this change has not been easily made. Couples have found themselves concerned with caring for and supporting a growing family, while simultaneously in the midst of a transition in their occupational role as Unification leaders or members. The life of faith is no longer the simple total involvement and communal life-style that was possible for single people. Sometimes the heart is torn between one's love for one's spouse and children and the sacrifices made in the religious life. This is the painful experience of many Unification parents who have gone to the mission field to do evangelical work (for months or even years), leaving their dear ones in the care of others. Some, with absolute faith, have made many sacrifices for the sake of God's Providence, including tempo-rarily working apart from spouses and children. However, for others, the desire to provide the best of everything in a material sense may introduce a new conflict into a seemingly absolute faith. This, we feel, is one of the areas of greatest potential conflict for Unification couples.[6] It is not easy to maintain the same level of commitment after being married. Many Unification couples have done so, but not without much personal and familial sacrifice.

The Interim Ethic: the Process of Restoration

At this point it seems appropriate to express something about the difference between our ideals and everyday reality. Most Unification members are idealistic people; therefore, every discrepancy between ideal and practice is painful, and is difficult to explain without an in-depth study of the role that *restoration* plays in the Divine Principle. This aspect of our belief system is among the most misunderstood in sociological circles. We will use an hourglass diagram in our explanation.

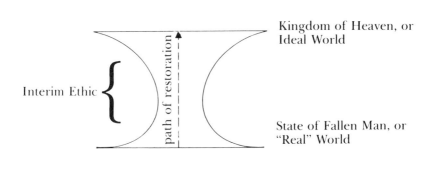

From a sociological point of view, it is easy to observe the two broadest parts of the hourglass. The "real world" is the world as we know it. It is composed of contemporary social institutions, personality theories, even religions. The "ideal world" (at the top of the hourglass) is the world we are striving to attain. It is the ideal taught in the Divine Principle. The core of this world is the God-centered family, out of which a God-centered society with God-centered institution is envisioned to grow. How do we get from the bottom of the hourglass to the top? By the path of Restoration! It is deeply religious and requires faith and sacrifice. It necessitates a self-denying interim ethic. In the narrow opening of the hourglass lies the re-birth experience—the stripping down of the trappings of the old world, the shedding of everything which, though good in itself, may hinder the process. One could liken it to the Biblical reference to a "camel going through the eye of a needle."

Unlike a single born-again experience, we see marriage (indeed, the religious life in general) as a lifetime process which begins when a person first hears the Divine Principle and joins the church. Often the life seems spartan to others; certainly it is sacrificial. But there is also the gradual rebuilding of a fuller life. In the ideal world— the kingdom of heaven—we believe that all institutions and levels of society, as well the individual, will be restored. Until that time we are in the process of becoming restored. We believe that as more individuals are restored, the path broadens and individual maturation becomes shorter and easier.

For the early Blessed couples it was painful to pioneer the path. We made, and still make, many personal and collective sacrifices. Careers, ties with parents and friends, time with children, ambition, wealth, and leisure are often sacrificed. Our lives are not our own, but are viewed as being for the sake of others, which requires broadening the path—with the hope that the Kingdom can come in the next generation. Our tears, and the tears of our children, are the most precious gift we can offer humanity. For us the deepest pain comes, not in the making of the offering, but in being misunderstood. Knowing the ideal for which we are striving makes every deviation from that more intense. We are not zombies without feeling, nor do we lack desire, at times, for easier ways of life. But, we believe that we are paying a redemptive price for humankind which will allow God a working base from which to bring the Kingdom of Heaven on earth.

Conclusion

One point that stands out is the strong emphasis in the Unification Church on faith and spirituality. It is something which transcends, but is present in, daily human relationships. The challenges of life are given meaning and are experienced from the perspective of one's total life of faith as growth-producing. We, as a couple, have chosen this course for ourselves and our family because we believe that we are living at a turning point in history. We believe that because of God's blessing, our children are born into this new providential era and a new lineage. Unlike us, they are free from original sin and the need to go through such a difficult restoration process. Of course, they also are responsible for their own spiritual growth and are affected by the influences (both good and evil) of their environment.

Our desire to have the optimum situation in which to raise our children, and at the same time participate in the restoration, is often a source of tension and conflict. It is here that couples sometimes face a crisis of faith and marital conflict. A personal example would be fitting here. We discussed our answers to a questionaire Nora had prepared for Unification couples. One question dealt with the tension between commitment to one's family and commitment to the Church which is the foundation of that marriage and family.[7] One possible response read: "In a situation where my spouse is having a struggle of faith, I would continue my commitment to the church even though my spouse could not continue in the church." Nora was somewhat surprised that (as a third choice) Hugh chose this doctrinal answer, rather than another response which stated: "Our marriage and family ties are very strong, and if in conflict with church responsibilities, we have chosen or would choose to protect the family bond and have a less demanding relationship with the church." Hugh was surprised that Nora, if faced with no alternative but a choice between him and the Church would choose to stay with him in order to keep the family intact, even if it meant externally leaving the Church community. Of course, the question is hypothetical; neither knows what his or her choice would be if such a situation were to arise. Fortunately, although some tension is always present between these two priorities, few couples have been faced with such an extreme choice. Based on our contact with other couples, we feel that most of them strongly value their family, as we do, and would go to great lengths to keep it intact. Our responses may reflect the tendency for each individual to apply in his own way the two great commandments, to love God with all one's heart and to love one's neighbor (especially one's children and spouse) as oneself. These are the marriage of the vertical and horizontal; the two are inseparable.

NOTES

1 "True" is a favorite word of Unificationists. In this context it means to be ideal, perfect and mature.

2 Sex is not itself sinful, since God intended man and woman to procreate, but only within the confines of a God-centered and sanctioned, marital relationship.

3 He had no bride who could represent (in addition to his mother) the feminine aspects of the Creator.

4 Anne Edwards, "Marriage, some practical concepts," *The Blessing Quarterly,* Vol. 1, no. 2. (Summer 1977): 61.

5 "Home church" is the name given to the concept of making one's home in the community a central, spiritual hub.

6 It might also be noted that some other religious communities have avoided this problem by banning marriage and remaining celibate.

7 The question and possible responses were as follows: Blessed marriage and families are a fundamental and external bond of great spiritual significance, according to the Divine Principle. Also, our affiliation with, and contribution to the church, are of great spiritual value. These two commitments are not always equal in strength. Please check the phrase or phrases which best describe your feelings. If you check several, rate them 1, 2, 3, etc.

☐We are confident and secure in our marriage and are willing to make the sacrifices which may be required for the higher purpose.

☐Our marriage and family ties are very strong, and if in conflict with church responsibilities, we have chosen or would choose to protect the family bond and have a less demanding relationship with the church.

☐When conflicts come up between church commitment and my family, I usually choose or would choose to sacrifice my family even though my spouse would find this very difficult to live with.

☐In a situation where my spouse is having a struggle of faith, I would continue my commitment to the church even though my spouse could not continue in the church.

Celibacy, Virtue, and the Practice of True Family in the Unification Church

Tom Walsh

In the recent work entitled *After Virtue,* Alasdair MacIntyre argues that in order for the concept of virtue to be intelligible there is required "some prior account of certain features of social and moral life in terms of which it has to be defined and explained."[1] For MacIntyre the idea of virtue is meaningful only when understood in terms of some social project, as, for example, one can best understand Aristotelian virtue theory only when there is some acquaintance with the community ideal of the *polis* and its project. In this sense the *Nicomachean Ethics* and the *Politics* are correlative, with the virtues functioning as meaningful within a particular political and social context. MacIntyre's argument, however, is not simply that sociology must precede moral philosophy or virtue theory. But rather, as I interpret him, that if we are to understand and, moreover, to formulate a theory of virtue, then we must attend first to those features of social and moral existence which allow certain virtues to take on meaning. In particular, for MacIntyre, these features include the notion of "practices," the notion of the narrative character of human and social existence, and finally the idea of a tradition.[2]

As I understand the nature of moral action, its distinction lies in its being purposive action directed toward some moral end or good, even when that moral good is understood as merely one's duty. In this sense I would assert that moral action is both intentional and teleological in character. Hence it follows that if one would enquire, for example, as to why the Moonies participate in arranged marriages or why they strive to live chastely prior to marriage, that some intelligible answer would be forthcoming; that is, if we assume the action to be moral, and not merely a kind of religious behavior. Now the answer that one receives may be far from persuasive, but nevertheless that answer should give an account which illuminates what is meant by, or internal to, the action.

This essay has as its project to interpret the way in which Moonies might, or perhaps should, understand and explain their own celibate action during the period prior to marriage. Following H. Richard Niebuhr's simple but now classic phrase, I shall be exploring the question, "What is going on?"[3] In approaching this exercise in interpretation I will, as has already been indicated, rely in significant ways on the insights into virtue theory afforded by MacIntyre. In fact his analysis of the "features of social and moral life" which render action in the context of virtues intelligible provides the framework for the design of this paper. As such I will employ the following format: An initial section will concern itself with the relationship between virtues, why Moonies see their celibacy as a *sine qua non* in regard to virtue, and what MacIntyre calls a "practice." I will attempt to show that the Moonie's "perfection of character" project, of which celibacy is a vital part, is a period for training in the virtues and predispositions which are correlative to and prerequisites for the "practice" of establishing a "true family."[4] Section two interprets celibacy, virtue, and the "true family practice" in terms of the narrative character of life histories as well as in terms of the story-formed character of communities. A third section will then attend to the relationship between virtues and a tradition, arguing that Unification seeks to train its members in the virtues appropriate not only to the construction of a "true family" but of a social world as well.

As should be obvious by now it shall be my argument that Unification lifestyle, and particularly its practice of premarital celibacy, is best understood in the context of virtue theory—albeit this tradition of thought, as MacIntyre points out, has enjoyed little popularity in modern times. And yet if indeed the new religious movements, and Unification in particular, represent anti-modern or even post-modern innovations, or in this case retrievals, then perhaps they are not best understood by employing modernist principles of interpretation. On the contrary, while the "rule of Unificationism" may differ in significant ways from the "rule" of the Athenian *polis* or the "rule of St. Benedict,"[5] there are nonetheless striking affinities. Certainly more similarities than one finds when sizing up Unificationism according to the standards of liberal individualism or Marxist collectivisms. I do not wish to argue that Unification is the rule of St. Benedict that will guide us through the "dark ages" of modernity, but, more modestly that while in many ways Unification has been an offense to the modern consciousness this may not necessarily be to its discredit.

To close this introduction let me also say that I do not presume to imply, much less argue, that all Moonies are virtuous. Nor do I wish to claim that the "oughts" pointed to in this essay are descriptive of the historical Unification community. It is my intention rather to portray the normative framework in accordance with which celibacy could be said to make sense, and why it might be a compelling option for some.

Celibacy, the "Perfection of Character" and the "Practice" of True Family

Allow me to begin this discussion with MacIntyre's lengthy and rather complex definition of a "practice,"

> By a 'practice' I am going to mean any coherent and complex form of socially established cooperative human activity through which goods internal to that form of activity are realized in the course of trying to achieve those standards of excellence which are appropriate to, and partially definitive of, that form of activity, with the result that human powers to achieve

> excellence, and conceptions of the ends and goods involved,
> are systematically extended.[6]

Perhaps an example will help clarify and unpack what MacIntyre means to tell us:

> In the ancient and medieval worlds the creation and sustaining of human communities—of households, cities, and nations—is generally taken to be a practice in the sense in which I have defined it.[7]

As I understand it a practice is a socially shared task which is something like a project. It is practical and constructive, but does not aim primarily at the acquisition of external or merely utilitarian goods. The practitioner, in turn, must comply with certain "standards of excellence and obedience to rules," the telos of which would be "goods internal to that form of activity." A practice is not merely some assortment of technical skills; the qualify of character in this sense is, in rank of importance, prior to skill.

As I interpret MacIntyre the virtues may be understood as just "those standards of excellence which are appropriate to, and partially definitive of" the practice. The virtues in effect constitute the possibility for, and indeed hold together, the social practice. In this same sense virtues are the standards of excellence, particularly as seen in terms of the standards which are to typify the character of practitioners, which prevent a practice from corrupting from within. In sum, while virtues are correlative to a distinctly envisioned social project or practice, i.e., they are derived from the idea of the practice and from the idea of the kind of individuals such a practice requires, these same virtues determine the quality and character of that community practice. Be reminded once again of the interrelation between Aristotle's *Ethics* and his *Politics*.

If I have expressed MacIntyre's position adequately, then it should be clear that it is in terms of the practice that the virtues become meaningful and virtuous action intelligible. The virtues are not derived arbitrarily but emerge logically as the *sine qua non* for the constitution of and participation in a practice.

Within Unification, I would assert, the task of establishing a "true family" is a kind of practice. The virtues appropriate to this task are to be cultivated during a period of what might be referred to as premarital apprenticeship, during which time one strives for "perfection of character." As a part of the "rule" or discipline for this course members are strictly enjoined to live chastely—engaging in no sexual relationships.

In a recent edition of the *Outline of the Principle: Level Four* it is stated that, "God's first blessing is man's ability to perfect his character." This person of perfected character is able "to share God's feelings as his own."[9] The function of celibacy in this spiritual quest is designed to prevent any lapse into sexual fixations or preoccupations, actions would would represent a detour from the path to spiritual maturity. In this sense celibacy functions, ideally, not as a repression of natural urges, but as sublimation. One foregoes certain indulgences in order that other facets, indeed virtues, of one's character may be shaped; with character being understood as that part of the self which is shapable.

From this perspective it could be rightly said that celibacy functions as a basis for a kind of self-realization. By this I mean that, according to Unification reasoning, it is only by giving one's undivided love and attention to God and to the service of humanity— and this entails at least for a time a postponement of sexual relationships, which for the Moonies equals postponement of marriage—that one can develop the virtues upon which the practice of true family depends. Of course, I am not arguing that celibacy is the virtue upon which true family depends; but rather, as Young Oon Kim states in *Unification Theology:*

> Without first perfecting one's love of God, true affection, concern for, and union with another human being is almost impossible, as the marital problems of our age clearly demonstrate.[10]

A quote from Herbert Richardson amplifies this point,

> The deepest insight from theology, I believe, is that men are created for communion with God and the universality of being, but that they cannot attain to this communion until they have

> overcome their narcissistic love of self . . . and are able to love
> all persons equally and fully. To overcome narcissistic love,
> the disciplines of virginity and celibacy have been, and will
> continue to be, essentially spiritual disciplines.[11]

Unification celibacy may be understood in this light as a discipline with a telos, what Kim has called "perfecting one's love of God." The discipline is designed neither to condition the self into a posture of disrespect for the body and its urges nor to foster a denigration-of-sex mentality. Rather it functions to constitute within the self a power that allows one not only to appreciate transcendental values but to fulfill transcendental *needs*. Celibacy, then, implies a recognition of a certain hierarchy of interrelated values and needs, a hierarchy whose apex and unifying thread is, for the Moonie, the "God-centered" love. To state this in Aristotelian terms one could say that celibacy operates positively towards the attainment of the *mean* of this God-centered love—mean being understood here not as a compromise between, or derivation from, certain vices, but as an ideal, one in terms of which vice may be viewed as a compromise or distortion—whose correlative vices would be either a self-centered love (merely concupiscence) or an other-worldly denigration of bodily existence. For the Moonie celibacy is an activity central to the pursuit and actualization of that mean.

Now I have thus far portrayed the Unification ethic of celibacy as a kind of eudaemonism. In many respects this is an adequate understanding, i.e., celibacy is practiced for the sake of some greater, long-run happiness. However, I would be remiss in my description of the Unification self-understanding if I failed to mention another dimension to the function of celibacy, that is, its relational or "heartistic" dimension. In short, celibacy also functions as an experience which opens the way for an understanding of what *Divine Principle* views as the broken-heartedness of God. In other words, through the course of celibacy, where one is to forego relationships which are sexually and interpersonally intimate, since the actual practice of family is deferred, one experiences often a sense of loneliness. According to Unification teaching, God, since the fall of his children, has been a miserable and lonely God, one who above all longs for true family. The God understood by the *Divine Principle* is not unlike the portrayal given in the book of *Hosea,* namely a God whose people have been led away by a "spirit of harlotry" (Hosea 4:2), and who laments. God's true family ideal was broken and betrayed by the Fall. Since then God in some sense languishes for a day of true family. It is to this heart, the broken heart of God, that Moonies look to understand in the course of their celibacy.

I have to this point tried to show that if the Unificationist's "true family" project is a practice, as defined by MacIntyre, then the period of premarital celibacy may be understood as a time devoted to the acquisition of virtues appropriate to the practice. While I have not delineated these virtues in any systematic fashion, and do not intend to do so in this context, they may be said to reduce generally to three types, namely the acquired moral virtues, pertaining to the management of the passions, the familial virtues of loyalty, filial piety, and obedience, and finally the theological virtues, namely, faith, attendance (service to God) and heart. Of these three types of virtues the so-called "theological" virtues are the most central. All however are interrelated and should come to manifest themselves in the person of perfected character, and all are constitutive qualities of anyone seeking to construct a true family. Given this understanding of the interrelatedness of the virtues, and given my analysis of celibacy as being an exercise related to a Unificationist's perfection of character project, I am disinclined to correlate the act of celibacy with any one of these virtues. Nevertheless, the most obvious candidate is the correlation between the discipline of celibacy and the moral virtue classically referred to as temperance, i.e., the control of concupiscence or lust. So at this point I would like to locate this virtue within its classical historical context.

As I understand the tradition of virtue theory, the two premier exponents are Aristotle and Thomas Aquinas. Of central importance to this tradition is the notion, as Stanley Hauerwas states it, that "an agent's being is prior to doing."[12] By this I mean to suggest that character, which is grounded in being or potentiality, is shapable. The shaping of the character is related to two factors which any theory of character must take into account. They are institutions and agency. By the first I mean to suggest that character is in many ways shaped by the nature of the institutions in the context of which an actor develops. We are, so to speak, thrown into a social world with an already existing culture; we are born into a family, a religion, a class, a race, etc. Given this feature of the human condition, any viable theory of virtue requires some theory of institutions which recognizes the social nature of the self. Again we are instructed by Aristotle's judicious treatment of virtues in the context of the household and the polis.

The other component to a theory of virtue is the theory of agency. Whereas a theory of institutions places emphasis on the social conditions which effect the emergence of selves as characters, and as such reminds us of the ways in which character is *shaped by* particular social contexts, the theory of agency stresses the autonomy of the actor, viz., the capacity for action. In many respects a theory of agency is more directly related to a theory of virtue. And by this I only mean to suggest that virtue theory, as I see it, understands that human acts are, so to speak, owned by the actor. And these acts are the episodes which accrue toward the construction of the character of a distinct self. One becomes what one is, i.e., one's character, by making decisions to act. Acts in this sense are self-shaping as well as world-shaping. Acts are practical; they modify what already is. In this way character is constructed by acts committed, according to distinct intentions, over time.

Aristotle describes agency in terms of efficient causation, such that "the moving principle is in the agent himself."[13] If one's act is the result of either ignorance or coercion then one's act is not distinctly moral, and not that of an agent per se. In other words the meaningfulness of a theory of virtue as it involves a theory of agency, requires a theory of freedom. As such freedom itself is not fully given with being, but rather is something that one acquires or enhances. For example, to be positively free to deliberate and act as a moral agent, one must have the capacity to employ one's rational capacities without their being unduly conditioned by sensuous interest, i.e., without their being determined and hence unfree. Freedom, conceived in the tradition of virtue theory, is dialectically related to virtue itself. That is, on one hand, freedom makes acts of choice possible; but as virtue is cultivated and particularly as the merely physical instincts are managed, one's freedom is enhanced. One goes from negative freedom, i.e., the capacity to will only as one desires, to positive freedom, i.e., the capacity to deliberate and choose a good among alternatives.

While freedom and agency are in certain respects the ground upon which virtue is constructed, they are also conditions furthered by the cultivation of virtue. Certainly within the Aristotelian and Thomistic traditions, not to mention the Kantian, true freedom and agency are equated with rationality, and one's having gained a degree of mastery over the passions. To be passionate like Kierkegaard's aesthete is not to be ethical, for the passionate one is passive to the a-rational and acts without the capacity to will otherwise. For Aristotle and Thomas the exercise of the truly human function is a possibility and not a necessity; the actualization of true human potential requires that one gain control of concupiscible and irascible appetites. Only upon this foundation can one employ the rational powers freely. Aquinas argues as follows:

> . . . when the passions are very intense, man loses the use of reason altogether; for many have gone out of their mind through excess of love or anger. It is in this way that passions draw the reason to judge in particular, against knowledge which it has in general.[14]

And concerning even natural law which Aquinas argues cannot be blotted out, he says,

> But it is blotted out in the case of a particular action, in so far as the reason is hindered from applying the common principle, on account of concupiscence or some other passion, as stated above. . . .[15]

For Aquinas as well as for Aristotle, the management of the passions stands as a virtue in relation to the practice of contemplation, i.e., intellectual virtue. Quoting again from Aquinas:

> ...the moral virtues belong to the contemplative life as a
> predisposition. For the act of contemplation, in which the
> contemplative life essentially consists is hindered both by the
> impetuosity of the passions which withdraw the soul's inten-
> tion from intelligible to sensitive things, and by outward
> disturbances. Now the moral virtues curb the impetuosity of
> the passions, and quell the disturbances of outward occupations.
> Hence moral virtues belong dispositively to the contempla-
> tive life.[16]

It is as if the passions, if left to their own designs, serve as a kind
of prejudice, something which blocks the proper exercise of a particular practice, in this case the practice of contemplation. In
Unificationism the practice which moral virtues serve would be
the expression of familial heart. In this sense the Unificationists
follow the tradition of Pascal and more recently such thinkers as
Max Scheler and Dietrich von Hildebrand. A quote from von
Hildebrand will illustrate my point about Unification nicely.

> To deny affectively as such the character of spirituality is a
> heritage of Greek intellectualism, which considered only rea-
> son and will to be spiritual. The affective sphere as a whole
> was held to be irrational and a characteristic which man shared
> with animals.[17]

Furthermore,

> It is high time that philosophy should do justice to the specific
> role of heart in morality.[18]

In Unificationism moral virtue functions not merely to liberate the
intellectual capacities, though indeed it is partially this, but to free
the sublimer affective capacities from certain prejudices. In essence
this marks a significant anthropological or moral-psychological difference between the Unification and the Aristotelian traditions; for
unlike Aristotle, Unificationism defines the distinguishing human
functions as the capacity to love and be familial. The passions are

to be brought under the dominion of love, and ordered within the practice of family.

I would like to underscore this last point, lest there be any confusion regarding either the Unification or the Thomist positions. While the passions are to be ordered or located in some proper position *vis à vis* the distinctly human function, they are not to be annihilated. A quote from Kenneth Kirk will I hope speak to the Unificationist as well as to the Thomist position:

> Perhaps his (Thomas) greatest contribution to ethics is the doctrine that the passions are to be ordered and harmonized, rather than extirpated; and it is from this point that he develops his massive scheme of the cardinal virtues.[19]

In short, it is not the argument of this paper that some kind of passionlessness is normative for the practice of the Unification marriage. What is normative, however, is the priority of ordered love, such that the passions are a function of one's heart, rather than the opposite. The importance of celibacy, even as understood within the context of an Aristotelian doctrine of the mean, is in achieving a particular mean, namely that the concupiscible appetites be ordered and relegated to their proper sphere of operation, the family.

I am aware that the assertions I am making regarding the proper location of sexual expression raises a number of important issues, and unfortunately they are issues which I shall not address here. My task here is to describe and explain the way in which celibacy functions and has meaning in relation to a particular practice. I am not attempting to persuade anyone regarding the universalizability or desirability of the practice.

The Story and the Narrative Quest

In the first section I defined my task as that of describing the discipline of celibacy within the context of virtue theory, and viewing it as a stage teleologically related to a particular Unification practice, namely true family. It is my hope that I have shown that celibacy is an intelligible moral act appropriate to the given telos of the community. In this section, in a somewhat briefer form, I wish to present the act of celibacy, the idea of virtue, and the practice within the context of the Unification story or narrative.

Frank Flinn in an article entitled, "The New Religions and the Second Naiveté," states,

> I believe that one of the unrecognized aspects of new religious movements is their recovery of life as story. . . . The new religious movements represent not simply the search for the Sacred but also the quest for the metaphoric richness by which the story of life can be symbolized and lived out.[20]

Flinn goes on to say that "*Divine Principle* reconstitutes the symbolic narrativity of the messianic story."[21] Flinn's point, which I find persuasive, is that some new religious movements are constituting a post-modern world view, one which has captured what Ricoeur calls the "second naiveté." This "postcritical" consciousness is conducive to the emergence of "story-formed communities," a term used by Stanley Hauerwas in a volume entitled *A Community of Character.*[22]

If indeed the Unification movement is largely a "story-formed community," and by implication a community of "story-formed" selves, then it merits our attention to examine the Unification story. To initiate this task I quote from a piece by Joseph Fichter, "Marriage, Family and Sun Myung Moon:"

> According to the theology of the *Divine Principle,* the revealed scripture of the Unification Church, God intended Adam and Eve to marry and have perfect children who would populate His physical and spiritual kingdom. This intention was frustrated when Eve was sexually seduced by the archangel Lucifer, committing the original sin of adultery and causing the spiritual fall of mankind. Her impurity was passed on in premature and illicit intercourse with Adam, causing the physical fall of mankind. Later, God sent Jesus to redeem mankind from sin. He accomplished His spiritual mission, but he was killed before He could marry and father a new race of perfect children. Our first parents threw away God's love; Jesus was

> prevented from completing the redemptive mission on which
> his heavenly Father had sent Him . . . The time has now come
> for the members of the Unification Church to establish per-
> fect families in love and justice and unity, which in turn will
> unify all races, all nations, all religions.[23]

Father Fichter's account of the story which informs the Unification
community is succinctly and fairly stated, and will serve adequately
for my purposes of locating celibacy within its setting in the story.

MacIntyre has suggested that the story which informs or forms
a community is significantly pertinent to the intentions and goals
of moral action. He says in fact that,

> I can only answer the question "What am I to do?" if I can
> answer the prior question "Of what story or stories do I find
> myself a part?"[24]

If MacIntyre is right, and I am convinced he is, then the Unification
story is the key to understanding Unification action. But MacIntyre
makes another point which I find equally compelling and important for the present analysis, and that is that not only are communities and selves to a great extent story-formed, but that the life of
each actor within the story is a story in itself. In short, each actor
or moral agent is an author of his or her own story. MacIntyre
states,

> Narrative history of a certain kind turns out to be the basic
> and essential genre for the characterization of human action.[25]

To sum up I would contend that one may adequately describe the
action of a Unification Church member, e.g., celibacy, as not only
a story-formed act, but as an act of an author-agent seeking to live
our a "narrative quest."

Let me first attempt to show that celibacy is a story-formed
activity. In Fichter's account of the Unification narrative he em-
ploys the phrase "premature and illicit intercourse" referring to
the Fall of Adam and Eve. As *Divine Principle* interprets it, the Fall
represents a failure on the part of the hero and heroine. The Fall is
not a tragedy in the classic sense of being a result of some peculiar

fate or inevitability; the Fall is a tragedy in the sense that it could have been avoided. Adam and Eve had no tragic *flaw* that undermined their "true family" project; theirs was rather a tragic *failure*. Of what did this failure consist?

On the level of behavior the Fall was the failure of constituting a family, i.e., relating sexually, without the proper qualifications; that is, they were yet babes in the virtues appropriate to the practice of marriage. Most importantly the relationship with God had not matured sufficiently. In this interpretation Unification is quite rigorist in that sexual relations are viewed as appropriate only for the practice of true family, which however is not to say only for reproductive purposes; family is interpersonal as well.

At an internal level the tragic failure which precipitated the Fall was lack of faith and loyalty to God, failure to trust that the promise of God, the three blessings, would be fulfilled. The Fall is really the failure on the part of God's children to remain loyal to God's word, and as a result a universal principle was violated. This violation was the disordering of love, or the misuse of love. This is the original sin. As a result the practice of family was instituted without the appropriate virtues—not the moral, familial, or theological. Furthermore, the family itself was not an institution capable of instructing or transmitting these virtues. Hence the need for Christ to institute the true family tradition.

In the context of this story one can, I trust, see the logic of celibacy as an appropriate part of the restoration or re-storying of the Fall. Celibacy is an act that attempts on one hand to heal the broken heart of God and on the other represents a practice itself conducive to the perfection of character. This was discussed in the first section. What is important beyond understanding that Moonies engage in story-informed action, is that Moonies also see themselves as involved in a narrative of which they are themselves the author. The true family is an object of a narrative quest. In this respect the agent is the author of his or her own autobiography. One's life is one's own. It is only a vision of the purpose and joy of a true family that makes celibacy meaningful and worthwhile. Hauerwas has stated:

> . . . what young people properly demand is an account of life
> and the initiation into a community that makes intelligible
> why their interest in sex should be subordinated to other
> interests. What they, and we demand is the lure of an adven-
> ture that captures the imagination sufficiently that conquest
> means more than the sexual possession of another.[26]

Many young people have found the Unification story persuasive
in a way that makes celibacy meaningful.

Hauerwas's usage of the term "adventure" is important. It speaks
not of cool rationality, something which I fear the very tone of
this paper conveys, but of vision, of dangers (at times, after all, it
is dangerous to be a Moonie), of a goal that is both very transcendental and yet very historical. And to achieve the goal of the quest
one must be well trained and equipped with those skills and virtues without which the *telos* becomes inaccessible. Like Adam and
Eve one can fail the quest. With this in mind MacIntyre's definition
of virtue takes on added meaning.

> The virtues therefore are to be understood as those disposi-
> tions which will not only sustain practices that enable us to
> achieve the goods internal to the practices, but which will also
> sustain us in the relevant kind of quest for the good, by ena-
> bling us to overcome the harms, dangers, temptations and
> distractions which we encounter, and which will furnish us
> with increasing self-knowledge and increasing knowledge of
> the good.[27]

In this section, with the help of Flinn, Hauerwas, and MacIntyre,
I have tried, in terms of what might be called narrative analysis, to
make Unification celibacy and virtue acquisition more intelligible.
The pursuit of God's love and the true family is a narrative quest
and an adventure in which celibacy plays a distinct and important
role. Moving now to a third section I would like to comment on
the theory of institutions which the practice of celibacy, the theory
of virtues, and the Unification *telos* implies.

Toward a Post-Modern Rule or Tradition

Throughout the course of this exposition I have often referred to the inextricability of a theory of virtue from a theory of institutions. On more than one occasion I have mentioned Aristotle in an attempt to underscore this point. If indeed a theory of virtue implies a correlative sociology or political theory, then we must ask what kind of social tradition is inherent in the Unification theory of virtue.

In keeping with other sections let me begin with MacIntyre's position on the relationship between virtue and tradition.

> The virtues find their point and purpose . . . also in sustaining those traditions which provide both practices and individuals with their necessary historical context.[28]

As I interpret it, a tradition is an intergenerationally transmitted view of the good, and of those conditions of community which facilitate the achievement of that good, and which imply a particular social structure. I would argue that the Unification tradition, unlike either liberal individualism or Marxism, suggests a communitarian social order.

Sang Hun Lee, author of *Explaining Unification Thought,* made the following statement:

> The collapse of the order of love is closely connected with today's disorder in sexual love. Sexual love should be the realization of God's second blessing—the establishment of a family centered on God's love—but today many people have no such idea. In addition, mass communication scatters sexual stimulation and promotes immorality and free sex. The collapse of the order of sexual love necessarily leads to the collapse of order in the family, society, and world.[29]

Lee not only suggests, but insists Unification's sexual ethic has a political and social dimension; so much so that he argues that "the key to solving world, national, social and family problems lies in solving problems between husband and wife."[30] The organization of sexual conduct is not merely construed as a matter of personal morality, though indeed it includes this, but as a public matter. In taking the position that sex is a political issue, Lee does not stand alone. Certainly most feminists, while perhaps offended in certain ways by Lee's conclusions, would agree with his assumptions regarding the political dimension of sexual ethics. Also Stanley Hauerwas has sounded a note in some ways similar to Lee's.

> Any attempt to reclaim an authentic Christian ethic of sex must begin by challenging the assumption that sex is a "private" matter.[31]

Hauerwas adds that:

> Our children have to see that marriage and having children, and the correlative sexual ethic, are central to the community's political task. For only then can they be offered a vision and an enterprise that might make the disciplining of sex as interesting as its gratification.[32]

Earlier I mentioned liberal individualism and Marxism as modern traditions. As I see them, both relegate sex ethics, just as they do religion, to a private sphere. Sex ethics then becomes a matter of indifference for social ethics. I would contend that each of these modern world views fails to adequately consider the primordially familial character of the self. Both fail to attend to the role which the family plays in character-formation and world-formation. Furthermore, each had failed to consider the fragility of the family as an institution and that its dissolution bodes poorly for the future of a civilization.

Liberalism in the West has all too often focused on the importance of liberty and free enterprise, both as regards commercial transactions as well as sexual transactions. The only criterion for moral legitimacy is that the transaction be between consenting adults. In this way the shaping of a social world is left to an "invisible hand," a belief in the inevitability of a harmony that eventuates from the rational pursuit of self-interest. Courtship and mating are based on a romantic self-interest model. Sexuality is less for the sake of a "practice," than it is a means for the gratification of the interests of consenting adults. Family is characterized according to a utilitarian model rather than a teleological model.

The weakness of liberalism's sexual ethic lies in its individualism, and in many respects its hedonism. For these two features lead to a dissolution of the family as a tradition. When the family does not produce external utility it is best disposed of. If the dissolution of a marriage is a decision of consenting adults, then it is believed that no one is the worse off. However, with the disposability of family arises the fact, as Christopher Lasch points out, that it no longer functions as a "haven in a heartless world."[33] In fact, the very virtues which that "heartless" modern world celebrates are in many ways inimical to the traditional family.

Marx cogently diagnosed the alienation that plagued the people of a newly industrialized modern world. But while Marx's theory of institutions, especially economic ones, was offered as a way out of an alienating system, there seems no question that alienation is alive and well in the Marxist societies. In portraying human conditions in a macrosocial way, focusing strictly on a theory of economic institutions as the locus of alienation and exploitation, Marx failed to address the issue of the family. Marxists are indeed usually quick to denigrate the so-called "bourgeois family" as merely a bastion of classist traditions. Furthermore, sexual virtue is often understood as a form of bourgeois ideology.

Whereas the tendency of liberalism has been toward an ethic of individualism, the tendency of Marxism has been toward a kind of statism. In both, ironically, bureaucracy attempts to supplant family; what Lasch calls the "socialization of reproduction."[34] Neither could be viewed as offering a communitarian ethic, that is, an ethic which places its emphasis upon the importance of local forms of community—face to face communities. Unificationism, on the other hand, advocates a kind of familyism that could indeed be characterized as within the communitarian tradition. Young Oon Kim has stated that, "A family centered ethic avoids the extremes of both individualism and collectivist statism."[35]

The point to be made here is that Unification in its family-centered social ethic represents a form of communitarian social theory. In this respect it differs from both an atomistic individualism and a statist Marxism. In fact, Unification differs from the ethos of modernity itself. This is apparent in its stress on virtue, its recovery of *mythos* as Flinn tells us, and its insistence on the "natural law" of the family as an institution. In these respects Unification is post-modern and yet traditional. However, I do not think that Unification understands itself merely as recovering some glory from the past, and in this sense it is hardly "conservative." Modernity, rationality, and technology are not viewed as mutants to be rejected. They are, however, to be reconstituted within a particular normative framework. I have only begun this essay to touch on the character of that normative framework, particularly as it deals with the topic of celibacy and the importance of true family.

NOTES

1 Alasdair MacIntyre, *After Virtue* (Notre Dame, Ind.: Notre Dame Press, 1981), p. 174.

2 Two chapters from *After Virtue* are of a particular pertinence to the format and general stance of this paper. In these chapters MacIntyre addresses the topics referred to as "practice," the "narrative unity of the human life," and tradition. These chapters, fourteen and fifteen, are "The Nature of the Virtues," and "The Virtues, the Unity of a Human Life and the Concepts of a Tradition."

3 Richard Niebuhr argues in his classic work *The Responsible Self* that the first question to be asked in any kind of ethical reflection of deliberation is the hermeneutic or interpretive question, viz., "What is going on?" Once having asked this question and explored the phenomenon one can begin to put together an appropriate or fitting response.

4 The notions of the "perfection of character" and the "true family" are drawn from *Outline of the Principle: Level Four,* particularly the chapter on "The Principles of Creation." Perfection and "true" family mean essentially having the right relationship with God, and are not meant to imply anything superhuman.

5 MacIntyre refers to "the rule of St. Benedict" as an example of a local form of community which preserved the tradition of the virtues through the dark ages.

6 MacIntyre, p. 175.

7 *Ibid.*

8 *Ibid., p. 177.*

9 Chung Hwan Kwak, *Outline of the Principle: Level Four* (New York: Holy Spirit Assn. for the Unif. of World Christianity, 1980), p.24.

10 Young Oon Kim, *Unification Theology* (New York: Holy Spirit Assn. for the Unif. of World Christianity, 1980), p. 121.

11 I have quoted Richardson from Gabrielle Brown's *The New Celibacy* (New York: Ballantine Books, 1980), p. 36.

12 Stanley Hauerwas, *A Community of Character* (Notre Dame, Ind.: Notre Dame Press, 1981). This passage is taken from an article in this collection called "The Virtues and Our Communities: Human Nature as History," p. 113.

13 Aristotle's *Nichonachean Ethics* 1110b15, ed. Richard McKeon.

14 Thomas Aquinas, *Summa Theologica* I-II, 77, 2.

15 *Ibid.,* I-II, 94, 6.

16 *Ibid.,* II-III, 180, 2.

17 Dietrich von Hildebrand, *The Art of Living* (Chicago: Franciscan Herald Press, 1965), p. 107.

18 *Ibid.,* p. 183.

19 Kenneth Kirk, *The Vision of God* (London: Longmans, 1941), p. 386.

20 Frank K. Flinn, "The New Religions and the Second Naiveté": Beyond Demystification and Demythologization," in *Ten Theologians Respond to the Unification Church* ed. Herbert Richardson (Barrytown, N.Y.: Unif. Theo. Seminary, distr. Rose of Sharon Press, 1981), p. 54.

21 *Ibid.,* p. 55.

22 Hauerwas, pp. 9-36. This is an essay entitled "A Story-Formed Community: Reflections on Watership Down."

23 Joseph Fichter, "Marriage, the Family and Sun Myung Moon," in *America* (27 October, 1979), p. 227.

24 MacIntyre, p. 201.

25 *Ibid.,* p. 194.

26 Hauerwas, p. 195.

27 MacIntyre, p. 204.

28 *Ibid.,* p. 207.

29 Sang Hun Lee, *Explaining Unification Thought* (New York: Holy Spirit Assn. for the Unif. of World Christianity, 1980), p. 237.

30 *Ibid.,* p. 102.

31 Hauerwas, p. 177.

32 *Ibid.,* p. 183.

33 Christopher Lasch, *Haven in a Heartless World: The Family Beseiged* (New York: Basic Books, 1977).

34 *Ibid.*, pp. 18-19.

35 Kim, p. 78.

Crisis of Single Adults: An Alternative Approach

Michael L. Mickler

Introduction

A year prior to the convening of the New ERA conference on "Family Values and Spirituality" in Jamaica in February 1982, a group of more than four hundred church leaders, including some of the best known and most active proponents of single adult ministries in the United States, met in Dallas where they attended workshops and general sessions designed to study the problems and challenges of ministry to single adults. The three day conference was called SALT I, "an appropriate name," according to *Christianity Today,* "for those who consider that the nuclear family was a bomb in the 1970s and that, as a result, single adults will continue to proliferate in the 1980s" (Maust, 1980). SALT I (Single Adult Leadership Training), the first national interdenominational gathering of its kind, is evidence of expanding single adult ministries in the United States since the mid-1970s, much of which had been popularized by Robert Schuller's Garden Grove (California) Community Church where single adult memberships rose from 200 to 1,300 in 1974-78. "SOLO Minstries," a division of *SOLO* magazine—originally a publication of Schuller's Garden Grove Church—was organized as a resource agency in 1979 and a year later planned SALT I. During that same period, *SOLO* magazine, a bi-monthly magazine aimed at "Positive Christian Singles," increased its circulation from 1,200 to 12,000 prompting some SALT I participants to speak of "a coming, larger 'single ministries' boom." One conference organizer asserted that the singles movement was "becoming as strong as Youth for Christ in the late 1950s and early 1960s" (Maust, 1980).

   While such hype may smack of contemporary evangelical entrepreneurship, marketing singles as the newest brand of religious consumers (one only need refer to the sudden Christian growth industry of single pen pal clubs, tour groups and newspapers aimed at Christian single adults), SALT I, to its credit, also faced some of the hard issues of singleness. Foremost among these, at least at Dallas, was sexuality. Conference leaders recognized that many people join singles groups for "relationships with the opposite sex," and described those "looking for an accommodation for their promiscuity" (Maust, 1980). A 1979 survey conducted by one SOLO Ministries staffer of 203 formerly married and "born-again" Christian adults within a singles program in a large California church found that only nine percent of the men and twenty-seven percent of the women remained celibate after their divorces (Smith, 1979). Another hard issue was that of divorce, including the problem of "divorced persons who rush into a second marriage and find this relationship also on the rocks" (U.S. census figures report that 59 percent of second marriages versus 37 percent of first marriages fail. A final hard issue was the status of single adults in the churches. With the growth of single ministries, one perceived danger was that of "singles becoming self-centered 'in-groups'." Here, SALT I leaders made it clear they "were not building a church for singles." As one organizer put it, "We're the family of God, not the singles of God" (Maust, 1980).

   While SALT I exhausted neither the possibilities nor the problems of single adult ministries, the very targeting of single adults raises questions of single identity in contemporary culture. I intend to explore some of those questions in this paper. In the first section, I will survey the contemporary situation of single adults in the United States. Utilizing U.S. Census Bureau statistics and psychological literature on single adults, I will profile America's single population and highlight the central ambiguity of the contemporary situation: that is, the discrepancy between increased social acceptance of singleness as a lifestyle and systemic psychological maladjustment among single adults. In the second section, I will locate the source of this discrepancy in the current inadequacies of the two predominant models of "being single"; namely, "non-vocational" singleness of modern culture and "vocational" singleness of the Western Christian tradition. In the third section, I will suggest that one appeal of the new religions which proliferated throughout the 1960s and 1970s involved creation of a viable single identity and lifestyle. Taking the Unification Church as a case in point, I will show how it has revitalized contemporary models of singleness while at the same time attempting to integrate "being single" and "being married" within an overall model of wholeness.

The Contemporary Situation

There is no question that the previously ignored single adult assumed a new visibility in the 1970s. There were two major reasons for this. The first and most obvious was the fact of increased numbers. According to the 1970 census, single people were one third of the adult population of the United States, if adulthood was defined as beginning at age 18. That is, out of 133,313,480 adults, 44,508,113 were living without spouses in 1970. By 1980, the number of single American single adults had increased to more than 50 million with nearly 20 million "non-family" households (people living alone or with an unrelated person)—this latter figure a 66 percent increase since 1970. In terms of visibility, these figures are compounded in that single populations tend to congregate in major urban centers—over one half of the *total* populations of Boston, San Francisco and Washington, D.C.; and over 40 percent of the *total* populations of St. Louis, New Orleans, Cleveland, Chicago and Los Angeles are single adults. Thus, by dent of numbers alone, single adults are a social force of considerable proportion. The other major reason for the new visibility of single adults in the 1970s was increased acceptability of singleness as a lifestyle option. According to anthropologist Herbert Passim of Columbia University: "For the first time in human history the single condition is being recognized as an acceptable lifestyle for anyone. It is finally being possible to be both single and whole" (Edwards and Hoover, 1974).

Despite increased numbers and acceptability, the contemporary situation of single adults is not without complexity and problems. In the first place, the single adult population of the United States is by no means homogenous but reflects a "kaleidoscope pattern of subgroups differing from one another as much as from married adults" (Davis and Coleman, 1977). At least four subgroups are clearly distinguishable: the "Never-Married" who were 22,379,107 in 1970; the "Divorced" who were nearly 5 million in the same census; the "Widowed" who were 12 million in 1970; and the "Separated"—a catch-all category including couples separated, though not divorced for financial or other considerations, and those with spouses in the military, prisons or mental hospitals—who were 2,763,044 in 1970. Besides the significant differences among the four subgroups, there are additional differences within each subgroup making any notion of "common-cause" highly unlikely. For instance, although 10 million of the "Never-Married" in 1970 were 18-21, the majority of whom would marry before the age 25-29, there were 6 million people forty and above who had never married and with whom the younger age brackets would have limited resonance. Gender is another differentiating factor with there being twice the number of single divorced women as single divorced men and five times as many single widowed women as single widowed men. Differing economic and social statuses further complicate the situation, rendering a diverse set of attitudes and perceptions that belie any simple or single-minded approaches to the "singles movement."

A review of the psychological literature on single adults also shows the complexity of the contemporary situation. Ironically, although the 1970s witnessed increased social acceptance of singleness as a lifestyle, research indicates limited self-acceptance among single adults, themselves. A 1975 *Psychology Today* article stated that: "All the married groups—men and women, over thirty and under, with children and without—reported higher feelings of satisfaction and good feelings about their lives than all the unmarried groups— the single, divorced, or widowed" (Campbell, 1975). Other studies reached similar conclusions (Bradburn & Caplovitz, 1965; Glenn, 1975). Some studies equate singleness not only with lower rates of life satisfaction but also with higher rates of mental instability. Studies of both in-patient and out-patient mental institutions, for example, indicate that single adults are more prone to mental illness than married adults, and that single men are more prone than single women (Bachrach, 1975; Gove, 1972a). Maladjustment appears to be especially pronounced in the single male. In studies of the single community, single men are classified as more psychologically impaired (Srole, Langner, Michael, Kirkpatrick, Opler & Rennie, 1962), and experience more life stress (Uhlenhuth, Lipman, Balter & Stern, 1974). They commit more suicides (Gove, 1972b), and have higher mortality rates (Gove, 1973). Research on marital status, according to one recent study, has led to two major theories that explain the data. The "selectivity" approach holds that maladjustment in the single population is the result of natural selection so that those who are emotionally unstable or maladjusted are less likely to marry. The "reactivity" approach holds that maladjustment is the result of the social role of singleness. Although the theories are not mutually exclusive, research lends greater support to the reactivity hypothesis (Thiesen & Cooley, 1979).

Whatever the validity of these theories, psychiatric research highlights the key ambiguity in the contemporary situation of single adults in America: that is, the ambiguity between increased social acceptance of singleness as a lifestyle and systemic psychological maladjustment among single adults, themselves. In the following section, I will locate the source of this ambiguity in the inadequacies of the predominant models of "being single."

The Identity Crisis of American Single Adults

The discrepancy between increased social acceptance of single-ness as a lifestyle option and systemic psychological maladjust-ment among singles themselves is one symptom of the contempo-rary identity crisis of American single adults. Although this crisis affects all single groupings, a preliminary distinction must be drawn between those who are single by choice and those who are single by default. In distinguishing those who are single by default, I refer to those for whom singleness is a secondary, or unavoidable, lifestyle option. They may have wanted to marry, but didn't and think they have been passed over because they are not worth having. They may come to singleness out of a sense of guilt and failure over a broken marriage, or they may come in anger or feel useless and discarded after the death of a loved one. For all of these people, any identity crisis remains primarily on a personal level. For those who are single by choice, however, the crisis exists on a broader level. That is, it signifies the current inadequacies of the two pre-dominant symbol-systems for "being single": "non-vocational" singleness of modern culture and "vocational" singleness of the Western Christian tradition. I will locate the indemnity crisis of American single adults in these two symbol systems.

Non-Vocational Singleness: The Model of Self-Fulfillment

"Non-vocational" singleness is rooted, most fundamentally, in the ideal of self-fulfillment. Singleness, divested of transcendent meaning, offers itself as the lifestyle best suited to meet this over-riding ideal. With values of individual freedom, self-expression and self-awareness, "non-vocational" singleness is a particularly modern phenomenon. It has two dominant expressions: libertine and ascetic. In its libertine mode, the thrust is toward an experien-tial dimension of self-fulfillment. Singleness, here, symbolizes un-limited possibilities. Specific images might include a plurality of "non-binding" relationships or travel opportunities, the goal being able to live a less repressed, more open, and aware existence. In its ascetic mode, however, the thrust is less toward experience and more toward success as a means of self-fulfillment. Repression, in fact, could be a positive value as singleness here affords the opportunity for a much more single-minded devotion to self-fulfillment, usually in the form of a career. Whereas the libertine model spotlights multiple and varied personal involvements, the ascetic mode of "non-vocational" singleness tends to cut off relationships as distractions, or worse, as implying the possibility of failure. Unlike the libertine who can chalk up failure to "experience," the ascetic is interested in only one possibility, that of success.

The key problem and source of the contemporary identity crisis of "non-vocational" singleness is that the surrounding culture has co-opted its basic values within competing symbol-systems. The question in the late 1960s and early 1970s became: "Why be single when one can have an open marriage?" In contrast with stable family patterns, "non-vocational" singleness, while not abandoning its primary ideal of self-fulfillment, functions to offer the wider society fresh possibilities and enduring monuments of achievement. Submerged in a culture of narcissism, it has lost all cutting edge. The resulting identity crisis has given way to fragmentation and surprising new forms. Libertines, for example, have embraced "the new celibacy" or, moving in the opposite way, have decided that bearing (or having) a child is indispensable to one's self-fulfillment and thereby bolstered the proliferating ranks of single-parent families. More ascetic types have "gotten it" at est or picked up a mantra as a means of realizing inherent creative potential.

Vocational Singleness: The Model of Self-Sacrifice

"Vocational" singleness is tied to the ideal of self-sacrifice rather than self-fulfillment. Singleness, here, is a symbol for the lifestyle best suited for offering oneself to God. With its traditional values of poverty, chastity, and obedience, "vocational" singleness is rooted not in modern culture but in the Western Christian tradition. It, also, has experiential and ascetic dimensions. For the mystically oriented person the thrust is toward experience, though in this case, religious experience—traditionally, the variety of ways the self might be crucified with Christ. For the "lay" single, on the other hand, the thrust is less toward religious or mystical experience *per se* than toward missionary labor, church planting, service in behalf of the needy or oppressed and so on. Singleness, here, is a means to success, not in the sense of self-fulfillment but in the furtherance of God's work. In a similar way, external attachments are cut off, not for the sake of personal advancement, but for the sake of the Kingdom.

If the identity crisis implicit in "non-vocational" singleness is that its values have become those of the larger culture, the crisis in "vocational" singleness is just the reverse. That is, its values have been tied to the perpetuation of particular religious institutions and run the risk of irrelevancy. Traditionally, though upholding the ideal of self-sacrifice, "vocational" singleness functioned to offer the wider society examples of humanity and personal heroism. In contemporary society, with the religious sphere whittled down and secular organizations encroaching in the area of social service, "non-vocational" singleness, too, has lost its cutting edge, giving way to a closed system characterized by enforced celibacy. The resultant identity crisis, as in the case of "non-vocational" singleness, has led to fragmentation and new forms. Religious mystics have married or become Marxist revolutionaries. "Lay" singles, rather than missionizing, have become, with single adult ministries, the object of missions.

Another of the movements that won a number of single adults in the late 1960s and 1970s were the proliferating new religions. Part of the religious appeal of these new groups was the creation of a viable single identity and lifestyle. In the following section I focus on one movement, the Unification Church, and show how it has not only created a distinctive single lifestyle but attempts to integrate both "being single" and "being married" within an overall mode of wholeness.

An Alternative Approach

The Unification Church presents an anomaly to one investigating the contemporary situation of the single adult. On the one hand, it articulates a theological system that posits as its center-piece the ideal of the God-centered family. On the other hand, its appeal has been largely to single adults, and until recently single adults made up the bulk of its membership, especially in the United States. Thus, although the married state is perceived as normative, there exists a strong and significant tradition of single people in the life of the church. In this section, I examine that tradition; first, in terms of how the church has couched single life within an assemblage of symbols that integrate "non-vocational" and "vocational" singleness; and second, in terms of how the church has integrated this model of "being single" within a normative pattern of God-centered family life.

Integrating Non-Vocational and Vocational Singleness

One of the distinctive features of the Unification Church is the manner in which it has incorporated the single life within a symbol-system that integrates "non-vocational" and "vocational" singleness. On the one hand, it has evolved a communal basis of church life along with a mobile lifestyle and opportunities for educational and career development that model the ideal of self-fulfillment. On the other hand, by distinguishing "core" membership who dedi-cate themselves totally to God and "associates" who participate, often at some personal or professional cost, in broadly humanitar-ian projects, the church incorporates the ideal of self-sacrifice. Be-cause these dual emphases are central to single identity in the church, it is worthwhile to consider them both at greater length.

Non-vocational singleness: Apart from an explicitly "religious" orientation, the church has couched singleness in a symbol-system that affirms the ideal of self-fulfillment. Singleness here, as in the broader societal model, symbolizes the lifestyle best suited to real-ize that ideal and has both experiential and ascetic dimensions. Of primary significance in the experiential mode of self-fulfillment is the communal basis of church life. Here is the opportunity to "experience" a wide variety of personality types and, in many church centers to experience a broad sampling of cultures (generally European or Asian) in an international community. In short,

Unification Centers offer single adults opportunities for intimacy and self-enhancement within a supportive environment. Aside from communalism (which the church seeks to institutionalize in its "home church" program), another experientially-oriented appeal to single adults is that of travel. Mobility is as much a part of church lifestyle as communalism, and is a special province of the single adult. To have participated in forty-day evangelical crusades in New York City or Washington, D.C.; to have attended an International Conference on the Unity of the Sciences in Los Angeles, Miami Beach and Korea or the New ERA conferences in Kauai or Montego Bay; to have fundraised in Wilmington, Delaware or Gary, Indiana; or to have gone tuna fishing off Gloucester, Massachusetts are all well within the range of possibilities. Related to this cosmopolitan appeal are the opportunities to interact with a variety of notables: from media to Nobel laureates, theologians, lawyers and government officials. For more ascetic types, whose model of self-fulfillment hinges more on achievement or success, frequent in-church "competitions" in areas of fundraising, witnessing, lecturing, etc. offer stiff challenges and symbolic satisfactions. On the other hand, the proliferation of church and church-related organizations—often in conventionally secular fields and, in the case of businesses, often undertaken "from scratch"—offer ample career appeal and challenge.

Vocational singleness: In addition to the appeal to self-fulfillment, the church also has incorporated singleness in a symbol-system that affirms the ideal of self-sacrifice. Singleness here, as in the traditional model, symbolizes a lifestyle optimally suited for a single-minded devotion to God. Furthermore, as in the traditional bifurcation between religious and lay, the church has evolved two separate expressions of "vocational" singleness: that is, "core" and "associate" membership. For "core" members, primary thrust is toward religious experience, that is, the variety of ways one might "experience God's heart." In this setting, traditional vocational norms of poverty, chastity and obedience are integrated with what might otherwise be viewed as "non-vocational" aspects of single life within the church. For instance, though one be singularly successful in business or in the solicitation of funds, all monies are public. Similarly, though single adults experience the intimacies of communal life, the thrust is *agape* not *eros,* and one's sexual desires also are offered up. Finally, although one may have wide ranging travel opportunities, they are not always of one's choosing and may call for the sacrifice of a venture barely begun for the sake of a "higher purpose." For "associates," the thrust is less toward religious experience *per se* than toward identification with the church's broader religious, social, cultural and political initiatives. Here, the church affords the opportunity for a wide range of single adults to participate with some personal or professional cost, in larger humanitarian, and explicitly non-sectarian, issues and goals.

Integrating Singleness and God-Centered Family Values

If the Unification Church is able to couch the single life within an assemblage of symbols integrating "non-vocational" and "vocational" singleness, the question remains how the church integrates its model of "being single" within a normative pattern of God-centered family values. The answer to this question is two-fold. On the one hand, "being single," as practiced in the church, is foundational for family life. On the other hand, family or married life is an extension of the single state. In order to treat these dual responses, it is best to deal with each in turn.

Singleness as foundational for family life: One of the reasons "vocational" singleness within the church is able to retain its cutting edge is because it is yoked not only to the ideal of self-sacrifice but also to the ideal of corporate and personal fulfillment. Notions of fulfillment within the Unification context, however, generally are based on a family model; that is, the development of "parental" heart, the establishment of an "ideal" family and the projection of parental consciousness and family values to ever widening social spheres. Both the single state and family life are thus integrated into a larger "model of wholeness." Moreover, within the Unification context, singleness is seen as foundational for family life, not only spiritually (that is, in the development of "parental" heart), but also structurally in that one's "spiritual" children are the foundation for one's physical children.

Marriage as an extension of the single state: If singleness, within the context of the church, is seen to be foundational for family life, family life is seen to be an extension of the single state. This is evident, quite literally, in the frequent separations of married couples. Although patterns vary, couples after marrying typically take up separate missions that may last up to three years although there are examples of separations for the purpose of mission work lasting ten years and more. In a more symbolic sense, family life within the church is an extension of the single state in that it, too, is "vocational," that is, consecrated to the service of God. Moreover, as singleness is foundational for family life, the family is foundational for the establishment of "home church" or what might be described as a God-centered community. By, thus, relativizing both single and married states in the name of more inclusive social spheres, the Unification Church posits a "model of wholeness" that avoids attributing a false sense of ultimacy to either "being single" or "being married." Hence, it diffuses the dichotomization of ideal types which have led to coercive models of enforced celibacy or coercive social pressures to "get married."

REFERENCES

Bachrach, L. "Marital Status and Mental Disorder: An Analytical Review." *National Institute of Mental Health,* 1975, (3, series D).

Bradburn, N.M., and D. Caplovitz, *Reports on Happiness.* Chicago: Aldine Publishing Co., 1965.

Campbell, A. "The American Way of Mating." *Psychology Today.* August, 1975, pp. 37–43.

Davis, A. and Coleman, L. "The Single Person in Contemporary Society." *Review and Expositor* Winter, 1977. pp. 33–42.

Edwards & Hoover. *The Challenge of Being Single.* New York. Hawthorne Books, 1974.

Glenn, N.D. "The Contribution of Marriage to the Psychological Well-Being of Males and Females." *Journal of Marriage and the Family,* 1975, 37, pp. 594–601.

Gove, W.R. "The Relationship Between Sex Roles, Marital Status, and Mental Illness." *Social Forces,* 1972 (a), 51, pp. 34–44.

Gove, W.R. "Sex, Marital Status and Suicide." *Journal of Health and Social Behavior,* 1972 (b), 13, pp. 204–213.

Maust, J. "SALT I Gives New Visibility to Single Adult Ministries." *Christianity Today,* 7 March 1980, pp. 56-58.

Smith, H.I. "Sex and Singleness the Second Time Around." *Christianity Today,* 25 May 1979, pp. 16-22.

Srole, L., *et al. Mental Health in the Metropolis.* Rev. ed. New York: Harper & Row, 1975.

Thiesen, N.L., and B. B. Cooley, "The Psychological Adjustment of the Single Male Adult Compared with Married Males and Single and Married Females Aged 25-34." *Journal of Psychology and Theology* 7 (Fall 1979), pp. 202-11.

Uhlenhuth, E.H., *et al. "Symptom Intensity and Life Stress in the City." Archives of General Psychiatry* 31 (1974), pp. 759-64.

Women: Guilt, Spirituality and Family

Patricia Zulkosky

A woman knows guilt for most of her life. She is guilty if she is too assertive; she is guilty if she is too feminine and therefore seductive. She is guilty if she is too brilliant, too articulate, too successful. If she becomes pregnant, she is at fault. If she chooses not to have children, she is guilty at best of denying her true femininity; at worst, of murder. If her children are maladjusted—if they fail at school, get involved with drugs, or exhibit inappropriate behavior it is her fault. And, if her marriage fails, if her husband loses interest and chooses the attention of another, it is because she has fallen short.

And, guilt is taking its toll. If violence against women has been recorded in footbinding, gynecological mutilation, rape and pornography, it is also being etched into the secret lives of women who turn against themselves in self-hatred; who lose themselves in alcohol, drugs, starvation diets—or in the frenetic activity of trying to please everyone else.[1]

Guilt has emerged as a common theme in the lives of my female clients and friends. It appears to be especially acute as women find themselves trying to live up to the myth of the American middle-class woman and wife which calls for fulfillment through an identity derived from her husband and children. The social isolation

women experience promotes the feeling that something is wrong
with them personally; they just have to try harder or resign themselves to an unhappy situation. Only recently have women been
sharing their stories and pain with each other and finding that they
are not alone in their experience. This sharing is the impetus for
the current in the women's movement that is calling for women to
name their experience and to seek change. There has emerged a
deep awareness of the interrelationship between individual women's
experience and social systems such as the family, religion and other
institutions. In this paper I will review the role of Christianity in
the formation of woman's guilt and discuss its relevance to
Unification theology and lifestyle. Then, I will discuss some of
the changes in the family system that may result from and support
the new identity of women, as women emerge from lives of guilt.

Valerie Saiving's 1960 essay "The Human Situation: A Feminine
View" set forth the premise that the vision of the theologian is
affected by the particularity of his or her own experience as male
or female.[2] She argues that the theological position which defines
sin as pride and virtue as sacrificial love (as held by Reinhold Neibuhr
and others) fails to illuminate woman's experience and further reinforces what might be considered "woman's sin" of self-forgetfulness
and self-negation.[3] Sue Dunfee further expanded this concept in
her development of woman's sin as the "sin of Hiding":

> Inasmuch as woman has accepted the name of "other" to the
> patriarchal culture; inasmuch as she has accepted a role, a place,
> a name without realizing her human freedom to name herself,
> she has been guilty of hiding. And, inasmuch as she has poured
> herself into vicarious living; inasmuch as she has denied her
> sense of self in total submission to husband/father/boss or in
> total self-giving to children, job or family, she has been guilty
> of the sin of Hiding. As she has been afraid to dream a dream
> for herself as well as for others, and as she has trained herself
> to live a submerged existence, she has hidden from her full
> humanity.[4]

The result of this misnaming of women's sin is the perpetration
of patterns of bondage and repression that result in guilt. Dunfee

argues that our understanding of guilt is rooted in our concept of the nature of sin and in the way religion names and proclaims forms of sin. While awareness of sin and guilt is balanced by the promise of forgiveness and love of God in Christianity, the guilt of woman does not seem to have known this same redemptive promise. Rather than guilt leading to the confession of sin and resultant forgiveness, guilt has led woman into the very cycle of bondage to guilt and patterns of destruction that the Christian faith is supposed to shatter. "Thus by encouraging woman to confess the wrong sin, and by failing to judge her in her actual sin, Christianity has both added to woman's guilt and failed to call her into full humanity."[5]

Both Saiving and Dunfee recognize that Christianity's contribution to the problem of woman's guilt is compounded by Christianity's call for women to emulate the virtue of self-sacrificial love which is synonymous with her sin. By making self-sacrifice, the inverse of pride, the paradigm of an authentic life, Christianity has given religious validation to the situation of oppression of woman.

> As long as the highest human virtue is self-sacrifice, and as long the long-suffering, totally self-giving wife/ mother is the symbol our tradition uplifts as true woman, then woman cannot answer the call to accept her human freedom without knowing the guilt of being named by her tradition, as well as by herself, as assertive, self-centered, unfeminine—and finally as a sinner. A theology which recognizes pride as the primary form of sin and which fails to understand that the sin of Hiding is an actuality hiding under the guise of self-sacrifice, and which fails to develop a teaching that the call of God to full humanity is the call into freedom to name oneself, to assert one's selfhood, and to know pride in one's self, seeks to perpetuate woman's bondage to her hiddenness. Furthermore, because self-assertion is equated with the sin of pride, the knowledge of her desire to be a self is often expressed by a woman with guilt and anxiety. Thus the need to be a self is placed in opposition to being the good woman—the good wife and mother—whose total devotion to others is her virtue. Not

only then does woman know the guilt of submerged desire that puts her into hidden conflict with the virtues she is called upon to emulate, but that desire itself creates a state of guilt and anxiety within her. As long as the sin of pride remains *the* sin and as long as the sin of Hiding remains an un-named sin, woman is caught in a double bondage to her guilt.[6]

As a consequence, woman, cut off from herself, tries to strangle impulses to be both a woman and an individual in her own right as she speaks of such temptations as sin or as temptations to sin. She is the woman who constantly apologizes for having her own thoughts and who in her guilt hides her creativity because it seems too much like self-assertion. "She is the woman who is consumed by a guilt she can never assuage through total self-sacrifice because deep down it is a guilt goaded on by an even deeper sense of guilt— the guilt of not being a self."[7]

It is important not to underestimate the power of religious concepts such as sin and virtue in a woman's experience of life. Religious symbols order human experience by providing an overarching framework within which to understand human life. By providing a picture of the ultimate context, religious stances integrate human experience primarily by encouraging commitment to specific values and goals. An overarching religious framework is not arbitrary addendum to an integrated human life but the very structure which provides a coherence and direction to our lives. Much of this orientating task is accomplished through stories.

Carol Christ points out the importance of stories in the introduction to her book, *Diving Deep and Surfacing.* "There is no experience without stories. There is a dialectic between stories and experience. Stories give shape to experience, experience gives rise to stories."[8] Stories provide orientation to life's meaning; they are boundaries against which life is played out. Woman has lived in the interstices between her own vaguely understood experience and the shapings given to the experience by the stories of men. How much of women's experience has been surpressed in order to fit into the stories of men?

The recognition of these incongruencies expanded as Valerie Saiving, Mary Daly, Shelia Collins and others began to argue for "experience as a crucible for theology."[9] It was only as women began telling woman's stories from a woman's point of view, and as women recognized experience as the grist of theological reflection that analysis such as that developed by Saiving and Dunfee began to emerge. Telling stories led to the recognition of common experiences and then to new female-oriented theological reflection as woman set about the task of naming herself and her experience.

This theological reflection based on woman's experience seems to be a catch-22, however. On one hand it releases a burst of freedom and empowerment as women "hear each other into speech."[10] On the other hand, terror emerges as the altered vision of reality forces woman to redefine her most basic commitments and values which often call upon her to upset the status quo. Thus the heroic and spiritual quest to confess the sin of Hiding is both challenging and threatening to women. The challenge to the would-be female hero is not the movement from arrogance or pride to humility as it is for the male, but rather to move from humiliation to self-affirmation and identity. The real question is whether or not Christianity can accept the challenge to convict woman of her real sin.

In summary I have said that guilt is a dominant feature of woman's experience. It is generated by the unsuccessful attempt to conform to the prescribed role model of being submissive, family-oriented and self-sacrificial. Further this role model is embedded in both the praxis and theology of religious institutions and as such has carried over into secular praxis and thought.

To evaluate the applicability of the sin of Hiding to woman in the Unification Church both the theology and the praxis must be considered. The theological consideration, based on *The Outline of the Principle, Level 4,* will focus on an explanation of sin and virtue in comparison to the concept of sin as pride and virtue as self-sacrifice presented earlier. The experiential discussion will focus on oral tradition, written tradition other than the *Divine Principle,* and my personal experiences as a woman in the Unification Church.

The Unification view of sin, particularly of original sin, bears

closer relation to the Catholic strain of thought which views sin as
concupiscence than to the Protestant strain which understands sin
as pride. In this sense, across-the-board comparisons cannot be
made. However, Unification theology maintains the destructive
image of woman as temptress that was reflected and perpetuated
by Christianity's interpretation of the Fall.[11]

> Since a tree reproduces itself by its fruit (which bears the seeds)
> and man reproduces by a sexual relationship, then the Fruit of
> the Tree of Knowledge of Good and Evil symbolizes the sex-
> ual love of Eve. The fact that Eve ate the fruit which Satan
> persuaded her to eat means that she committed fornication
> with Satan. Since eating something means to make it a part of
> our flesh and blood, Eve's giving Adam the fruit of good and
> evil means that Eve caused Adam to fall through this same act
> of illicit love (p. 44).
>
>   Eve's sin was the root of sin, which bore fruit when Cain
> killed Abel (p. 144).

While these statements have not been developed in the oral tradition of the Unification Church in as explicitly sexist ways as
Tertullian, Barth and others have done and continue to do, the
tradition does not dispel the myths or images either.

    In Unification theology, sin is an "act or thought which violates
'Heavenly law'" where Heavenly law is defined as "the principle as
it applies to proper human conduct" (p. 51). Sin is most commonly understood as four fallen natures: (1) not loving as God
loves; (2) leaving one's proper position; (3) reversing the order of
rule; and (4) multiplication of sin (p. 53).

    The Unification understanding of virtue is the inverse of its
understanding of·sin. The "Principle" as it applies to proper human
conduct is best summarized in the Principles of Restoration which
includes both restoration through indemnity (the condition that
must be met in order for something to be restored to its original
position or state, achieved by the reversal of the process which led
to the loss of the original position or state (p. 107) and the Foundation for the Messiah. Without reviewing the entire *Divine Principle*

understanding of the goal of creation, the process of the fall and the history of restoration, it is enough to say that all things that were lost at the fall of man [*sic*] need to be restored through the indemnity condition for removing the fallen nature. If we call Adam's position a mediator's position between someone in the position of servant (archangel position) and God, then someone in the servant's position (each fallen person) must: (1) love a person in the mediator's position, (2) receive God's love through someone in the mediator's position, (3) be obedient to and submit to a person in the mediator's position, and (4) learn God's way from a person in the mediator's position (p. 110). In short, fallen man [*sic*] must love, serve, and obey the person chosen by God to fill the mediator's position, with the goal of saving the world.

This view of virtue is perhaps best expressed in the song from Unification hymnody named "Call to Sacrifice."[12]

> Come unite the world you soldiers of Truth,
> chosen by God to carry His Word.
> Till the world proclaims Him ruler of all,
> every soldier must go forward to fight.
> Offer God your life and desire,
> uniting both body and soul.
> We shall be the soldiers who can fulfill,
> everything for God by doing His Will.
> Chorus:
> Join the fight, for the Lord
> sacrificing all that you have.
> Join the fight, win the world,
> We will see—Victory.

When we move to the praxis level of evaluation, a survey of official texts of *Divine Principle,* developments of the Principle such as those by Young Oon Kim, *Unification Theology and Christian Thought,* and *Unification Theology,* Unification hymnody, and books of brief excerpts from Rev. Moon's speeches such as *A Prophet Speaks Today,* we find nearly exclusive use of sexist language such as male imagery for God, and masculine pronouns and generic nouns that operate to enforce masculinist attitudes. Though the criticism of sexist language is trivialized in the Unification Church, there is an ever-growing mass of evidence from linguists, psychologists, feminists and others who recognize that words are symbols that profoundly and unconsciously affect us. Our thinking about God is important because it colors our self-image and interaction with others. To illustrate, I am reminded of a cartoon of a girl-child writing a letter: "Dear God, Are boys better than girls? I know you are one but please try to be fair." Women have just as much right as men to think of themselves in the image of God and to think of God as similar to them.

The Unification response is that it views God as being both masculine and feminine. Unificationists therefore feel they have the potential solution to some of the theological problems related to a traditional view of a "male" God. But what is the value of a view that holds God is both masculine and feminine, if it is not embodied in the theology, liturgy and devotional practices of the church? On the contrary, it may be detrimental.

A parallel situation is found in the Mormon Church which has a feminine image of God, a Heavenly Mother, equal in power and glory to a Heavenly Father God. But everyone still refers to God as "He." Prayers are addressed to God the Father, never to God the Mother. A Mormon colleague, Gale Bolling, made the astute observation that the Mormon concept of God as Heavenly Father and Heavenly Mother is one reason why Mormon women do not take so readily to feminism. Bolling explains:

> Mormonism has the "advantage" over a system that conceives of God in solely male terms in that women do not feel like outsiders. The image of deity and of religion as being a male club which excludes women is avoided. Mormon women never experience the shock that non-Mormon women do when they realize men are more like God than women are.

The same may be true for Unification women.

A second finding of the survey of Unification texts was the obvious lack of references to women. While the texts do not make blatantly negative remarks about women or contain statements defining the role of women, neither do they develop or even mention the role of women in providential history. Given the prominent role assigned to woman at the fall, woman's experience is painfully missing from the history of restoration.[13] In fact, lack of female presence in the providence and the use of generic language, might give one the impression that women do not exist. This is one piece of evidence to support Sonia Johnson's observation that to live in a patriarchy means that the underlying assumption of one's entire world view is that anything of any importance is done by men.[14] Women have even been blinded to their non-existence.

Feminist theologian Mary Daly points out many devices available to both men and women for refusing to see the problem of sexism.[15] One way is trivialization. For instance, "Are you on the subject of women again when there are so many important problems?" Another way is particularization as illustrated by, "The feminists' problem is their unresolved resentment and anger; it is their personal problem." Still another way is spiritualization, the refusal to look at concrete oppressive facts. And the method of universalization is to reply, "But isn't the real problem human liberation?" Often these words are true but are used to avoid specific problems of sexism. Humor can also be a weapon of extraordinary power. Women are often silenced by the fear of being labeled as not having a sense of humor when they no longer find certain jokes funny or when they perceive them as offensive and painful.

Let us return to the technique of universalization long enough to respond to the comment that the Church is not oppressing women because it requires the same self-sacrifice and obedience from both men and women. While it is true that the same devotion is required from both men and women, the implication of this demand differs according to social position and training. The demand of self-sacrifice from a one-down group such as women, functions to keep them in a subservient position. On the other hand, the demand to sacrifice is beneficial to men who stand in a one-up social position because it encourages them to temper their prideful self-serving behavior encouraged by our society. In this sense, the church is better for men than it is for women. Let it also be recognized that men have far greater opportunity to be placed in positions of leadership. Women state leaders, regional fundraising commanders, graduate students and department heads are few and far between.

In short, the harbor of the theological concept of God as both male and female, the use of devices to prevent recognition of sexism and the lack of references to women in the restoration process all add up to a kind of hidden sexism—at least it is hidden to many members of the Unification Church. It has been necessary for members to lower substantially their threshold of awareness in order to deny oppression. Hidden sexism is much more dangerous than blatant sexism because it is more difficult to recognize and point out the enemy and to demand change. Robin Morgan declared: "The subtlest and most vicious aspect of women's oppression is that we have been convinced we are not oppressed. We have been blinded so as not to see our own condition."[16]

In the meantime, women continue to experience the pains of patriarchy alone and without understanding. The most readable and enlightening expose of the pains women experience under patriarchal religion is Sonia Johnson's book, *From Housewife to Heretic*.[17] She uses her experience and story to illustrate many experiences which I have also had in the Unification Church such as: divide and conquer techniques, exalted feminine rhetoric, the use of women to keep other women in their place, the appropriation of the church viewpoint as personal viewpoint without serious reflection and decision, reliance on male authority for direction in personal lives, holding the woman (the victim) responsible for feelings of worthlessness and depression, and compartmentalized thinking.

In conclusion, I feel there is adequate theological and experiential evidence to say that the sin of Hiding, and the guilt derived from the sin remaining unnamed, is a feature of women's experience in the Unification Church. It was my experience.

Can the Unification Church be responsive to the needs and pains of its women?

There are many things that could be done to strengthen the presentation of the Principle to make it more inclusive and applicable to women. Care could be taken to replace generic terms with inclusive terms, the role of women in providential history could be developed and more information about Mrs. Moon and other strong women in the church could be made available to members of the church to serve as role models. Efforts could be made to develop the understanding of the feminine aspect of God and to incorporate this understanding in the theology, devotion and hymnody of the Church. Perhaps the Principle could be taught using only female references to God as a consciousness-raising effort. These are a few obvious suggestions. A women's task force could be initiated to further explore the concerns and to make suggestions.

Will the Church respond? Will it be enough?

Some women are not so optimistic about the usefulness of patriarchal Christianity or Unificationism to solve the dilemmas women face. Instead, they are turning towards woman's experience, literature, stories and dreams as alternative sources of spirituality and identity. For these women the problem of guilt is not solved by renaming the sin and calling for repentance, but by rejecting the traditional notion of sin and evil. They are urging women to look deeply within themselves and society for meaning in life. The searching and sharing experience of hearing each other into speech is critical to this movement. Woman's spiritual and identity quest is seen as integrally related to the telling and hearing of women's stories.

The function of story is to provide orientation and meaning to life's flow. Until recently women have lived with the problem of being in a world where women's stories have rarely been told from a woman's perspective. The spiritual growth that emerges from the interaction of story and experience has been thwarted. Women need to develop the resources that will facilitate the spiritual quest of awakening to the depths of our souls and our position in the universe. Woman's experience must be the matrix out of which theological questions are formed and answered.

In *Diving Deep and Surfacing* Carol Christ documents this quest as depicted in literary heroines as they grew to understand themselves and to sense their own power and value in the world. She does not claim there is a universal spiritual quest for all women, but rather that there is religious meaning in uniquely female experiences.[18]

Shelia Collins suggests that the content of women's theology is the personal life history, the concrete daily experiences, dreams, frustrations, hopes, fears, and feelings of women who share struggle for life and for self-actualization. The theological form consists in storytelling, personal biography, poetry, song, dance, myths, images and symbols which emerge from a communal theologizing process.[19] Religious development should spring up and out from within, rather than break in upon the person from without. There is a diversity of form and content to woman's spirituality. It is not necessary for women to share the same myths, stories, and experiences in order to share community. It is important that women share the process of creating and reflecting on imagery.

This process often begins by turning inward. Naomi Goldenberg suggests the loss of one's father, whether through physical death or through psychological growth away from his authority, is an event that generally precedes serious introspection and inward psychic movement. She goes on to theorize that "since introspection does follow the death of the father's, then death of father-gods could mean the onset of religious forms which emphasize awareness of oneself and tend to understand gods and goddesses as inner psychic forces."[20] Goldenberg notes that persons who have outgrown the father god tend to place their gods within themselves and to focus on spiritual processes whose value they experience internally. Perhaps the psycho-religious age will be a mystical one which will emphasize continual observation of psychic imagery.[21]

Christ also stresses the mystical nature of woman's spiritual quest.[22] It is ineffable, transient, insight producing and leads to integration with the powers of being. It leads to new self-awareness and self-confidence. Christ is clear that it is important for a woman to name her experience so that others may find validation in their experiences. This mystical experience provides the insight that woman's power stems from her clear understanding of her rootedness in nature and in her own personal past and also provides a sense of identity that can reduce guilt.

As we have seen, the inward process can be stimulated by the declining influence of the father or by naming the mystical experience. In a related way, Jung believed that people are engaged in spiritual activity when they follow the transformations of dream or fantasy.[23] He developed instructions for dreaming the dream onwards through the method of active imagination so as to provide spiritual insight and meaning to life.

Up to this point I have been talking about story, myth, mystical experience and dream. Each is separate and yet interrelated. Each arises from, and reaches down into, the depths of a woman as both cause and effect, which is why they can transform guilt. All of these experiences are "imaginal aspects" of a psychic picture that a woman works to weave into reality. Spiritual depth and progress may depend on the ability to see tangible aspects of imaginal things and to act on them.

Transformation through the inward path is complemented by the theme of the "watcher" which Carol Christ finds in Doris Lessing's novels. The watcher is the part of a woman that observes, understands and becomes conscious of the deepened dimensions of experience. It is a receptive intelligence that specializes in waiting with purposefulness. It transcends conscious control and yet the woman learns to trust that whatever happens, wherever she goes, the process of living will provide her with opportunities to deepen her insight. The conscience arises from within rather than being imposed from without. Christ observes that:

> An observing, connected, deepened consciousness is the source of the heroine's prophetic power. As she understands what is happening in herself, in the children, and in the world in which she lives, she comes to understand what will happen as a development of what is already happening.[24]

This organic prophecy is a part of spirituality wherein the personal also becomes the social and the political. The spirituality and identity of the woman is distilled from her concrete experience. "All that is visible must grow beyond itself, and extend into the realm of the invisible. Thereby it receives its true consecration and clarity and takes firm root in the cosmic order."[25]

In this discussion, guilt is reduced as women find that it is not their individual problem that they can't conform to the mythic ideal, but that it is a shared problem imposed by existing religious and secular societies. In this way the personal becomes the political, and women gain the impetus to strive for the recognition of alternative values. Guilt is no longer debilitating, but becomes empowering within the context of a support system. This approach allows women to develop a new self-image—based not on the self-sacrificial role of woman that Christiantiy has come to value—but in women trusting their own personal and community experience.

But Christ, Goldenberg and others take the argument still further, claiming it is not possible for women to construct a new role through limiting themselves to psychological process. Women need a female role model, the goddess, as an affirmation of the legitimacy and beneficence of female power. Guilt cannot be removed in the existing patriarchal system.

> Religions centered on the worship of a male God keep women in a childish state of psychological dependence on men and male authority, while at the same time legitimating the *political* and *social* authority of fathers and sons in the institutions of society. The damage done to women by exclusively male symbolism in religion and culture is both psychological and political; women feel their own power is inferior or dangerous and they therefore give over their will to male authority figures in family and society.

Madonna Kolbenschlag states that matriarchal religious experience provides an antidote to many of the excesses of patriarchal experience:

> It exorcises archetypal images through a process of renominization; it overcomes transcendent instrumentality in immanence; it derationalizes religious experience through recovery of mys-

ticism and the "numinous"; it replaces clerical elitism with
the authority of the individual; it demystifies transcendent religion by identifying divine power within natural energies.[27]

Christ suggests three possible meanings to the symbol of the
goddess: (1) the Goddess as divine female, as personification who
can be invoked through prayer and ritual, (2) the Goddess as symbol of life, death and rebirth energy in nature and culture, in personal and communal life, (3) the Goddess as symbol of affirmation
of the legitimacy and beauty of female power. Each explanation
can be appropriate for different individuals as they make the symbol primory while allowing for different interpretations. Regardless of the meaning one chooses the Goddess still serves the same
functions: (1) the affirmation of female power, (2) the affirmation
of the female body, (3) positive valuation of the will, ("A woman
is encouraged to know her will, to believe that her will is valid,
and to believe that her will can be achieved in the world").[28] and
(4) the revaluation of mother-daughter relations and women's
heritage. Goddess imagery provides one role model and positive
image of womanhood to enable women to escape from the bondage of guilt.

Regardless of the approach taken to minimize guilt, it is a necessary movement for modern women. I hope it is clear that the guilt
of which I am speaking is not the guilt that arises from being
guilty of a crime, but is the guilt a woman feels as she becomes
aware that her inward promptings which call her toward full per-
sonhood extend beyond or fly in the face of traditional social roles.
Perhaps she is guilty of the social crime of upsetting the status
quo. The guilt emerges in countless ways since the decision to
assert one's self is a decision that affects the people she cares about—
husband, children, family. Because of a family's organic interdependency and its unconscious structure, it is often difficult for one
person to change and grow unless the whole family system changes
in directions that support the woman's growth or unless the woman
leaves the family and establishes a new network of support. This
problem is compounded by the need for society to change to sup-

port a changing family structure. In this context I want to discuss the impact of woman's growth on the family.

Families are the basic system of "people making" in all human societies. A family is a primary social organism with a distinctive identity or personality of its own, which is more than the sum of its parts. There is an organic interdependency such that the functioning of any one part of the system reflects and influences the interaction of all parts of the whole organism. The behavior, attitudes, values, and patterns of relating of individual family members are shaped by the family structure and social expectations. These include unconscious family rules, expectations, values, taboos, beliefs, patterns of communication, and distribution of power among its members. This dynamic structure can frustrate or facilitate the growth of all its members. Therefore, we need to look at some of the dynamics that influence the process of family growth.

Virginia Satir has identified four family dynamics that encourage growth. First, each member feels and supports each other's self worth. Second, persons communicate in clear, direct and honest ways. Third, the implicit rules are fair, flexible and open to negotiation as the family's situation changes. Fourth, families are open systems that have a broad system network beyond themselves.[29] Though these qualities may seem obvious, they are often extremely difficult to implement, especially in the face of change. A family can go through the motions of change while attitudes and expectations remain rigid, leading to still more guilt.

Calling women into account for their sin of Hiding necessitates the development of a new symmetrical family where there is a minimal division of work along sexual lines. Until recently, it has been popularly thought that men and women have complementary psychological needs and conjugal roles. The male was the provider and the female was the nurturer. This led to the misconception of viewing persons as half-persons who are dependent on the other, rather than promoting the more balanced view of two whole persons relating in mutual interdependence. Furthermore, the process of overvaluing the role of the provider has led to the undervaluing of other significant roles of men such as husband, father and human being. Nurturing should not be defined as mothering but as parenting. Emerging from hiddenness for women involves developing their strong, assertive and rational potentials and integrating them with their other skills.

Another concept that needs modification is that of the home as haven or escape from the world at large. It cannot successfully stand as the sole sanctuary of moral nurturance and emotional strength. We need to let go of the exclusivity of marriage by recognizing that one person cannot meet all of the needs of another. We need more friends, networks, and involvement beyond the couple, balancing time spent together, with others, and alone. In order for this to work, our understanding of work has to be modified so that it too can be a source of nurturance and emotional strength. Far reaching changes on every level of social interaction are needed for women to grow beyond the social guilt they are now experiencing.

Kolbenschlag feels that women are at the center of this spiritual and social transformation. She summarizes some of the signs that distinguish a woman in the process of authentic liberation: (1) their capacity for ethical choice will increase, (2) an increased capacity for religious experience will parallel development in ethical maturity, (3) the woman will accept responsibility for her own inner life, (4) the concept of sin and virtue will undergo radical inversion; we will be required to do no harm to no one and to no thing, (5) there will be a recognition and transmutation of anger, (6) there will be a convergence of the two powerful energies of politicization and contemplation.[30]

The dimensions of change I have outlined in this paper are but a very few of the dimensions that will need attention as women take or receive permission to emerge from Hiding. The needed changes are so extensive that we might do well to look at utopian novels for possible visions, rather than discuss each dimension individually; though we need both the vision of another way of relating and the mechanism by which we can change the existing system. This is our community task.

NOTES

1 Sue Dunfee, "Beyond Violence, Beyond Guilt," for the conference "Beyond Violence—Facets of a New Vision," 6-7 Nov. 1981, Claremont, Calif., p. 1.

2 Valerie Saiving, "The Human Situation: A Feminine View," *Womanspirit Rising,* ed. Carol P. Christ and Judith Plaskow (New York: Harper & Row, 1979), p. 25.

3 *Ibid.,* p. 37.

4 Dunfee, p. 8.

5 *Ibid.,* p. 2.

6 *Ibid.,* pp. 8-9.

7 *Ibid.,* p. 11.

8 Carol P. Christ, *Diving Deep and Surfacing: Woman Writers on Spiritual Quest* (Boston: Beacon, 1980), p. 5.

9 Shelia Collins, *A Different Heaven and Earth* (Valley Forge, Pa.: Judson Press, 1974), pp. 33-45.

10 Nelle Morton, "Hearing into Speech," A Sermon given at Claremont School of Theology, 27 April 1977, p. 1.

11 Elizabeth Clark and Herbert Richardson, *Women and Religion* (New York: Harper & Row, 1977); Mary Daly, *Beyond God the Father* (Boston: Beacon, 1973), pp. 44ff.

12 "Call to Sacrifice," *Holy Songs* (New York: Unification Church), p. 20.

13 The two brief references to women in restoration history are found in *Outline to the Principle: Level 4* (New York: Holy Spirit Assn. for Unif. of World Christianity, 1981), on p. 144 paragraph F, which refers to Rebekah's role in Jacob's mission, and on p. 196 which refers to the need for an "Eve" country in WWII.

14 Sonia Johnson, *From Housewife to Heretic* (New York: Doubleday, 1981), p. 376.

15 Mary Daly, *Beyond God the Father* (Boston: Beacon Press, 1973), p. 5.

16 Robin Morgan, *Going Too Far* (New York: Village Books, 1978), p. 96.

17 Johnson, p. 376.

18 Christ, *Diving Deep,* pp. 3-4.

19 Collins, p. 208.

20 Naomi Goldenberg, *The Changing of the Gods* (Boston: Beacon, 1979), p. 41.

21 *Ibid.,* p. 120.

22 Christ, *Diving Deep,* p. 22.

23 *Ibid.,* p. 67.

24 *Ibid.,* p. 71.

25 Mary Ester Harding, *Women's Mysteries* (New York: Harper Colophon Books, 1971), p. 151.

26 Carol P. Christ, "Why Women Need Goddesses," paper presented at American Academy of Religion Convention, 1977, p. 3.

27 Madonna Kolbenschlag, *Kiss Sleeping Beauty Goodbye* (New York: Doubleday, 1979), pp. 188-89.

28 Christ, "Why Women Need Goddesses," p. 14.

29 Howard Clinebell, *Contemporary Growth Therapies* (Nashville: Abingdon, 1981), p. 220.

30 Kolbenschlag, pp. 193-96.

Relations in Progress: Paradigm for Education and the Family

Diana Muxworthy Feige

Introduction

How many of us have ever sat on park benches watching and idealizing what seems to be the simple, joyful play of a few children? We sit there wondering what it would be like to return to that innocence and apparent simplicity of life—would it not be wonderful, we think and fantasize. Even scripture reminds us that "unless you turn and become like children, you will never enter the kingdom of heaven" (Matthew 18:13). "Those were the days, my friends, we thought they'd never end." Fantasies ripple by and we long to play as the children play.

Yet, when some of us leave those park benches and go into the halls of academia, an examination of that simplicity of childhood takes on new, more complex forms. Under the dissecting microscope of the academic, the bubble bursts. What seems so simple and spontaneous suddenly, with some initial regret and apprehension, appears to be quite complicated and not so spontaneous, not so innocent. Peter Laslett *(The World We Have Lost)* and Philippe Ariés *(Centuries of Childhood)* have pointed to the complex matrix of childhood experiences. The authors of *All Our Children* express surprise at the traditional miopic understanding of the context in which children grow:

> Some traditional American views, we conclude, severely hamper our national efforts to help children and parents. They obscure the *'ecology of childhood'* [my emphasis]—the overall social and economic system that exerts a crucial influence on what happens to parents and children (Keniston, 1977: xiii).

And Dr. Clarissa Atkinson in a recently published article "American Families and 'The American Family': Myths and Realities," notes that "myths about family are as complicated, ambiguous, and significant as myths about God—and very closely related" (Atkinson, 1981: 11). The most powerful myth is that of a Fall—the fall of that once wonderfully stable and Eden-like American family:

> It may be comforting to believe that there was a time when personal lives and family relationships were stable, but the fact is that we cannot locate such a time in the past any more than we can in the present (Atkinson, 1981: 11).

All of this is to say that it is not easy to be a child. For all the fantasizing and idealizing that we would like to do, upon closer examination it becomes necessary to understand the "ecology of childhood," the complex, heavily organized world into which a child is born and through which it will quickly learn how to behave.

This paper is about this social organization of behavior—specifically, the social organization of family life. It is about theories that describe this organization, their contribution to what Marilyn Ferguson in *The Aquarian Conspiracy* (borrowing from Thomas Kuhn's *The History of Scientific Revolutions*) has called an emerging paradigm shift, and Unification thought's relationship to these theories and paradigm shift. Believing that paradigms, as "frameworks of thought," "scheme(s) for understanding and explaining certain aspects of reality" (Ferguson, 1980: 26), not only permit us to think, but also frame how and what we think, and how we experience the world, I write this paper in the hope that it may help us envision, think, talk, experience, and construct family life in more fulfilling ways.

The Social Organization of Behavior

It is always exciting to me to find that the thinking and experiences of different persons are related—one, then, becomes the complement of the other. Nancy Friday's story *(My Mother/My Self)*, for example, is not so different from Lois Hood, Ray McDermott and Michael Cole's telling of Adam's story ("'Let's Try To Make It A Good Day'—Some Not So Simple Ways"). And L.S. Vygotsky's explanation of the dependence of psychological processes on social interaction *(Mind in Society)* is a fine complement to Hood, *et al's* formulation of a psychology of person-environment interactions. Each in his/her own way tries to understand the dynamic inter-play between the individual and society; each wants to understand what happened to make us what we are.

Nancy Friday begins her story with the confession that she always lied to her mother, as her mother always lied to her:

> How young was I when I learned her language, to call things by other names? Five, four—younger? Her denial of whatever she could not tell me, that her mother could not tell her, and about which society enjoined us both to keep silent, distorts our relationship still (Friday, 1977: 19).

' Adam's story is that of a Manhattan school child who has been tested, diagnosed, and labelled as having a "specific learning disability" (Hood, 1981: 158). It is the story of a young boy's attempt "to make it a good day." It is also an "account of why the good of Adam's day sounds so tenuous, how he tried so hard in the face of this, the consequences of this trying, and all the trying by the other children and adults that make up Adam's environment from one moment to the next"—an account of "how Adam's disabilities are socially organized" (Hood, 1981: 155-56, 159).

Already one sees the juxtaposition of personal life stories with theoretical explanations of their occurrences and outcomes. For Vygotsky's, Friday's and Adam's stories are more than just one person's story. Their stories are an integral part of every person's development, a process of internalization, "the internal reconstruction of an external operation" (Vygotsky, 1978: 56). This "internalization of socially rooted and historically developed activities is the distinguishing feature of human psychology" (Vygotsky, 1978: 57). It is what distinguishes the human from the animal. Furthermore, "human learning presupposes a specific *social nature* [my emphasis] and a process by which children grow into the intellectual life of those around them" (Vygotsky, 1978: 88).

This process translates all that is interpersonal into that which is intrapersonal:

> Every function in the child's cultural development appears twice; first, on the social level, and later on, on the individual level; first, between people (interpsychological), and then inside the child (intrapsychological) (Vygotsky, 1978: 57).

Psychological processes, to summarize Hood, *et al.,* are therefore developmental, dynamic, continuously undergoing change, and socially embedded. And for Vygotsky, what happens socially on the outside organizes the person on the inside.

Finding it unnecessary to "postulate internalization in order to describe (the) children's behavior," Hood, *et al.,* build upon Vygotsky's emphasis on developmental, socially embedded processes to begin constructing what they call a psychology of person-environment interactions. They write:

> While internalization may be a proper gloss on what people become more able to do as they grow from infancy to adulthood, our data show that in interpersonal situations most psychological functions remain to a large extent in the inter-personal level.
>
> We seek to build on Vygotsky's work by emphasizing the ways in which psychological processes constantly undergo change, and are *actively maintained,* as a function of ever-changing socio-environmental circumstances (Hood, 1981: 157-58).

In this context, then, Adam's story (and probably Friday's) is the story that everyone in Adam's environment constructs together. His "disability" is everybody's disability in the sense that they all cooperate, collaborate in creating, manifesting, and maintaining Adam's "failure."

Consequently, the question "why is Adam a failure?" needs to be drastically revised. In Albert Scheflen's perspective (interaction analyst), the "why" ought to be converted into a "how"—the meaning of a behavior being found in the *relation* between the behavior and its context. "We gain this information," he explains, "from perceiving the structure of behavior—from perceiving the composition of its elements, qualities, and cues in a system of relationships, programs, and institutions" (Scheflen, 1974: 181). We understand how behavior means by immersing ourselves in a "context analysis" which preserves the wholeness of events and recognizes the complex networks of reciprocal relationships that are negotiated in any communication (Kendon, 1979: 69). What is studied is "always a relationship or an infinite regress of relationships. Never a 'thing'" (Bateson, 1972: 246).

Thus, a perception of human communication emerges "in which people are seen as participants in complex systems of behavioral relationships instead of as isolated senders and receivers..." (Kendon, 1979: 69). The assumptions are that: "(1) the process of communication is a continuous one... (2) the behavior of people in face-to-face interaction is functioning in systems of reciprocal relation... (3) since all behavior is always a possible source of information, we cannot, at the outset of an investigation, exclude any aspect of behavior from the possibility that it may be functional in the communicative system" (Kendon, 1979: 71). Hence, the title "context analysis"—a vision of communication (and behavior) that perceives the "circularity of communication patterns" (Watzlawick, *et al.,* 1967: 46), that insists on studying interactions in context, that holds the *"behavioral relationship"* (Kendon, 1979: 67) as the focus of analysis.

Given Vygotsky's idea of social embeddedness that all higher functions originate as actual relations between human individuals, Hood's and McDermott's idea of the social organization of behavior as contexts for learning, and Scheflen's perception of communication as negotiated processes of information gaining reciprocal relations, the question "Why is Adam a failure?" is rephrased to read "How does Adam's behavior come to be, mean what it is?" These perspectives inform us that in order to ask the right questions one has to take into consideration where the answers are going to be found; asking the right questions is as, if not more, important as finding the right answers. The question is rephrased and the locus of attention shifted. With the new question, Adam's "disability" is not to be located simply inside Adam's head, the result of some completely personal, private perversity. It is, rather, "to be found and described as part of the contexts in which the disability(s) is made manifest to the people who notice it, suffer with it, and try to repair it" (Hood, 1981: 159). It is a shared phenomenon:

> Adam's learning disability is as much in the world as in his head, not just in the sense that the world is passively there as a medium of expression for the disability, but because the world can be described as a field of forces which organize Adam as a display board for the weaknesses of the system in which he is immersed (Hood, 1981: 159).

New questions subsequently emerge which are more sensitive to the complexity of contextual relations. For example: *What is Adam's task environment?, How do Adam and his friends, parents, teachers, etc., deal with his "problem"?* and, more specifically, *How are Adam's "failures" noticed?* Answers to these questions, from the above perspectives, would need to take into account, finally, what Mc-Dermott has called the way the participants "'make sense' of each other and hold each other accountable, given the resources and limits of their community" (McDermott, 1977: 198). The scenario is that of a dynamic dance, each participant defining, creating, maintaining the tempo, rhythm, form of the dance.

The Zone of Proximal Development: Its General Description and Implications for an Understanding of Family

General Description

The preceeding discussion serves as prelude to a discussion of what Vygotsky called the zone of proximal development. According to him every child embraces two developmental levels—the actual developmental level and the potential developmental level. The first is that "level of development of a child's mental functions that has been established as a result of certain already completed developmental cycles" (Vygotsky, 1978: 85). An example would be what a child has scored on a math quiz. The latter is that which the child exhibits when s/he is aided by an adult, that which s/he latently holds waiting for guidance in order to come into fruition. The zone of proximal development is the difference between these two:

> It is the distance between the actual developmental level as determined by independent problem solving and the level of potential development as determined through problem solving under adult guidance or in collaboration with more capable peers.

It is that which

> defines those functions that have not yet matured but are in the process of maturation, functions that will mature tomorrow, but are currently in an embryonic state (Vygotsky, 1978: 86).

In other words, the zone of proximal development defines that which is still a "bud," rather than a "fruit" of development. It "characterizes mental development prospectively" (Vygotsky, 1978: 86-87), inviting in the educator and others a sensitivity for what the child potentially holds, his/her emerging capabilities:

> The mere exposure of students to new materials through oral lectures neither allows for adult guidance nor for collaboration with peers. To implement the concept of the zone of

proximal development in instruction, psychologists and educators must collaborate in the analysis of the internal ('sub-
terranean') developmental processes which are stimulated by
teaching and which are needed for subsequent learning
(Vygotsky, 1978: 131).

Implications for an Understanding of Family

I am again excited to find a marvelous integration of ideas taking place. What I see as I read Vygotsky, Hood, McDermott,
Scheflen, etc., is a series of connections, a series of wonderful
"aha" moments that connect now with still another body of
literature. This new integration marries thinking about socially
organized zones of proximal development with that of families as
educative systems.

If it is true that "properly organized learning" can stimulate development that would otherwise go unnoticed, then it follows that
the task of the educator is to nurture this zone of proximal
development. I propose that Vygotsky's suggestions for the class-
room be taken as equally applicable to the family. It is possible, for
instance, to substitute "the family" in the following sentences for
Vygotsky's reference to learning and teaching. The substitution
makes an interesting matching of ideas:

> an essential feature of learning (the family) is that it creates the
> zone of proximal development; that is, learning (the family)
> awakens a variety of internal developmental processes that are
> able to operate only when the child is interacting with people
> in his environment and in cooperation with peers (Vygotsky,
> 1978: 90).

> teaching (the family) represents the means through which de-
> velopment is advanced; that is, the socially elaborated con-
> tents of human knowledge and the cognitive strategies necessary
> for their internalization are evoked in the learners (children)
> according to their 'actual developmental levels' (Vygotsky, 1978:
> 131).

This substitution implies that Vygotsky's assumptions about

learning, teaching and the zone of proximal development may also apply to the theme of the family as educator. The overarching thesis is, simply, that "'good learning' is that which is in advance of development" (Vygotsky, 1978: 89)—thus, the attention of the educator is on what the child does only to the extent this points to what the child can do. These potentials, in turn, mature only in relation to an external social environment. Some of the assumptions to which this thesis leads are: (1) focus is on *interaction,* specifically the individual-in-interaction (on what the individual can do, both when alone *and* with the assistance of others— that which is done alone successfully is used as a sign for what can be done with assistance), (2) stress is thus given to *context,* (3) importance is also given to *process, how* education is organized, not only *what* education is organized; and (4) attention is on the process of *transformation,* it being necessary for the educator to be sensitive, flexible, open to change, growth, to invite the child to educate him/her, to inform him/her of the next step.

To propose that the family is to serve as a zone of proximal development is to propose that family interaction be seen as a contributor to the quality of the context that affects development. As Lawrence Cremin in *Public Educator* has pointed out, the family is not the only factor in the "ecology of education," but it is certainly an important member of the "configurations of education" that mold our lives (Cremin, 1976: 27-53). The family is both a physical context *and* a state of mind, a social environment *and* an orientation. It is a context, outer and inner, that may provide all its members with a supportive network of interactions that is sensitive to the latent capabilities of individuals. It is a context where individuals interact and in that interaction inform one another, organize one another to "do" *family. And in the "doing," education proceeds.

*I borrow this phrase from Charles O. Frake, *Language and Cultural Description* (Stanford, Cal.: Stanford Univ. Press, 1980).

Hope Leichter and Lawrence Cremin's articles in *The Family as Educator* and *Families and Communities as Educators* are helpful in explaining how this occurs. Cremin defines education as the "deliberate, systematic, and sustained effort to transmit, evoke, or acquire knowledge, attitudes, values, skills, or sensibilities, and any learning that results from the effort, direct or indirect, intended or unintended" (Cremin, 1979: 137). Inherent in such a definition is a vision of an educational process that proceeds across a host of individuals and institutions. This definition also clearly focuses attention on the relationships among several educative institutions and on the effects of one institution's efforts on those of another" (Cremin, 1979: 137). Thus, the focus is on what he calls "linkages," the connections, integrations, the dance that takes place among the varied institutions that educate.

Leichter uses this definition to help her in thinking about the family as an educative system. She takes this to "include not only deliberate processes but also those processes that are at the margins of awareness" (Leichter, 1979: 5). Seen in this light, education is a "lifelong process that may take place in a variety of settings and that needs to be understood as it takes place in each of these settings" (Leichter, 1979: 6). It is a process that takes place on multiple levels simultaneously. "Both the content of learning and instruction and the process of learning and instruction must be understood. Of particular importance are the processes of learning to learn, or what has been called deutero-learning or meta-learning" (Leichter, 1979: 6). Furthermore, education is a process in which affective and cognitive learning are intertwined in each and every setting. "One cannot presume, for example, that affective learning takes place at home and cognitive learning in the school. On the contrary, both aspects must be understood in both settings" (Leichter, 1979: 6).

The conception of education is again one that is dynamic, recognizing the rich interchanges which take place across and within educative institutions. This dynamism may appear never ending, impossible to handle scientifically. Leichter therefore suggests several approaches to research. These include the concept of the family as an educative system and the process oriented approach to the study of the family.

The key words are system and process. These ought to come as no surprise for they have been so much a part of the previous discussion. System is used here simply to refer to the idea that "in a system of interdependent parts, a change in any one relationship will have an effect on all other relationships" (Leichter, 1979: 18). The emphasis is on connections, relationships, interdependencies, reciprocating influences:

> If one applies this image to thinking about the family's relation-
> ship to other institutions that educate, it suggests that it is not
> sufficient merely to look at the family's values as compared
> with the school's values at a given moment in time; one might
> look rather at the way in which communication between fam-
> ily and school serves to modify the values and perspectives of
> each (Leichter, 1979: 21).

The family is an open system, a system with permeable, not closed boundaries. Thus the heavy emphasis on the family-in-relationship, both from the point of view of the relationships within the family and between the family and other educative institutions. Thus also the heavy emphasis on "contextual rigor":

> that is, the rigor that derives from placing the analysis of specific
> relationships in the context of other significant relationships
> and influences and in the process considering the cross-pressures
> that stem both from within the family and from without
> (Leichter, 1974: 25).

The model is one in which grandparents educate parents who in turn educate grandparents, etc. Sister educates brother who edu-cates sister who educates brother, and so forth. The family influences the school which in turn influences the family. The family-school configuration influences the church which in turn influences the family-school configuration. There is no direct, linear cause and effect relationship. It is, as Watzlawick states, a circular pattern of relationships, each a beginning and an end, continuously in motion, in process, in transformation. Incorporating Hood's, McDermott's and Scheflen's thinking, we may say that it is a vision of the family organizing the individual who in turn organizes the family. R.D. Laing puts forth a similar idea when he writes: "The family may be imagined as a web, a flower, a tomb, a prison, a castle. Self may be more aware of an image of the family than of the family itself, and map images onto the family" (Laing, 1972: 6). And, Hood and others would add that the family continues this process by mapping images onto the individual—each reciprocally organizing the other.

This model of the family requires a particular approach to research. It needs an approach which is like a vision, a particular perspective, or lense through which to observe its subject. It needs an approach which sees wholeness and not separate, independent entities. Its sensitivity must be toward relationships-in-process, "the shifting character of interactions throughout the life cycle," "the continuous process of change and development within the family, both for adults and for children" (Leichter, 1974: 27, 43). Its focus, therefore, is not on outcomes, but rather on process— "the moment-to-moment processes of education within the family and . . . the more general processes by which the family mediates educational experiences elsewhere" (Leichter, 1974: 29-30).

Concerned with the educational interactions occurring within the family, this approach might incorporate the following agendas in its research: "language interaction within the family," "the organization of activity in space and time," "memory as an interactive process," and "the processes of evaluating and labelling" (Leichter, 1974: 31-39). Each of these agendas would provide a description of how the family mediates educational experiences, i.e., how the "family members translate and interpret educational experiences for one another" (Leichter, 1974: 40). Each would be a part of the scheme developed by Hood, *et al.,* McDermott, and Scheflen, for each would describe the ways in which family members inform one another of who they—the individual and the family—are and in so doing, mutually construct environments in which to grow (or not grow). As such, the family may serve as a zone of proximal development, as an educative system.

Emerging Paradigms: Brief Description and a Coming Home for Unification Thinking

Brief Description

Until now I have been presenting some current models of family and education theory, focusing primarily on showing their underlying connections. I shall now briefly summarize the recurring themes I have pointed out and then put them in the context of Marilyn Ferguson's encouraging thoughts on "learning the emergent paradigm" (Ferguson, 1980: Chap. 9).

The threads which have been woven together are these: (1) from Vygotsky we noted the importance of social environment on development, the emphasis on the social birthing of potential; (2) from Hood, *et al.*, McDermott, and Scheflen we derived a psychology of person-environment interactions, a view of development that stresses the importance of understanding behavior in context, within the network of events, relationships in which it is manifested and maintained; and (3) from the Cremin, Leichter dyad we begin to see the function that the family serves as one such dynamic, interdependent, organizing network. The shared notions (regardless of differences) are those of interaction (the individual-in-interaction, the-family-in-interaction), relationship, interdependency, connection, linkage, configuration, context, circularity, development, change, transformation and process.

The scenario they weave is one of *relations-in-process,* a perspective that nicely complements Ferguson's description of the differences between the "old paradigm of education" and the "new paradigm of learning" (Ferguson, 1980: 289-91). The old paradigm focuses on *content,* "acquiring a 'right' body of information, once and for all," on learning as a *product,* or "destination," and on the "one-way-street" of teacher instructing student (Ferguson, 1980: 289-91). The old paradigm understands learning to be a series of "methods of instructions ... teachers, literacy, math, grades, achievements" (Ferguson, 1980: 288). It emphasizes the external world, considering inner experiences "inappropriate in ... [a] school setting" (Ferguson, 1980: 289).

The new paradigm looks, instead, to the nature of learning, "the processes by which we have moved every step of the way since we first breathed" (Ferguson, 1980: 288). It focuses on "learning how to learn, how to ask good questions . . . and be open to and evaluate new concepts . . . " (Ferguson, 1980: 289). Hence it stresses *context* over content and emphasizes learning as a *process,* a journey in which the teacher learns from the student. "Learning," in this perspective, "is transforming." "Think of the learner as an open system—a dissipative structure, . . . interacting with the environment, integrating it, using it" (Ferguson, 1980: 291). The hope is for a "transpersonal education" that recognizes the "transcendent capacities of human beings," that "celebrates the individual and society, freedom and responsibility, uniqueness and interdependence, mystery and clarity, tradition and innovation. It is complementary, paradoxical, dynamic" (Ferguson, 1980: 288). Without needing to regurgitate "right answers" as the only evidence of a good education, the individual-in-transformation is challenged to explore his/her inner and transcendent powers, to be a learner, transformer for a "new world" (Ferguson, 1980: 285-91).

Coming Home: The Family and Unification Thinking

By now the reader is likely to be saying to him/herself "I've heard that before." For me, as a Unificationist wanting to better understand her community's thinking and actions, the reading of these themes is a coming home, a feeling of "they are playing my song." The themes are not merely repetitious lyrics—they complement one another and, better yet, provide me with a context for understanding Unification thought and praxis. My experience is similar to that of Harvè Varenne during his ethnographic studies of an American town: "It dawned on me that I was living a sort of improvised baroque concerto with various instruments playing the theme and answering each other" (Varenne, 1977: 9).

Most importantly, the discussions of the social organization of behavior, zones of proximal developments, families as educative systems, and learning as transformation provide a framework, a paradigm, for comprehending what families and education are about.

They are like eye glasses that we put on in order to see, experience the world, lyrics we use to sing our songs, themes we create to play our concertos; through them we envision and, thus, organize our lives. A paradigm shift involves a con-version—a willingness and ability to see in new ways. What these theories and Unificationism offer, I suggest, is a paradigm shift, a way of looking at and experiencing the world and, for our purposes here, a particular way of perceiving and experiencing family.

My intention in this final section, then, is to describe how a Unificationist (or, at least, how I as a Unificationist) thinks about the family. My contention is that *how* we think affects *what* we think which in turn affects our experiencing of the world. I shall begin by describing the paradigm a Unificationist uses to envision and experience family life.

If one spends any amount of time within a Unification environment there are certain themes—ways of thinking—which one notes keep emerging. These themes are in the written and oral tradition: *Divine Principle* speaks of them, Rev. Moon speaks of them, the members speak of them in their daily conversations and use them for making important decisions for their life. They are constructs that are not so different from those already presented here.

First and foremost, there appears a *relational* kind of thinking. Every thing, every person, every event is thought of in relation to some other thing, person, event in space and time. Thinking is strongly contextual, both in terms of placing moments in relation to some historical event of the past or event yet to come, and in terms of recognizing that one's actions affect others. The individual is embedded in the family, the family is embedded in society, society in the world, the world in the cosmos. The model is one of circular chains of interconnections, stimulating and responding to one another: "Without give and take action, no being or thing can exist, act, and multiply" (*Divine Principle Study Guide,* 1973: 18).

Thus it comes as no surprise to hear that "no man is an island." The con-version that takes place in accepting the Unification paradigm is one that involves recognizing (maybe first intellectually and then experientially) what David Spangler of the Findhorn community has aptly called our "intrinsic relatedness"—our inborn relatedness to each other, the buds and the trees, the past, the present, and, especially, to God. And the family is crucial to Unification thinking and life precisely because of this recognition.

The family is the place—again, both physically and otherwise— wherein this relatedness and embeddedness is first experienced. Rev. Moon has called it "God's universal textbook" (Moon, 1982: 9); Rev. Chung Hwan Kwak has described it as the "fundamental foundation for the fulfillment of God's love on earth" (Kwak, 1982: 15); Dr. Moses Durst has called it "God's university" (Address at Unification Church Wedding, 1982). They have given the family such eminence because it is conceived of as that place, that network, wherein we each discover our God-given relatedness to everyone, everything, to God Him/Herself. It is a primary context in which we discover our selves by discovering our ability to share in this relatedness; it is a primary network in which our character, "growth of the heart," (Lee, 1975: 14) matures in its ability to think, feel *with* God, humanity, and the creation.

This emphasis on the individual-in-relationship, the family-in-relationship, brings with it a sensitivity to the importance of *context.* As important as the family may be, it is also understood to be a part of the larger configuration of educative systems. Thus the recent emphasis on "home church as the base of the kingdom of heaven" (motto for the church for 1979). Every Unificationist knows that, at one point or another, his/her family, ideally, is to settle into a community and serve that community as wholeheartedly as possible. To not do this is to deny one of the basic principles of creation—our intrinsic relationships and shared responsibilities. To do this is to find freedom in fulfilling these basic laws. Our wedding vows remind us of this:

> Would you pledge to observe heavenly law as an original man and woman, and should you fail, pledge to take responsibility for that?
>
> Would you, as an ideal husband and wife, pledge to establish an eternal family with which God can be happy?

> Would you pledge to inherit heavenly tradition and, as the
> eternal parents of goodness, raise up your children to be exam-
> ples of this standard before the family and world?

> Would you pledge to be the center of love before the society,
> nation, world, and universe based upon the ideal family?

The church logo on our wedding bands, representing the reciprocating dynamics of the principles of creation, daily remind us of
this.

"Social relations," as in the views of Vygotsky, Hood, McDermott, Scheflen, and Leichter are, therefore, the essential, primary,
"contexts for learning." Our "social embeddedness" becomes our
joy and our curse. Well organized, appropriately oriented, it can
nurture the "original nature" of every person; badly organized,
poorly directed, as in Adam's case, it can inhibit, malform this
potential. And nowhere along the way should any Unificationist,
poignantly aware of this embeddedness, find blame in the "perversity" of any one individual or group of individuals. Adam figures
will emerge in our communities and it will be our responsibility,
with our paradigm of circular interconnections, to not blame Adam
or his parents for his "failure." It will be our responsibility to note
the complexity of his environment and work to help reorganize it.
And if that is not possible, at least to be careful of not laying
blame where it cannot be laid.

This requires, as in any con-version or paradigm shift, the wear-
ing of a new pair of lenses—lenses, as in Leichter's model, that
sees wholes and not parts, connections and not separations, or as
in Bateson's theory that sees "relationship or an infinite regress of
relationships. Never a 'thing'" (Bateson, 1972: 246). And it is also
a con-version, grounded in the principles of creation, that is patient with regard to time, sensitive to process. All growth, these
principles state, happens relationally and through time. The body
grows automatically under healthy conditions and the spirit or heart
grows also when the individual attends to his/her responsibility
for being-in-relationship.

Growth, physical and spiritual, occurs in stages:

> Every being needs time to reach a state of maturity or
> perfection *(D.P. Study Guide,* 1973: 37).

> Man is meant to fulfill God's love throughout his life. First,
> before marriage, or before blessing, each brother and sister
> needs to experience the fulfillment of God's parental love.
> Second, we need to experience the fulfillment of the love be-
> tween husband and wife. And, thirdly, we need to experience
> the fulfillment of children's love in our lifetime (Kwak, 1980:
> 15).

The "growth period" is that time during which we take responsibility for fulfilling our potentials, educating our character ("growth
of heart"), our goodness (loving service to humanity), and genius
(perfection of our inborn creativity) (Lee, 1975: 7-8, 14-17). Growth
is a transformative process, requiring the patience and attention of
every family member, every person-in-relation with the family, no
matter how wide the network might be.

Thus, families are learning environments, loci for learners-in-
transformation. Stagnation is troublesome. As "open systems,"
family members grow in relation to each other and in service to
the world around them, relationally and developmentally. This point
of view is similar to the "transformational worldview" that Jack
Drach (1982: 2) presents in contrast to what he considers the
"prevailing worldview":

Transformational Worldview:

Life is a matter of contributing, through myself and others,
to the universe. Therefore, in that service, I must realize
my fullest potential of body, mind, and spirit.

I am unique, but I am also one with the human species.
Therefore, the degree which I can successfully connect my
full potential to the potentials of other human beings in the
service of the universe is the measure of my success.

Prevailing Worldview:

Life is a matter of survival in a hostile environment.
Therefore, I must produce food, property and children to
enhance my security.

Other human beings are separate from me. Therefore, I
must compete with them for the power that assures my
security . . .

To say that from a Unification perspective the family serves as a zone of proximal development is to add a dimension to the idea of proximal development which I am not sure Vygotsky would wish to include. This is the dimension of spirit, which Ferguson and Drach also mention. Unificationism speaks of spirit and "original nature." The latter may be briefly described as the "true character of man created by God" (Lee, 1973: 128), that part of the human being that is "seeking God and thus to attain the purpose of goodness" *(D.P. Study Guide,* 1973: 5). This is to say, then, that in Unification thinking the family may serve not only as a zone of proximal intellectual, psychological development, but also as a zone of proximal spiritual development. We are not only socially embedded, as Vygotsky apparently believes, but are also, as the *Aquarian Conspiracy* suggests, "embedded in nature" (Ferguson, 1980: 29) and in addition in a spiritual reality transcendent of nature.

REFERENCES

Atkinson, Clarissa. "American Families and 'The American Family': Myths and Realities." *Harvard Divinity Bulletin,* Dec. 1981.

Bateson, Gregory. *Steps to an Ecology of Mind.* New York: Ballantine Books, 1972.

————. *Mind and Nature: A Necessary Unity.* New York: Bantam Books, 1980.

Cole, Michael. "The Zone of Proximal Development: Where Culture and Cognition Create Each Other." Published in a journal for the Center for Human Information Processing, La Jolla, Calif., 1981.

Cremin, Lawrence. *Public Education.* New York: Basic Books, 1976.

————. "Family-Community Linkages in American Education: Some Comments on the Recent Histography." In *Families and Communities as Educators.* Ed. Hope Leichter. New York: Teachers College Press, 1979.

Divine Principle Study Guide. New York: Holy Spirit Assn. for the Unif. of World Christianity, 1973.

Drach, Jack. "Report." *Association for Humanistic Psychology Newsletter,* July, p. 325. As quoted by Marilyn Ferguson. "Transformational Worldview." *Leading Edge Bulletin* 3, no. 1 (August 1982).

Ferguson, Marilyn. *The Aquarian Conspiracy: Personal and Social Transformation in the 1980's.* Los Angeles: J.P. Tarcher, Inc., 1980.

Friday, Nancy. *My Mother/My Self.* New York: Dell Publishing Co., 1967.

Hood, Lois, Ray McDermott, and Michael Cole. "'Let's Try to Make It a Good Day' —Some Not So Simple Ways." Paper prepared for a conference at the Center for Psychosocial Studies, Sept. 1981.

Kendon, Adam. "Some Theoretical and Methodological Aspects of the Use of Film in the Study of Social Interaction." In *Emerging Strategies in Social and Psychological Research.* Ed. G.W. Ginsberg. New York: John Wiley Press, 1979.

Keniston, Kenneth and the Carnegie Council on Children. *All Our Children, The American Family Under Pressure.* New York: Harcourt Brace Jovanovich, 1977.

Kwak, Chung Hwan. "Ideal Family." *The Blessing Quarterly,* Autumn 1981.

Laing, R.D. *The Politics of the Family and Other Essays.* New York: Vintage Books, 1972.

Lee, Sang Hun. *Unification Thought.* New York: Unification Thought Institute, 1973.

Leichter, Hope, "Some Perspectives on the Family as Educator." In *The Family as Educator.* Ed. Hope Leichter. New York: Teachers College Press, 1974.

————. "Families and Communities as Educators: Some Concepts of Relationship." In *Families and Communities as Educators.* Ed. Hope Leichter. New York: Teachers College Press, 1979.

McDermott, Raymond P. "Social Relations as Contexts for Learning." *Harvard Educational Review.* 17, no. 2 (May 1977).

—————, and David R. Roth, "The Social Organization of Behavior: Interactional Approaches." *Annual Review of Anthropology* 7 (1978).

Moon, Sun Myung. "Blessed Family." *Today's World,* 3, no. 7 (July 1982).

Scheflen, Albert E. *How Behavior Means.* New York: Anchor, 1974.

Spangler, David. Lecture given for the Symposium on the Coevolution of Science and Spirit, New Dimensions of Consciousness, New York, 1978.

Varenne, Hervè. *Americans Together, Structured Diversity in a Midwestern Town.* New York: Teachers College Press, 1977.

Vygotsky, L.S. *Mind in Society: The Development of Higher Psychological Processes.* Cambridge: Harvard Univ. Press, 1978.

Watzlawick, Paul, Janet Helmich Beavin, and Don D. Jackson, *Pragmatics of Human Communication: A Study of Interactional Patterns, Pathologies, Paradoxes.* New York: W.W. Norton and Co., 1967.

Marriage and the Family in Unification Church Theology

Frederick Sontag

The Family's Role In Salvation

The family has a central place in most societies and in some religions. Religious conversion often involves leaving the biological family to join a new family group. Thus, it is not unusual for a new religion to be formed around a new notion of the family. In fact, one key to understanding a religious novelty is to see what is unique or special about the way that new religion regards the family. Loyalty is often transferred from one family form to another. When the Roman Catholic nun leaves her earthly family, for example, she becomes "the bride of Christ."

In traditional Christianity, the Trinity may be considered as a "family concept." Certainly, Father, Son, and Holy Ghost are intimately related. You must understand the bond of relationship between the members of the Trinity if you want to grasp the uniqueness of Christian belief. Furthermore, the relationship between the Father and the Son is crucial to salvation. Unless the Son is filled with the power of the Father and can act for him, any promise of salvation will lack the force needed to back it up. The Old and New Testaments are full of references which trace a line

This article is reprinted from *Update* 6, no. 3 (Sept. 1982): 74-95, with the permission of the publishers.

of descent from Abraham or Isaac. The issue at stake is how God acts to provide salvation or to keep his covenanted promises. Father-Son relationships are frequently used in speaking of God, and family analogies often illustrate how God relates to his people. Obviously, what the believer has in mind is the idealized model of the family, not actual families with their myriad difficulties. Given the importance of the family in that Judeo-Christian tradition, why should a stress on the family in the doctrine of the *Divine Principle* be special or occasion surprise? The reasons are the novelty of the doctrine and its centrality to the whole program of the Unification Church.

The first thing to note is the fact that the Unification marriage ceremony, or blessing, is not simply one important sacrament in the church. It is the only real sacrament. The general public is either surprised or shocked to learn that members of the church, after an appropriate period of probation, are matched to each other by Rev. Moon. As a variation of the traditional Oriental system of arranged marriages, however, it is not a surprising custom. It is quite common in Korea, from whence the Unification movement emerged. In addition, the family plays a central role in their doctrine of salvation. Thus, whom one marries can never simply be a matter of casual personal attraction. Because properly based marriages are crucial if the church is to realize its religious goal, members must be matched according to that goal.

Second to that odd practice of mass marriages, the interested outsider is likely to be intrigued by the church's expression "True Parents." To those families who agonize over the defection of a child from their home to a new identification with the Unification Church, the phrase can be an occasion for outrage. It is often taken as a slur that implies a failure on the part of the biological family. Similarly, those who hear members call Rev. Moon "Father" may be offended because they think it represents a claim to divine status and usurps a title reserved for God. Given the concept of True Parents and the centrality of the "restored family" in their program of salvation, however, it is a natural thing for Unification members to see Reverend and Mrs. Moon in the role of archetypal parents. How, then, does that newly inaugurated family function to provide our long sought for salvation?

Briefly put, the Unification Church takes more seriously than most other Christian sects the image of Jesus as the new Adam. Unificationists focus on the Genesis story, and they aim to fulfill, or to restore, the Adamic ideal. God's proposed family could not be established in the beginning due to Adam and Eve's sin, followed by Cain's total defection from God's plan. Thus, from the Unificationists' perspective, the establishment of the ideal family which Adam could not accomplish is left for later generations to complete. As the new Adam, Jesus remained without sin, but those around him (particularly John the Baptist) failed to support him at a crucial turning point in his ministry. That forced Jesus to abort his full mission, that is, to establish a new ideal family. Consequently, the completion of God's plan depends on trying once again to establish an ideal, sin-free (or non-sin prone) family line. If we take the Garden of Eden story seriously, as Unificationists do, human salvation depends upon our ability, at long last, to actualize the plan that God inaugurated there. Not unexpectedly, Garden of Eden references abound in Unification Church songs, and Reverend Moon's home in New York is called "East Garden."

To restore the lost heavenly garden, we must find new original parents, ones who can point out the way that leads us to freedom from the burden of sin that has infected humanity since Adam and Eve threw God's plans into chaos. Can such a pure family first be established and then graft others into the new line? True Unificationists believe it can be done as each new couple is grafted into the bloodline of the True Parents. Reverend and Mrs. Moon have been called upon to inaugurate the new community and to serve as model parents and family. God exempted Mary, the mother of Jesus, from inherited sin. But that is no longer given to us gratis; the way for us to achieve perfection is outlined in the Principle. Jesus was like unto us, "save without sin," which enabled him to serve as a savior. Now the inauguration of God's plan involves restoring the ideal family, that is, one free from the tendency to turn away from God which is to sin. Most doctrines in Judaism and Christianity state the program of salvation more individualistically. The notion of the Holy Catholic Church as the bearer of the keys to the kingdom which they guard for the faithful is not the same as the notion in Unification doctrine of the family as the vehicle of salvation. The issue is: Can salvation—God's action to save us—be mediated by a restored, sin-free family structure?

The Family in the Official Doctrine

The casual reader of *Divine Principle* might not recognize the importance of the family in Unification thought. It stands out clearly only to one who is familiar with the life and practice of the movement. Like many other religious groups, actual practice has developed independently from its doctrinal base. Nevertheless, the importance of the family can certainly be found in the chief text. The Introduction to *Divine Pinciple*[1] chastises established Christian groups for their corrupt behavior, tracing it to a contradiction between the spiritual world and the physical world. True belief, therefore, is intimately linked to physical and behavorial practice. A new truth has been revealed, we are told (p. 9), which obviously involves new physical relationships, not just new spiritual beliefs. The aim of that new revelation is to unite all religions, but the family turns out to be the key to achieve that goal of ecumenical unity. All of that becomes clearer when we read that brotherly love can only be achieved "under God as our parent" (p. 10).

Parent imagery is strong from the beginning of *Divine Principle* and permeates all Unification life and practice. Chapter one opens with the *Divine Principle* account of creation. The centrality of reciprocal relationships is stressed, and the male-female relationship is primary among them. God has dual characteristics. That brings him much closer to a human image than mystical notions which stress a transcending unity in the divine nature do. Much is made of the notion of "the four position foundation" (p. 33) which unites God, husband and wife, and their offspring. In fact, that imagery is central to all Unification life and practice. Marriage, in that sense, is simply the chief physical exemplification of the

Unificationists' spiritual perception of the core of reality. Since sin disrupted that four position foundation, its restoration must lie at the heart of the plan of salvation. Obviously, that cannot be accomplished by God acting alone. He is involved, but reestablishing the broken relationship depends equally on human participation and constant cooperation. God has revealed the new truth and the way to restore our lost status in this latter day, but all of it will fail unless we join in the effort.

Husband and wife must unite together before they can hope to stand before God. A relationship with God (the subject) begins first with the individual (the object—p. 33). Men and women stand at the center of creation, although the ultimate center is God. If Adam and Eve had not fallen, "they would have become a central body dominating the created universe" (p. 38). It is important to note that the whole account in *Divine Principle* begins with Adam and Eve. Consequently, Jesus' coming and his mission are interpreted on that basis, not the other way around. If humans can become objects of the love of God, they need not fall again as Adam fell. That means that it is possible for us to attain deity (p. 43). Such is the core of the doctrine and the chief aim of all church practice. Marriage is simply the outer embodiment of the spiritual goal, but it is important because spirit and body must be united. There can be no spiritual salvation without its physical counterpart. The "kingdom of heaven" means that God's commands are conveyed through the True Parents (p. 46). When successful, that causes all those taken into the family to work toward one purpose. It would appear, therefore, that the Unificationists' major goal of achieving the unity of all religious peoples is dependent on building that new family structure.

Love is spoken of as parental, conjugal, and childlike (p. 49). The central Christian notion of love is first expressed in family symbolism. Had Adam and Eve not sinned, they would have created a family that realized God's purpose. Thus, our every problem is symbolized in Adam and Eve's failure, and our every hope of success rests on overcoming it. Jesus' mission can only be seen in that light and with that objective in mind. Such a belief provides an obvious rationale for why it is thought that Jesus' purpose was to come, marry, and establish the true family at last (the doctrine that probably shocks traditionalists most). We should have dominion over all things—a power lost by Adam and Eve—and restoring that dominion is our "portion of responsibility" (p. 59). Humanity is the mediator and the center of harmony between the worlds (p. 59). It is crucial, in that case, to organize a religious counterpart based on that image. "Jesus came as a perfected man in flesh and in spirit" (p. 60) is now understood to mean that he was perfectly suited to establish the restored family in Adam's lineage and in that way could overcome the age-old sin of not centering life on God.

Since Christians have always looked forward to God's inauguration of the kingdom of heaven, they can understand the central importance of the restored family line when *Divine Principle* reports, "The Kingdom of God in Heaven can be realized only after the realization of the Kingdom of God on earth" (p. 62). Some Christians have looked away from the earthly life toward the heavenly city. But for the Unificationists, just as for Marx, the earthly kingdom must first be realized as a condition. Thus, Unification thought puts equal stress with Marxism on eslishing a new earthly society. For the Marxist, that will come via a new economic order spreading its reform throughout society. For the Unification movement, the restored family serves as the center for that reformation. Whereas *Divine Principle* parallels Marxism in many ways, it deviates from Marxist ideas in counting on a spiritual reform to accomplish its goals, and it expects that new spirit to be established first in a new family line.

Just as sin came to Adam through the corruption of family relationships and an illicit use of sex (Chaper two—"The Fall"), so our route to overcome sin must be through those same channels. Unificationists have no notion of "grace" in the usual sense of a free gift of God. Their account is more like Anselm's theory of atonement where God demands payment in kind, and his justice does not allow him to overlook sin without restitution. God cannot forgive freely and unconditionally; rather, he sets up conditions which, if men and women can meet them, offer us the possibility of a new life. But the prescribed road must be pursued carefully or the whole divine plan will be delayed once more. In that program, the family that can progress toward sinlessness (because it is centered on God and follows the way prescribed in *Divine Principle*) is central to the success or the failure of the whole human effort.

If "man's portion of responsibility" were not so crucial, and if God could simply restore us by a unilateral divine act, establishing new family relationships would not take on such supreme importance. But because salvation is partly dependent on human cooperation, and because the earth must be restored before heaven can be opened to us, the importance of establishing and spreading a new family-parent relationship looms large. The informal name the Unificationists use for their movement is the "Unified Family," and they think of their whole effort in those terms. Acceptance of the doctrine as it is outlined is important, but only because it is the blueprint for the program of earthly restoration. Most converts will report that it was the people and the warmth of the family relationships they observed that first attracted them to the church. The affection showered on novices is not pure surreptitious PR, but rather an attempt to demonstrate the loving bond which should exist between all members of an ideal family.

It is pointless to speculate as to whether the centrality *Divine Principle* gives to the family was originally borrowed from Eastern or Confucian notions of family bonds. No religious beliefs are free from cultural influences, and all doctrine reflects some notions present in the society in which it is formed. We are so familiar with Western interpretations of Christianity that Eastern motifs stand out more glaringly to our eyes. To a Korean, such an interpretation does not seem at all strange. The Unificationists' goal is to unite all forms of Christianity. Could their doctrinal interpretation, which is slightly more Eastern, have possible advantages over our usual Westernized forms? Certainly we have neglected the potential theological advantage of making the family central in religious life. Ironically, we agree more often with secular groups on the necessity to engage in earthly reform projects.

Adam and Eve could not have fallen "if they had become hus-band and wife after their perfection, and extended into God's di-rect domination through their absolute love" (p. 83). Adam fell because he centered on Satan instead of God, but that was due to his immaturity and the fact that he had not reached the perfected, or invulnerable, stage. It easily follows that our need is to raise husbands and wives in a protected line until they reach the stage of perfection in which they are no longer vulnerable to sin. Each couple must follow church rules (for example, sexual abstinence) until they have matured sufficiently to withstand temptations to sin. But if Adam failed because he could not remain free from sin long enough to reach the point of perfect union with God's love (thus becoming invulnerable), how can we later creatures of sin hope to escape the trap of falling while we are still immature? The answer involves the centrality of *Divine Principle* as a document and why receiving that new revelation was so important. The men and women who studied Scripture before this century could not have fully understood God's "principle" of operation. Now that he has given full "principle" to us in a new revelation, we have a manual we can follow to safety.

How can we raise children who might follow Satan and protect them until they reach the safety of maturity? The answer rests within the bonds of the restored family and the new spiritual par-ents who have been called to inaugurate that line as "man's last best hope." We are offered a way via *Divine Principle* and the new family "to make Satan come to a natural surrender" (p. 85). God has given us a new revelation of the route to use for such an impor-tant accomplishment, but it is the men and women who live in that new spiritual/physical relationship who will accomplish those goals. The Kingdom of God will be realized on earth; earth will not be abandoned for heaven. It is projected that, once absolute goodness is established in society, conflict will cease (paralleling Marx's classless society). But there is no freedom apart from the "principle," (p. 91) since ignorance first led Adam and Eve to turn away from God and to center on Satan. In turn, it causes us to leave our rightful position under God in the family.

We have the power to "restore the original nature of creation by the power of principled love" (p. 94). Revolutions in society will continue until that happens. Restored family love is the Unificationist's counterpart to the social ownership of the means of production for the Marxist. For both groups a newly discovered doctrine paves the way. An individual's body "comes to have deity" (p. 101), according to *Divine Principle*. Once men and women become God's temple and live according to the "principle," they can by no means commit sin. Both Marx and the *Divine Principle* have discovered the origin of sin, as well as the formula to root it out and change all of mankind. Since these are the "Last Days," our time is an exciting one—the inauguration of a new age in which God's first blessing to mankind is restored (p. 121). But we must find the True Parents "through whom all men can become children of goodness through rebirth" (p. 123). A person becomes a Unification Church member if he or she acknowledges Reverend and Mrs. Moon to be those model True Parents.

Whatever his importance was in establishing God's spiritual kingdom in his own day, Jesus is not as central in the present age as are the True Parents. They are at the center of our current hope to escape the bondage of sin in these Last Days. It's often been said, largely by way of criticism, that Unification thought lowers the status of Jesus. For the establishment of God's spiritual kingdom, without which the way would not be open for us today, Jesus is supreme. But, through no fault of his own, he was blocked and could not establish the needed "family centered on God." In our present age, the True Parents hold the key to our ability to overcome sin and create the kingdom of heaven on earth. That is the only way the final kingdom of heaven can ever be established. The family and the earth come first. Anthropology before theology. Christ and the Holy Spirit together are, of course, the True Parents of mankind (p. 123), but in the Last Days we need to discover what new focus that relationship will take; that is, the people living among us who embody the "principle."

According to *Divine Principle,* God moves and restores by degrees (p.124), not all at once or by divine fiat. It is important for us to recognize that very different perception of divinity and its mode of operation since it explains why the progress in family reconstruction is so slow. God moves by degrees, and restoration is achieved by indemnity (that is, repayment of the debt incurred in sin). Although every bit of progress is hard fought, in the time of the Second Advent "all men will come to live harmoniously in the garden as one family" (p. 129). That phrase illustrates the cultural role the new family plays in the salvation drama. The symbol of the new family replaces the centrality of the crucifixion and resurrection. Those traditional aspects of Christianity are included, but they are reinterpreted. The crucifixion represents Jesus' failure to found an earthly family, and the resurrection becomes a symbol of God's plan to restore the divine family.

New Revelation is the Key

A theme of evolution and progress is built into that plan. If it were not so, there would be little reason to believe that the future could be different from the past. "Man is gradually being elevated in his spiritual and intellectual standard as history progresses" (p. 120). We know there is nothing inevitable about that, however. We failed to meet God's program in the past, and we can do so again. Our only advantage in the present day is the receipt of the "principle." Now we can clearly understand how God operates to restore humanity and join him in that effort with full knowledge. The revelation of the details of that plan, which could not be clearly discerned before, is itself one more indication that we are ushering in the Last Days when God will bring to fruition his plans to restore mankind and the family.

Thus, a great deal of the credibility of that plan of "salvation through the restored God-centered family" depends upon the assertion that a "new truth" has appeared (p. 131). Even the Bible is rated as a bit out of date, given the appearance of new scientific truth. Here again we find a parallel with Marxism. Whereas the

Bible expresses truth, it is not held to be the final truth itself. The Enlightenment has had its effect on the philosophy of the "principle." We must now expect God and religion to keep pace with a higher standard of truth. Even Jesus is viewed as not having been able to say all that he wanted to say before the crucifixion (p. 132). The way is thus open for a higher truth to appear to complete what Jesus was forced to leave incomplete. If one is tempted to reject that notion of the incompleteness of truth in the biblical record, consider that *Divine Principle* adopts that position partly to explain the divisions and quarrels that continue within Christianity (and among all religions) and also the failure of Christianity to complete its mission after centuries of trying. Because they have been operating on a not-yet-complete revelation which God has now supplemented, religions have failed to date to usher in God's kingdom on earth. But it is now possible to attempt that restoration project once more.

Another prominent notion in the Unificationists' whole program is that of "the central figure." "We must find the central figure of the new history, whom God has designated . . . " (p. 134). That idea is not a total novelty, but rather a special reading of the Bible that represents God as selecting a new central figure in each age, Jesus preeminent among the others. It is a free election on God's part and involves no foreordination. Discerning who among us is such a figure, however, is the major religious task of every person in any age, particularly in the Last Days. Any reference to the Reverend Sun Myung Moon as a messiah is usually misleading because *Divine Principle* understands messiahship as a non-divine role. Nevertheless, every member who joins the Unification Church must at one time have taken Reverend Moon to be the person through whom God has decided to move in these times. That is important to the formation of the new family since the chief function of the "central figure" is to form a new, pure family line as the vehicle of salvation.

In the Last Days the way has been opened for those who truly follow the newly revealed "principle" to "find the way to true salvation" (p. 136). Jesus was forced to take the way of the cross which opened spiritual salvation, but humanity's original nature has not yet been perfectly restored. We need to have the kingdom established on earth which means, to the Unificationists, the restoration of Adam's lost family. Although salvation must include the physical body, the notion of a new family line as the way to salvation comes about partly by rejecting a literal belief in the bodily resurrection. Such a miracle can no longer "satisfy the intellect of the modern man" (p. 165). Science has made the opening of the graves of the dead an untenable idea. The notion of a pure family line—first established, then gradually reaching out—is, however, something men and women can do for themselves under divine guidance. It eliminates the necessity of God breaking in with miracles. People can follow that plan without miraculous intervention, except for the assistance which members from the spirit world lend us. If their battle against demonic forces ends victoriously, they can then share that power with us.

Resurrection now means "to return to the Heavenly lineage through Christ" (p. 171). We leave the satanic lineage caused by Adam's fall primarily through the newly established family which is maturing to follow God's plan as Adam could never do. Since the spirit of a person can "grow and become perfect only through the physical body" (p. 173), the family and receiving the blessing in the mass-marriage ceremonies conducted by Reverend and Mrs. Moon are the necessary vehicles to restore the physical world. That must be done before we give any thought to heaven. We cannot leave the world of the body; we must move through it. We must follow the guidelines now given to us and try to get all the way through the periods of growth to reach perfection, as Adam never did. In Adam's day God's revelation was not yet complete, but "this is the last age in which man can communicate directly with God" (p. 177). "Now we see through a glass darkly," said Paul, "but then . . . " (1 Corinthians 13:12).

Those who know the "principle" and who believe in the coming of the Lord of the Second Advent will cooperate with him "in setting up the condition of indemnity . . . for the course of the providence of restoration" (p. 180). Although that begins with the individual, it must pass through family, national, and then worldwide levels in order to succeed (p. 187). Thus, it is easy to see that the formation of restored families, under the spiritual guidance and the blessing of True Parents, is the next and crucial stage after one's conversion. It is no wonder that the matching of couples, the strict sex mores, and the single sacrament of the mass-marriage blessing are the essential religious practices of the Unification Church. Without them, all else would fail. The family lies at the core of the doctrine and is the key to accomplishing the *Divine Principle* program. Consequently, an individual approach to salvation is unacceptable. Here again, as with Marxism, the Unified Family is a political, social, and economic movement, but its core is a spiritual principle.

God's will to accomplish his purpose in creation, which began with Adam, is unfailing; but the individuals elected to carry it out have not yet completed the task. God is not omnipotent in the traditional theological sense. "God's purpose of creation can be fulfilled only by man's accomplishing his portion of responsibility" (p. 197). Thus, the formation of new families is not merely a nice idea; it is that upon which the very success of God's original plan depends. The whole value of the microcosm cannot be complete without perfected men and women. First, however, the foundation of faith must be restored through indemnity or meritorious work. That is a course of repayment which people themselves set up as a condition, based on *Divine Principle* and the guidance of church leaders. According to the guidelines of *Divine Principle,* there must be a foundation of substance. But God cannot grant mankind grace unconditionally. Therefore, to create the foundation for receiving God's grace is a human act and responsibility. That foundation is the God-centered family, not the isolated individual praying or working alone. Communities are a necessity. A political and economic society centering on God's ideal must come into being. God does not work independent of history but through it, and the restored family is his instrument.

Marx and Engels on the Family

Having noted both the interesting parallels and the contrasts between *Divine Principle* and Marxist thought where the family is concerned, it is instructive to look at Marx and Engels's work on "The Holy Family." Remember that both groups adopt Hegel's notion of historical progression toward an ideal state. The Marxist ideal is materialistic and atheist; *Divine Principle* is spiritual, and it bases everything on a right relation to God. Marx and Engels thought metaphysics had lost all credibility and, like *Divine Principle,* they rested their confidence on a new scientific understanding. The Marx-Engels notion was that an individual must become "really human" since humans are truly social and develop their true nature only in society. Because people are shaped by their surroundings, with the right theory and the right surroundings they may become "really human," and the source of crime can be destroyed.

Marx formed a religion for the scientific era, a scientific humanism. *Divine Principle* forms a new religion based on a revised theory of the holy family, but it is no less oriented toward the restoration of mankind. Here is the source of *Divine Principle's* anti-communist stand, which at times leads Unificationists to vociferously oppose Marxism. Both groups propose to revamp humanity and society with the aim of restoring our true nature. Each has a newly developed formula and proposes to accomplish that goal by forming a band of dedicated followers. Each proposes a worldwide society, a new internationalism. One is materialistically based; the other depends on a new interpretation of Christianity. What increases the tension between them is that they do not have the same understanding of the new "science" which is to accomplish that goal and make possible what was not open to us before. The irony is that each requires the universal acceptance of the truth of their theory as a prior condition for accomplishing the task of the worldwide restoration of mankind.

Critique and Evaluation

We should begin by stating the positive aspects of the Principle's doctrine of the family since the Unification Church's rise as a new religion indicates that many people have found something satisfying in it which they find missing in established religions.

(1) In a time when traditional family structure is under attack and disintegrating in many societies, the Principle's stress on family relationships is particularly attractive to some. The arranged selection of partners and the mass-marriage ceremony/sacrament are not traditional in the West. By way of contrast, however, the Unificationists treat the family as the center of the human fabric, and mother-father roles are accentuated as important. Marx and other secular doctrines desacramentalized the family and made it simply a matter of social convenience. In Marxism the central salvific institution is the party. If we must restore a religious role to the family as an institution, then that raises a fundamental question for present-day Western societies.

(2) In a time of racial tensions and national antagonisms wherein each small group asserts its autonomy, Unificationism or Unified Family marriages are quite often interracial. Anyone who did not see that racial tensions also exist within the ideal framework of the Unification Church would be blind, but it is true nonetheless that their theory works to build an international family. They are at least as successful as any other group in pursuing the goal of breaking down national racial barriers. Marxism also proposes to do that, and Christianity shed its provincial connections early in its history when it opted for a worldwide church. The Principle is a call to return to that goal of overcoming racial and religious barriers during a time of rising national antagonisms. Whether all religions will accept the Unification leadership is doubtful, but at least their aim is not to form an exclusivist religious in-goup. The Principle, as a counterproposal to a Marxist-atheistic internationalism, seeks to unite all religious strains under the common cause of restoring mankind.

Having thus commented on positive aspects of the Principle, let me mention several areas of critique.

(1) The chief flaw in the Principle's program is that the fulfillment of its idealistic cause is dependent upon prior acceptance of the rightness of its concept of the "completed testament." The history of religions, or of any theory-based enterprise, tells us that it is unlikely that all religious groups will ever agree on one theory by any means other than by violent revolution. We must also deal with the "scientific age" assumption involved in both the Principle and Marxism. Each believes something new has appeared in the modern age (due to the rise of science) that makes our intellectual climate different. The Principle is based on a new revelation concerning God's principle of operation which was not fully given until these Last Days. Marxists are no less apocalyptic. They feel we have reached a turning point (that is, events have come to such a climax) that gives us the opportunity to "make all things new." The Unificationist follows the new Principle, the Marxist a dialectic of materialism . At that point each reader will have to observe the present situation for him- or herself and ask if he or she finds that mankind has reached such a decisive turning point so that what was once impossible is now possible.

(2) More difficult, and also more central and baffling still, is the question of whether God does in fact operate as the Principle outlines his divine program. I see no reason why God could not do so. The Principle gives us a perfectly possible and even plausible theory, and it is much more capable of extension and analysis than many theologies which undergird successful religions. That God prizes and supports family relationships is quite probable. Even though some have abandoned it, that notion was once widely adopted by many religions. But the heart of the issue is whether God uses the family as an instrument of universal salvation. I cannot accept that myself, partly because I do not see salvation as being dependent on any human course of action, whether as outlined in the Principle or by Marx. The Principle remolds the story of Jesus according to theories which change his intentions from the way they have commonly been understood. Of course, it is possible that we could

not have understood Jesus' mission rightly until the coming of the "Completed Testament," as the *Divine Principle* says. Be that as it may, to attribute a family aim to Jesus' mission requires us to believe in a divine plan of salvation carried out by humanity. I do not see that God acts in that way. And, if that is not God's chosen mode of operation, the question of reinterpreting Jesus' mission becomes a moot point.

(3) In the end, the question of our role in and responsibility for the divine plan of salvation looks as the largest issue, just as the question of whether a new economic program can usher in the classless society did for Marx. The Principle parallels the American social gospel in that both rely on human beings to accomplish, in a new age, what mankind previously could not do. The Unificationists' assumption that there is progress in history is crucial, too. There is also the important question of whether God does operate within the cycles of human history to accomplish his purposes, as the Unificationists' assume. Hegel and all "progress theories" think that is so. Marx did, too, but he needed the aid of a practical, applied metaphysics, not God. Both Marx and the Principle stress the absolute need for the chosen elite to act out the new theory and put it into practice. Unificationists often say that what is unique in their life is that they are "living out what they believe," which is also a claim of the Marxist. But communism is a political-economic theory and so, obviously, has a chance to gain control of societies, by violent revolution if necessary. But can a spiritually-motivated new religion hope to have the same public effect? They lack a new economic theory (except for their support of capitalism and their ventures into various business enterprises), and they disavow any use of aggression. The Principle must, therefore, depend on marriage and the restored family to carry out its plan. The appearance of the new central figure is, in addition, no less important for accomplishing God's purpose.

As with Marxism, we can suspend our final judgment of the Unification movement until we can inspect its public record after a trial period. Unlike the mysticism of John of the Cross, the Principle's projects will be quite easily visible if they succeed. Even if they do not alter society in a manner easily open to inspection (as many revolutionary proposals of a sweeping nature do), the Unificationists may achieve less obvious, beneficial effects. For instance, their system of arranged and God-centered interracial marriages seems to create quite stable homes, even if the restoration of all humanity is not thereby ushered in. If they can create a stable Unified Family on an international basis, that will be, in itself, an accomplishment of some religious significance. Of course, the children of those marriages (including Reverend Moon's 13) may begin the cycle of sin and salvation all over again, rather than achieving perfect union with God within the bonds of the restored family. Nevertheless, if an ideal is not fully accomplished, that is no reason to fault what it can do to improve our human lot.

NOTES

1 *Divine Principle* (Washington, D.C.: Holy Spirit Assn. for the Unif. of World Christianity, 1973). All page references are to that edition.

Marriage as Eschatological Type in Unification Theology

Frank K. Flinn

In his article, "Marriage, Family and Sun Myung Moon," Joseph Fichter, S.J., wrote: "There has been much comment and criticism of the theological, political and economic aspects of the Unification Church, but very little has been said about the positive value implications in regard to marriage and family."[1] The aim of the present essay is to attempt to fill in the glaring lacuna which Fr. Fichter has detected in the prevailing critiques of the Unification Church. The lacuna is glaring because, in my study of and experience with the Unification Church, the teachings and practices concerning marriage and family are the keystone to the edifice of Unification theology. And the axis of the keystone is centered on the eschatological and messianic meaning with which Unification theology endows marriage and family. Furthermore, the attraction which the teachings on marriage and family holds for the young adults joining the church must, I believe, be seen in light of the crisis in the modern conception of marriage and the family.

Marriage, Family and the Crisis of Modernity

The word "crisis" has become a buzz-word in our time, so it is

This essay is a translation and amplification of my lecture "Die Ehe as eschatologischer Typ in der Vereinigungstheologie," delivered at the Forschungsinstitut für Neuen Religionen, University of Marburg, Nov. 8, 1981.

incumbent upon me to make clear how I am going to use it. Most often, the word is applied to situations or conditions of existence, for example, an economic crisis, or a political crisis. I am not addressing the crisis in the conditions of existence which beset marriage and family in modernity. The conditions are all too obvious and prevalent in those societies now in the grip, or about to be in the grip, of the technological moloch. Rather, the crisis I wish to address is the crisis in the *conception* of marriage and family—a conception which arose in modernity, which is concomitant with the conditions, and which legitimates those conditions. This does not imply that the idea generates the conditions or that the conditions generate the idea but that the idea and the conditions dialectically reflect one another. Much has been written about the conditions of marriage and family in modern life but little about the conceptual undergirding of those conditions. This is so because it is most difficult to stand outside one's own or to critique one's own from "within the within" in which we live, move and have our being. Much of what goes by the name of critique (e.g., "the end of ideology") is nothing but a rationalization and disguised legitimation of the conceptions of the status quo. One way of standing outside one's own, if only for a fleeting moment, is to recollect what our ancestors thought concerning marriage and family.

According to the classical thinkers, marriage and family are institutions which exist by nature as opposed to convention. The ancients believed that human beings were naturally propelled to enter into marriage, family and wider social and political relations. Their reasons for having this opinion were never more starkly nor more simply stated than by Socrates in the *Republic* (367b 5-7): "Well, then, a city, so I surmise, comes into being because it so happens that each of us is not self-sufficient but stands in need of many things." Beginning with this humble premise on the natural insufficiency, and hence natural sociability, of isolate humans, Socrates proceeds to "found in speech" three cities. The first, the "city of sows," is dedicated to satisfying solely the physical needs of humans. It fails because humans seem to want something more than meat; they want relishes, too (372d). Because humans want "more" the city of sows, where self-interest and the common good coincide, degenerates and gives rise to the "feverish city" in which self-interest and the good come into conflict through greed and acquisitiveness. The contradictions which arise in the feverish city, in turn, motivate the quest for the City of Beauty, the best regime *(politeia),* wherein the tension between service and reward (or "obligations and rights"), and between the good and self-interest is mediated through justice. Plato frankly admits that this third city, which strives to bring out what is highest in humanity, is imaginary and fantastic, indeed, improbable of achievement. The city where perfect justice reigns cannot be supposed to exist anywhere on earth but only as a "pattern laid up in heaven for the man who wants to see and for the one seeing to found a city within himself" (592b).

Plato is frequently called an idealist. It would be far more accurate to call him an ideaist. The perfectly just regime is not an ideal which can be targeted as the goal of history but an idea or paradigm by which we may measure the presence or absence of justice in any earthly regime whether it be aristocratic (rule by the best), oligarchic (rule by the few), democratic (rule by the many) or tyrannic (rule by the one). An ideal, by contrast, can be entertained only within the framework of the historicized and secularized eschatology in the age that goes by the name "progress." Ideas are discovered and above us; ideals are realized and in front of us. Failure to acknowledge this crucial distinction entails the failure to recognize the crucial break wrought by all modern thinkers against the ancients, especially on the question of the natural inclination of humanity to live in families, tribes, cities and nations.

Modernity commences with a conscious break with antiquity. According to the moderns, the ancients—including the classical political philosophers and the Christian thinkers—aimed too high. The ancients expected too much of human nature. The conscious break was, in the words of Leo Strauss, "a "lowering of the standards."[2] Modernity has even a dedicatory text to which all subsequent modern thinkers refer with conscious, if incautious, approval. The text comes from chapter fifteen of Machiavelli's *Prince:*

> Many writers have constructed imaginary republics and prin-
> cipalities which have never been seen nor known actually to
> exist. But so wide is the separation between the way men
> actually live and the way they ought to live, that anyone who
> turns his attention from what is actually done to what ought
> to be done, studies his own ruin rather than his preservation.[3]

If we may say that classical anthropology was founded on the assumption that humans are to take their bearings from human perfection or from how they ought to act, Machiavelli may be said to
have inverted this assumption and recommended the "realist" position that ethical and political teaching must be based on how humans in fact act. Machiavelli's presupposition might be called a
minimalist hypothesis which assumes that "all men are evil and
ever ready to display their vicious nature."[4] Thus he is forced to
"demythologize" the ancient "imaginary republics"—the City of
Beauty and the Heavenly Jerusalem—and to substitute the imitation of Socrates, who single-mindedly looked to the highest or
most god-like part of the soul, and the imitation of the Christ, the
God-Man, who single-mindedly obeyed the will of his Heavenly
Father, for the imitation of Chiron, the centaur who instructed
war-like Achilles, i.e., the Beast-Man.[5] In place of virtue, which
likens the soul to the Good, Machiavelli advances comfortable self-
preservation for the individual. His presupposition for political and
social teaching is undeniably solid; it is also unquestionably low,
for it is grounded on the emancipation of the—hopefully socially
useful—passions. The new Prince is recommended to mix virtue
with vice; or even better, vice with a reputation for virtue.

Because of the revolting character of Machiavelli's teaching, it
was both modified and mollified by subsequent thinkers who nonetheless agreed with him that the ancient political thinkers aimed
too high.[6] The ancients taught that the search for virtue requires
the containment of the passions. The moderns teach the idealistic
and utopian belief that the right political order can emerge from
the skillful emancipation of the passions. The emancipation takes
various forms: glory (Machiavelli), power (Hobbes, Bacon), ac-

quisitiveness (Locke, Smith), and recognition (Hegel). The passions are private and individual, yet the moderns maintain that the passions are what most characteristically belong to human beings in the "state of nature." This contention, in turn, narrows the scope of the concept of the "natural" human, for it gives weight to individuals and their "rights" as against social beings and their "obligations." Thus the natural sociability of humanity is brought into doubt. In the "state of nature," according to Hobbes, there is no justice nor injustice but a "war of every man against every man."[7]

From the presupposition of the natural lack of self-sufficiency in human beings, classical political theory could easily derive the origin of society on the basis of nature. The moderns could make no such derivation, given the presupposition of individualistic self-preservation and the war-like "state of nature." If society had no "natural" origin, then it had to evolve artificially or by convention. This artifice, the moderns named the "social contract." The social contract takes humans outside the state of nature and transforms them into the state of culture (Rousseau) or the state of civility (Hobbes). None asserted the artificiality of state and society more bluntly than Hobbes: "For by art is created that great LEVIATHAN called a COMMONWEALTH, or STATE, in Latin CIVITAS, which is but an artificial man; though of greater stature and strength than the natural, for whose protection and defence it was intended; and in which the *sovereignty* is an artificial *soul,* as giving life and motion to the whole body; the *magistrates* and other *officers* of judicature and execution, artificial *joints . . .* "[8]

One of the consequences of the modern conception that society originates by art rather than by nature is that all social institutions—including the intermediate institutions—came to be seen through the spectacles of the social contract. Thus even marriage as a permanent bonding of man, woman and offspring was restricted to a contractualist interpretation. Kant, for example, defined marriage as a contract for the reciprocal use of the genitals.[9] This contractual understanding of all social arrangements was never far from commercialism—always a preoccupation of the moderns. The modern concept of right itself is seen as an agreement between adults on the basis of a perceived "fair bargain." (Hence, it should come as no surprise that the rights of children, women and minorities—in other words, those who could not enter into "fair bargains"—have proven problematic and troublesome in all theories which hold to the contractual understanding of rights. The concept of rights, as taking precedence over obligations, was initially restricted to individual adult males who singly entered the primal social contract.)[10]

The contractual understanding of social relationships in modernity overwhelmed the earlier conceptions as *covenant* and as *sacrament*. In biblical literature, marriage is regarded as a covenant entered into not by two individuals striking a fair bargain, but by two families who form an alliance through their representatives, the bride and bridegroom.[11] Marriage in essence was trans-familial and trans-generational. The relational and trans-generational character of the matriarchal and patriarchal narratives in Genesis, for example, has been obscured by individualist and contractual narrowing of focus on individual figures like Abraham. A relational interpretation of the stories about Jacob and Esau would see their reconciliation as a partial inversion and mediation of the ruptured relation between Cain and Abel, i.e., as the restoration of the broken fraternal covenant involving not simply individuals but tribes and clans, shepherds and artisans. Though the fact is little recognized, the contractual interpretation of the Bible itself begins with the very moderns I have been citing. Hobbes, following the lead of his mentor Francis Bacon, was the first to systematically transform the biblical theory of covenant into a secular philosophy of compact or contract.[12] This transformation narrowed the meaning of covenant to intra-individual agreements by humans exclusively. Gone was the symbolic power of covenant, which on the one hand, could include Israel's relation to the earth as well as express God's marital relation with the people (Isaiah 54: 3-6—"Your Maker is your husband . . . For the Lord has called you/Like a wife forsaken and grieved in spirit/Like a wife of youth when she is cast off"). The apparent magnification of the role of humankind, or should I say *man*kind, in the social contract theory led paradoxically to a radical narrowing of the horizon. A contract effects relations between humans; it suggests nothing of humanity's beholdenness to the earth and the heavens, nor indeed, to divinity itself.

The quarrel between the ancients and the moderns can be highlighted with a number of sharp statements. The ancients thought that human beings were social by nature; the moderns by convention. In ancient political theory the end of society was not the political *per se,* but human excellence or the likeness of the soul to God; in modern theory the focus shifts from ends to origins (animal passions), from final causes to efficient causes of the political order. In ancient theory duties, based on natural insufficiency of individuals, preceded rights; in the modern theory of the "state of nature" there are perfect rights but no perfect duties.[13] In modern thought, justice does not consist in complying with standards apart from human will but in fulfilling contracts. Especially among the English-speaking contractualists there emerged the view that out of the satisfaction of private vices, notably acquisitiveness, there could emerge public good as if by some "invisible hand" of a commercial "providence."[14]

One of the chief consequences of the contract theory of human relationships is that intermediate institutions—family, church, guild, etc.—lost their theoretical undergirding. In classical political theory institutions were defined by their ends or purposes. Modern theory, taking its cue from modern natural science, defines institutions not from their ends but from their origins. Hence, the modern preoccupation with the "state of nature" as opposed to "natural law" and the narrowing of the origin of origins to the state of isolated individuals in nature. In Locke's case, the prepolitical individual is nothing more than a potential enterpreneur. All subsequent or "higher" institutions, particularly the family, do not have self-defined purposes but serve to protect the rights, especially property rights, which the individual does not forego upon entering the social contract.[15] Modern socialist counters to the excessive individualism of contract theory did not and could not restore the intermediate institutions to their proper autonomy. Rather, the aims and purposes of smaller partnerships were swallowed up in an exclusive collectivism. Ironically, even the putative rights of individuals are also being consumed in late state corporate capitalism. In the market economy the interest in individuals is only as "consumers" who are pitted against the "mega-individual" of the bureaucratic corporation, which, as we have recently seen, becomes more an end in itself and can shirk even low-level patriotism with political impunity. The recent "mergers" of such renowned educational institutions as Harvard, MIT, and Washington University with transnational and transpolitical petrochemical corporations, which will get first dibs on patent rights, is a perfect illustration of the evisceration of an intermediate institution of its autonomy in late modernity.

Marriage and family, which suffered the added disillusionment of Freudian critique, could hardly have been expected to escape the constraining forceps of modernization. Either the family was viewed as a way station on the child's journey to full rights (Locke) or as the idyllic refuge of intimacy between a passionate pair (Rousseau).[16] At worst, the family has been thought of as the primary instrument of oppression. One would have thought that the prevailing religious traditions could have ameliorated the tide of confusion created about the family in the modern contractualist view of human relations, but, as George Grant has noted, there exists an "intimate and yet ambiguous co-penetration between contractual liberalism and Protestantism in the minds of generations of our people" which has coincided with the confluence between "modern positive science and the positivist account of revelation in Calvinism."[17]

Indeed, the dominant driving destiny of calvinistic Protestantism was the private, inward opening of the unjustified individual before an infinite and transcendent deity. This positing of faith as individualistic inwardness opened up the possibility of sundering religion as the cumulative tradition of a faith community from faith as the personal orientation of the believer toward the divine. The positivist conception of religion as individual faith terminated in Alfred North Whitehead's famous definition of religion as "what the individual does with his own solitariness."[18] Such a half-truth blunts the cutting edge of religion as concerned with public justice, peace and hope. For all its dynamism, modern faith could not be a mainstay for communal and corporate institutions like the family since it cut itself off from the dialectic with the cumulative religious tradition and, in fact, contributed to its demythologization and de-construction. Indeed it was the paragon of modern, subjectivized faith who wrote that " 'the individual' is the category through which, from a religious point of view, our age, our race and its history must pass."[19] In full accord with this concept of faith as solitariness Kirkegaard could also proclaim that "erotic love and marriage are really only a deeper corroboration of self-love by becoming two in self-love..."[20] Whatever the more basic disagreements between contractual positivism and subjectivizing existentialism, they both reveal themselves as the common, if feuding, offspring of Hobbes when it comes to the priority of the individual and the omission of the communal at the starting point of social philosophy.

To a certain extent the history of modernity has been the history of capital I's and capital We's, isolate egos and mass institutions, autobiographies and industrial revolutions. The small-case we's have come in for short shrift except as they illuminate the I and the We. Among these intermediate collectivities are marriage and family, whose real history lies hidden beneath "studies" of sexuality, economics, technology, politics, etc. As Rosenstock-Heussy has said with great force, marriage is not an event of the everyday market-place but the telling moment in which speech becomes both revelation and destiny:

> The bride speaking her decisive "Yes" or "No" before the altar uses speech in its old sense of revelation, because her answer establishes a new identity between two separate offspring of the race and may found a new race, a new nation. We are so dull that we rarely realize how much history lies hidden in marriage, and how the one word spoken by the bride makes all the difference between cattle-raising and a nation's good breeding.[21]

Part of the very crisis of modernity is that the speech of marriage has been muffled, if only because speech itself is no longer revelation.

New Religions, Marriage and the Family

Marriage and family are unique institutions. Governments vary radically and there has been no government that could be called truly universal. With a few variations which are comparatively insignificant, marriage and family are similar the world around and are truly concrete universals. The family is an intergenerational bridge between past and future and the nexus where past heritages are interwoven to be either a blessing or bane for the future. Besides being the link between past and future, marriage and family are the nodes between nature and nurture, biological generation and cultural generativity.

Given the unique aspects of marriage and family, it is somewhat of a wonder that the family does not receive much discussion in 20th century theology. In the two major theological treatises of our century—Karl Barth's *Church Dogmatics* and Paul Tillich's *Systematic Theology*—marriage and family are hardly mentioned and much less seen in relation to the Kingdom of God. Barth, in particular, makes an amazing assertion:

> In the more limited sense particularly the idea of the family is of no interest at all for Christian theology. The families within the twelve tribes of Jacob are mentioned only infrequently and certainly play no substantial part in the outlook and presentation of the Old Testament.[22]

This type of theological reasoning comes from separating creation theology from redemption theology (redemption is the restoration of creation) and, frankly, flies in the face of biblical evidence. Indeed, a substantial number of stories in the Book of Genesis are devoted to displaying the ruptures in familial and tribal relationships (Adam/Eve, Cain/Abel, Noah and his sons) as well as the progressive mending of those relationships (Isaac/Ishmael, Esau/Jacob, Joseph and his brothers). Likewise, key elements of the patriarchal and matriarchal narratives are acutely focussed on getting spouses and having progeny. None other than Paul himself argued that the begetting of Isaac from the "dead" loins of Abraham and the "dead" womb of Sarah is a fore-sign of Jesus, raised from the dead (Romans

4:19-25). One can only ascribe this lacuna in contemporary theology to the unrecognized influence of contractualism, which left a wasteland between the autonomous individual and the corporate state.

In the wake of this vacuum there have been numerous attempts to revitalize the family idea in North America. These revitalization efforts can be broken down into three fundamental types: the family as commune, the "God-Flag-Family" movement characteristic of certain branches of fundamentalism, and sacramental renewal movements. The family commune type of movements attained notoriety beginning in the 1960s. Often they were indistinguishable from back-to-the-land crusades. In this they shared many features in common with the utopian socialist movements in the 19th century such as New Harmony, Oneida, etc. Most of these groups disintegrated, some were perverted, and others, like the Lama Foundation in Taos, NM, underwent a monasticizing reformation in order to give the group a firmer order and continuity. The Lama reformation indicates the weakness in most efforts of this type. The attempt to inaugurate newness meant not only the rejection of the bourgeois ideal of the "nuclear" family but also the sloughing off of any notion of the family as the mediator and transformer of past heritage. Indeed, family commune members often took little thought of their offspring's future.[23] The future-oriented "perfectionism" of 19th century utopian socialist movements had by the 20th century been liberalized into present tense "maximizing of human potential." Here, an observation of H. Richard Niebuhr hits its mark: "In the course of succeeding generations the heritage of faith with which liberalism had started was used up. The liberal children of liberal fathers needed to operate with ever diminishing capital."[24]

In contrast, the "God-Flag-Family" type of movement attempts to "re-pastize" the present. Thus Jerry Falwell sees the family in typical 19th century imagery as a "haven" in a "hostile environment."[25] This haven is characterized by well-defined roles: the man in the work force, the woman at home as the embodiment of "security and warmth." This notion of the family and home as a bastion of order and repose is a far cry even from the Puritan activist notion of the family as "a little church, and a little commonwealth" wherein family members were "fitted to greater matters in church and commonwealth."[26] What is incongruous about Falwell's project is that he seeks a political activist role for a conception of the Christian family which is anything but political.

Of a different order is a movement like Worldwide Marriage Encounter. Marriage Encounter started as a marriage preparation program and was expanded to serve as a marriage renewal program in the Spanish Catholic Church. It quickly spread to other countries and has been adapted by several Protestant denominations.[27] Marriage encounter both revitalizes and reinterprets the sacramental aspects of marriage for the general renewal of the church and society at large. It may be an adage that every sacrament has its day in the sun. In this time of decreasing enrollment among clerics and religious, the turn to the sacrament of marriage as the representation of the *communio sanctorum* for our time can be no accident.[28] Groups of "encountered couples" now form an infrachurch in North America not dissimilar to the "base communities" burgeoning in Latin America. The power of a movement like Marriage Encounter is that the theological heritage of the past is not simply negated but is reinterpreted with a view toward the future. Unlike the family commune movement, it does not start with a *tabula rasa*. Unlike the "God-Flag-Family" movement, it is not simply preservationist in its stance but seeks a transforming renewal beyond the white picket fence of the nuclear bastion.

Unification: Marriage and Family as Eschaton

Before discussing marriage and family in Unification theology, I need to make a few comments about the character of Unification theology itself. First, I see Unification theology as a Korean indigenization of a specific type of North American Presbyterianism known as "federal theology." This theology stresses the unity of mankind through "federal headship" with Adam in the creation and fall and with Christ in the redemption through imputation of

righteousness.[29] Unification gives this notion a planetary eschatological meaning by stressing interracial and intercontinental
marriages. (Here, I should note that "federal" is derived from the
Latin *foedus,* covenant, treaty.) Secondly, in Unification theology
relations rather than substances have primary place. This may relate to *yin-yang* notions in the East but it is also a metaphysical
principle at the heart of all federal theology, particularly in the
theology of Jonathan Edwards for whom the "consent of being to
being" constitutes the primary datum of the created order.[30]

Thirdly, Unification theology is a two Article theology, despite
the many subdivisions in *Divine Principle,* the bulk of the work is
divided between a theology of creation and a theology of restoration. These two Articles define the redemptive process, which is
seen not in content or substance terms but in relational terms with
respect to both the spiritual and physical orders. Creation is both
material and spiritual and likewise entails a dynamics of "give-and-
take" action (*DP,* pp. 28-31). The Fall of humanity is not simply a
solitary *act of disobedience* but a derailment of the dynamics of the
creation process and a *rupture of give-and-take relationships* between
the physical and the spiritual, between God and humanity, between
women and men, between children and parents, and between humanity and nature. Restoration, consequently, is not just the return of creation to is original status but the recapitulation and
restoration of the original dynamic of creative relationships. According to *Divine Principle,* Adam and Eve fell *relationally* on both
the spiritual and physical levels. Christ, with the Spirit, restored
creation on the spiritual level but not the physical. It is the function
of the Lord of the Second Advent and his Bride to bring about the

	CREATION		RESTORATION
	ADAM/EVE	CHRIST/SPIRIT	LORD/BRIDE
physical	−	−	+
spiritual	−	+	+

full restoration dynamics by bringing physical restoration into harmony with spiritual restoration (see Fig.).[31]

In the end, the Last Things (*ta eschata*) will be like the First Things (*ta prota*). But here we should note that, although *Divine Principle* speaks about all men coming to "live harmoniously in the garden as one family" (*DP*, p. 129), there is no simple nostalgia for paradise. Adam and Eve fell when they were immature, whereas the realization of the Kingdom of God on earth depends upon the full formation or maturation of the individual, growth through the family, and dominion over creation. The eschaton subsumes all the Alpha functions and brings them to completion in Omega time.

Marriage and family stand at the crossroads of Unification eschatology. The theologoumenon of the family is the Rome through which all the routes of Unification theology passes. As a theologoumenon, the idea of the family functions as a *condensed symbol* which operates on multiple levels. On the literal level, the family means the marriage of men and women and the raising of children, born without the effects of original sin but still liable to sin, in what the Unificationists call a "God-centered" way. On the moral or tropological level, the restoration of the family is seen as the catalyst for the restoration of all other social institutions to the "sovereignty of goodness" (*DP*, p. 122). This agrees with the Puritan idea of the family as a little commonwealth. On the allegorical or analogical level, marriage and family function as a kind of *meta-sacrament*. The Matching and Blessing ceremonies incorporate traditional aspects of baptism (salt, sprinkling with water), the eucharist (holy wine) and priesthood in as much as the Blessing amounts to ordination for bringing about the Kingdom of God on earth. On the anagogical level, the Three Blessings (*DP*, pp. 51-7) sketch out a kind of *process eschatology* for the realization of good character, good citizenship and good workmanship in the Kingdom of God.[32] This process eschatology is anchored in a teaching which may be called the *messiahship of the family*.

The question arises, how does the Unification theology relate to traditional Christian theology of the marriage? There is no doubt that all biblically-based religions place great value on the family as a means to salvation. However, none of the main Christian traditions has given marriage and family an eschatological significance. The beatific vision is still conceived by most Christians who hold to the coming of the Kingdom of God on earth as a vision of the individual *coram deo*. For Unificationism, that vision is focussed on God-centered families, which will become the catalysts for the unification of humanity on the tribal, national and world levels. A movement like Marriage Encounter can be viewed validly as something that is traditionally Christian in mode as well as content. The Unification theology of marriage and family falls, I think, within a biblically-based Christian *mode* but the messiahship of the family certainly is a different kind of *content*. We can see the continuities of mode and discontinuities of content, if we break down the above-mentioned tripartite Unification mythos of salvation history into its component parts.

Aside from the Confucian aspects of the principle of creation, the Unification treatment of the story of Adam and Eve (*DP*, pp. 64-91) may not be as "unorthodox" as some claim. The emphasis on the sexual aspects of the Fall, the paradoxical treatment of the role of the archangel (both literal and allegorical) may strike some as naive and, hence, in need of demythologizing, but traditionalists may always point to St. Augustine's grounding of original sin in concupiscence or carnal lust.[33]

With its treatment of Christ and the Holy Spirit, Unification without doubt runs into conflict with traditional Christianity, for it seems to challenge the once-for-allness of redemption in Christ. Furthermore, the claim that the Christ's mission was to raise up a God-centered family certainly challenges those wings of Christianity which staunchly defend Jesus' life-long celibacy. Here, some careful distinctions are in order. *Divine Principle* unequivocally states that Christ's and the Spirit's mission was indeed fulfilled as "*spiritual* True Parents" (*DP*, p. 127; italics added). For Unificationism the categories are not "once" vs. "twice" but complete vs. incomplete, and, granting the presupposition of a Kingdom of God *on earth,* one cane make an empirically valid argument that the physical restoration of creation is incomplete. Secondly, the early Christian arguments in favor of Jesus' non-married status were often tainted or at least tinged by the Neo-Platonic doctrine that the body is a prison (*soma* = *sema*). This can hardly be squared with a theology of creation that asserts the goodness of the entire created order, visible and invisible, material and spiritual. Little is known of thirty odd years of Jesus' earthly life, yet the argument from silence has been turned into an argument for anti-corporeal asceticism and celibacy.[34] In the known stories of Jesus' dealing with women there certainly is no evidence of avoidance tactics.

When the Unification treatment of the roles of Rev. and Mrs. Moon come into play, the question of Rev. Moon's own messianic function most often comes up. That Rev. Moon sees himself as a central figure in the messianic Last Days is without doubt. But he does not claim to be divine, and *Divine Principle* asserts that the dual aspects of divine masculinity and feminity are not reflected individually but only through the True Parents. Still, the role of women in the Unification Church and the special place of Mrs. Moon have yet to be given full theological reflection.[35] In the context of the content of traditional Christianity, the central motif of True Parents unqualifiedly strikes the discordant chord of "heresy." It is the point where Unification theology seems to depart from Christian content and bring in something entirely new. On the other hand, the theme of True Parents can be seen as a de-allegorization and concrete embodiment of the motif of Bride and Bridegroom, which was ever the source of theological reflection in medieval treatises. Moreover, it resurrects echoes of Milton's visions of the eschatological meaning of marriage. In departing from Paradise, Adam and Eve shed a few "natural tears" but soon another vision holds them:

> The world was all before them, where to choose
> Their place of rest, and Providence was their guide.
> They, hand in hand, with wandering steps and slow,
> Through Eden took their solitary way.

> (Paradise Lost XII.346-9)

Whatever one's ultimate judgment of the Unification movement, the symbolic complex of True Parents, the God-centered family and the restoration of the original principle of creation provide the Unificationists with a motivation that can be acted on in the here and now. As Fr. Fichter has pointed out: "The God-centered family is not merely a nice slogan or a spiritual ideal suggested by church leaders. It is the essential core of community among the faithful of the church."[36] The link between marriage and the Kingdom of God is something new in the Christian tradition. The restoration of the God-centered family as a type of the eschaton is a strategic metaphor calling for concrete action that links heaven and earth in the here and now. Whatever the Unification theology of marriage may mean, it is certainly one powerful answer to the raw contractualism that has infected the West.

NOTES

1 Joseph H. Fichter, "Marriage, Family and Sun Myung Moon," in *A Time for Consideration: A Scholarly Appraisal of the Unification Church*, ed. M. Darrol Bryant and Herbert W. Richardson (New York: Edwin Mellen, 1978), p. 139, reprinted from *America*, 27 Oct., 1979.

2 Leo Strauss, *On Tyranny*, revised and enlarged (Ithaca: Cornell Univ. Press, 1968), p. 110, n. 5.

3 Nicolo Machiavelli, *The Prince*, trans. A. Robert Caponigri (Chicago: Henry Regnery, 1963), Chap. 15, pp. 84-85.

4 Machiavelli, *Discourses*, Bk. 1, Chap. 3 in *The Prince and the Discourses*, intro. Max Lerner (New York: Modern Library, 1950), p. 117.

5 Machiavelli, *Prince*, Chap. 18.

6 See Leo Strauss, *What Is Political Philosophy? and Other Essays* (Glencoe, Ill.: Free Press, 1959), pp. 47ff.

7 Thomas Hobbes, *Leviathan*, ed. Michael Oakeshott (New York: Collier, 1967), Chap. 13, p. 101.

8 *Ibid.*, p. 19.

9 See Immanuel Kant, *Lectures on Ethics*, trans. Louis Infield (New York: Harper Torchbooks, 1963), pp. 166-67.

10 Note that the very notion of contract restricts itself to individuals in its primary meaning and only secondarily includes social groups.

11 See O.J. Baab, "Marriage," in *Interpreter's Dictionary of the Bible* (Nashville: Abington, 1962), pp. 284-87.

12 See Hobbes, Chap. 14, pp. 104-12.

13 See Leo Strauss, *Natural Right and History* (Chicago: Univ. of Chicago Press, 1953), p. 184.

14 Adam Smith, *An Inquiry into the Nature and Causes of the Wealth of Nations,* ed. Edwin Canna (New York: Modern Library, 1937), p. 423.

15 See John Locke, *The Second Treatise of Government* (Indianapolis, Ind.: Library of Liberal Arts, 1952), Chap. 5, pp. 16-30.

16 Rousseau's *Emile* may well be the first idealization of romantic love and of the nuclear family model. See esp. *Emile,* trans. Barbara Foxley (New York: Everyman's Library, 1969), Bk. 5, "Sophy, or Woman," pp. 321-414.

17 George P. Grant, *English-speaking Justice* (Sackville, New Brunswick: Mount Allison Univ. Press, 1974), pp. 62-64.

18 Alfred North Whitehead, *Religion in the Making* (New York: New American Library, 1974), p. 16.

19 Soren Kierkegaard, *The Journals of Kierkegaard* (New York: Harper Torchbooks, p. 133.

20 Kierkegaard, *Papirer* VII A190, quoted in *The Works of Love,* trans. Howard and Edna Long (New York: Harper Torchbooks, 1962), p. 361, n. 44.

21 Eugen Rosenstock-Huessy, *Out of Revolution* (Norwich, Vt.: Argo, 1969), p. 9.

22 Karl Barth, *Church Dogmatics,* trans. G.W. Bromily and T.F. Torrance (Edinburgh: T. & T. Clark, 1961), vol. 3, sec. 4, p. 241.

23 See John A. Hostetler, *Communitarian Societies* (New York: Holt, Rinehart and Winston, 1974), Chap. 2, "The Family: An Experiment in Group Marriage," pp. 6-20.

24 H. Richard Niebuhr, *The Kingdom of God in America* (New York: Harper Torchbooks, 1959), p. 194.

25 Jerry Falwell, *Listen America!* (Garden City, N.Y.: Doubleday, 1980), p. 123. For a critique, see Clarissa W. Atkinson, "American Families and 'The American Family': Myths and Realities," *Harvard Divinity Bulletin* 12, no. 2, (Dec. 1981-Jan. 1982): 9-13.

26 William Gouge, *Of Domesticall Duties* (London, 1621), quoted in Atkinson, p. 12.

27 See Fr. Chuck Gallagher, S.J. *The Marriage Encounter* (Garden City, N.Y.: Doubleday, 1975).

28 See Archbishop Raymond G. Hunthausen, "Pastoral Letter on the Sacrament of Matrimony," *Worldwide Family Spirit* 9, no. 5: 13-24. This is without doubt the furthest reaching document on marrige and family to be issued by a Roman Catholic prelate in modern times.

29 See esp. George Downame, *A Treatise on Justification* (London, 1639), selected in *Introduction to Puritan Theology,* ed. Edward Hindson (Grand Rapids, Mich.: Baker Book House, 1976), pp. 198-217.

30 Jonathan Edwards, "The Beauty of the World," in *Jonathan Edwards: Basic Writings,* ed. Ola Elizabeth Winslow (New York: New American Library, 1966), pp. 251-53.

31 See my treatment of this schema as an Aristotelian *mythos* or "plot," in "The New Religions and the Second Naiveté," in *Ten Theologians Respond to the Unification Church,* ed. Herbert Richardson (New York: Unif. Theo. Seminary, distr. Rose of Sharon, 1981), pp. 55-58.

32 See Franz Feige, "Die Betrachtung von 'innen'. Familie und Gesellschaft in der Vereinigungskirche," in *Das Entstehen einer neuen Religion: Das Beispiel der Vereinigungskirche,* ed. Gunter Kehrer (Munich: Kosel, 1981), 235-47.

33 Augustine of Hippo, *Enchiridion* VIII.23-7, in *The Library of Christian Classics,* vol. 7, ed. Albert Outler (Philadelphia: Westminster, n.d.), pp. 353-55.

34 See esp. William E. Phipps, *Was Jesus Married?: The Distortion of Sexuality in the Christian Tradition* (New York: Harper & Row, 1970), pp. 34-98.

35 See the discussion in *Lifestyle: Conversations with Members of the Unification Church,* ed. Richard Quebedeaux (New York: Unif. Theo. Seminary, distr. Rose of Sharon Press, 1982), pp. 113-24.

36 Fichter, p. 138.

Family, Spiritual Values and World Government

Gene G. James

The Unification conception of the family is central to Unification thought. Even the Unificationist's conception of God can be interpreted as modeled on their ideal of the family. They believe that since mankind which is divided into male and female was created in the image of God, He too must contain dual characteristics. And just as husband and wife join to give birth to offspring, God's dual characteristics must combine to bring about the world. Considered apart from creation, God may be said to be one, unchanging and eternal. Considered as Creator, God is universal energy which is generated through the interaction of His dual characteristics. Since God is originally one, and then divides and unites again in creating the universe, He may be said to be the four position foundation of all that exists.

Just as God is the four position foundation of all being, the family should be the four position foundation of human society. In an ideal family husband and wife come together with love for God and one another. Children are then born who are loved by God and their parents, and who in turn love God, their parents and one another. In such a family all activities would be undertaken for the glorification of God, the husband and wife would never feel romantic attraction for others, there would be no jealousy or rivalry, and each would place the good of others above his or her own good. Were society as a whole composed of such families, an ideal society would exist.

God intended for Adam and Eve to establish an ideal family. He bestowed three great blessings on them: to be fruitful, to multiply, and to have dominion over creation. To enjoy the first blessing they had to perfect themselves, dedicating their minds and bodies to God; to enjoy the second they had to give birth to children who loved God, their parents, and one another, and who would perfect themselves also; to enjoy the third they had to develop their knowlegde of creation and become its caretaker. Had Adam and Eve established such a family, and they and all their descendants enjoyed these blessings, there would never have been any crime, murder, racial hatred, religious persecution, economic rivalry or warfare. Science and technology would have been used to aid human beings in perfecting themselves and ruling nature, never as a means of destruction. The Kingdom of God on earth would have existed. Because man's body was not created to be eternal, death would still have occurred; but men having perfected themselves as spiritual beings would have joined God to live eternally in the Kingdom of God in heaven.

However, Adam and Eve fell before they established an ideal family. Lucifer, who had been created to serve man, was jealous of God's love for Adam and Eve and enticed Eve into a sexual act. Eve, feeling alienated from God and Adam, then entered into a sexual relationship with Adam thereby thwarting God's plan for them to establish a family only after they had perfected themselves and could help their children reach perfection also.

Lucifer's sins in bringing about the fall were: (a) failure to take God's point of view which would have made him realize God did not love him less because He also loved Adam and Eve, (b) jealousy of the love Adam and Eve received, (c) disruption of the divine order of dominion by dominating Eve rather than serving her as God had intended, (d) causing Eve to feel the same estrangement from God and Adam which he felt. Eve's sins were to: (a) engage in an act of unprincipled love—love not based on the desire to fulfill God's purpose in placing man on earth, (b) causing Adam to fall by engaging in a sexual act with him, and (c) failing to convey to her children the perfection she lost. Adam's sins were similar to Eve's—engaging in an act of unprincipled love, failing to perfect himself and failing to convey perfection to his children.

Adam's and Eve's disregard of God's will constituted the spiritual fall. Their illicit sexual act, which produced children who would not be brought up in an ideal family, constituted the physical fall. Because of their actions, all their descendants inherited tendencies toward egoism, selfishness and sexual lust which causes them to disregard God's will and the good of others. Man lost the ability to communicate directly with God which he had enjoyed before the fall. God's will, which is the absolute standard by which we should order our actions, was no longer apparent to man. Men no longer realized that "there cannot be any purpose of the individual apart from the purpose of the whole, nor any purpose of the whole that does not include the purpose of the individual."[1] They became alienated from God, nature and each other.

Instead of founding an ideal family centered on God which could serve as the four position foundation for the development of the Kingdom of God on earth, Adam and Eve's action brought about a family centered on Satan. God created the universe so that He could feel joy in beholding its perfection. However, the universe will not be perfected until man is perfected and the ideal family established. God's hope in creating the universe was that the love He felt for man would be returned. Only when man responds to God's love in the appropriate fashion, entering into a "give and take" relationship with Him, will God's will be fulfilled.

Unificationists believe give and take action to be a fundamental attribute of both God and all created things. God's creative activity is the product of give and take action between His dual characteristics. Both the organic and inorganic realms exhibit give and take actions. For example, animal and plant co-existence is made possible by the interchange of oxygen and carbon dioxide. And animal reproduction occurs because of give and take action between male and female. These types of give and take action occur automatically. But give and take action between human beings requires choice.

Men are created free and only if they make the right choices will the proper give and take relationships between them and God and between them and other men be established. "God created man so that man could reach his perfection only by accomplishing his portion of responsibility."[2] Whenever man fulfills his responsibilities he becomes beautiful in the sight of God. "In the relationship between God and man, God gives love as the subject, while man returns beauty as the object. Between man and woman, man is the subject, giving love, while woman is the object, returning beauty."[3]

As the foregoing passage suggests, different people have different responsibilities, giving rise to different types of beauty. "Between men, the beauty which a junior returns in response to the love of a senior is called 'loyalty'; the beauty which children return in response to the love of their parents is called 'filial piety'; the beauty which a wife returns in response to the love of her husband is called 'virtue'."[4]

Some men such as Abraham, Isaac, Moses, John the Baptist and Jesus have been singled out for special responsibilities. It is their task to pay indemnity for man's failure to live up to God's standards and to set up the conditions necessary for man to be restored to the state he enjoyed before the fall. Restoration must take place first at the individual level, then at the family, national and finally worldwide levels.

The first of the individuals chosen to play a central role in the restoration was Cain. Because he was the first born of Eve's illicit love, he was not as close to God as his brother Abel. "The Archangel fell because he failed to receive God's love through Adam, who was closer to God, as the mediator. The archangel intended to take Adam's position . . . Consequently . . . Cain, who was in the position of the archangel, should have taken the position to receive God's love through Abel, who was in the position of Adam, as the mediator . . . "[5] But instead of serving Abel as he should have, Cain murdered him. Since that time makind, seen from the perspective of restoration, can be divided into two types: Cain-type and Abel-type individuals. Abel-type individuals are closer to God than other people, having been chosen by Him to serve as mediators for the rest of mankind. They are recognized by their gentle characters and by the message they bring. If they are to fulfill God's will, Cain-type individuals must find an Abel-type individual and "obey him in complete surrender."[6]

Societies and nations may also be divided into Cain and Abel-types. In each historical age, God designates a central nation which plays the leading role in the restoration. These were Israel in the biblical period and Charlemagne's empire in the middle ages. They are the United States and Korea in the modern era. Although the ultimate goal of each central individual and nation is the same, their missions are different. The task during the 2000 years from Adam to Abraham was to restore communication with God through sacrifices and offerings, thereby reestablishing a foundation for the ideal family. The task during the 2000 years from Abraham to Jesus was for the Jewish people to accept and obey the Law of the Old Testament so as to establish a foundation on the national level. The duty of people living during the 2000 year period from Jesus to the Lord of the Second Advent is to believe in Jesus and to take his word to all peoples of the world, thereby establishing the foundation for the restoration on a worldwide basis. The duty of people during the final days after the coming of the Lord of the Second Advent is to follow his teachings and to help unify mankind so as to at last bring about the Kingdom of God on earth. Restoration will then be complete and God's purpose in creation totally fulfilled.

How do we know the last days are at hand? According to Unificationists we know this because: (1) the ability of man to communicate with God is increasing. Many people capable of spiritual communication are being born. (2) More people than ever before are seeking to perfect themselves, centering their lives on God. (3) Man's desire for freedom has grown to such an extent that he is willing to risk his life to obtain it. "This may be seen in the liberation of slaves, liberation of minority groups and liberation of the minor powers [from colonial regimes], together with the demand for human dignity, equality between the sexes and equality among all people."[7] (4) People are more than ever feeling a sense of kinship and oneness with one another. "Nations, too, are moving toward one worldwide structure of sovereignty, starting from the League of Nations, through the United Nations and reaching today for world government."[8] (5) We are more and more coming to realize the common economic interests of all people. "The world is now on the threshold of forming one common market."[9] (6) Science and technology required for man to assume his rightful dominion over nature have reached extremely high levels of development.

None of this is occurring without struggle. Although it is a mistake to think that God would send natural calamities during the last days, because Satan is resisting the coming of the Kingdom of God on earth, social and political conflicts are inevitable. Thus the modern period has been, and will continue to be, an era of struggle and wars. "Today is the Last Days beacuse it is the time of intersection, when . . . God and . . . Satan are confronting each other in the final battle."[10]

The mission of the Lord of the Second Advent is to "restore the foundation to receive the Messiah substantially, starting from family level, and gradually broadening it to tribal level, racial level, national level, world level and then to the cosmic level."[11] However, since Satan is resisting the coming of the Kingdom of God, the last days will also be a time of false prophets. How then can we recognize the Lord of the Second Advent?

First, he will teach that men should perfect themselves by seeking salvation through Jesus. "If and when fallen man unites with Jesus in a perfect give and take relationship, he will be able to restore his original nature, thus entering again into a give and take relationship with God and becoming one with Him."[12] It is because Jesus is the means or mediator by which fallen man receives salvation that he is called the way, the truth and the life.

Second, he will provide an interpretation of the Bible which will enable perfected men to agree about its message. This will allow one to see new truth that was not apparent before. In order for people to be receptive to this new truth, they must not be overly attached to conventional teachings. They must realize that the Bible is not a textbook to be read literally, that its most important truths are only revealed in parables and symbols. Since "inner truth" revealed through prayer, meditation and reflection on the Bible was not intended to conflict with "outer truth," discovered by our senses, the new truth proclaimed by the Lord of the Second Advent will also be compatible with the basic findings of science.

Third, because religious truth and scientific truth were not intended to conflict, the Lord of the Second Advent will work to unify the religious and scientific traditions which have hitherto been separate.

Fourth, he will preach economic reform, helping to bring about a worldwide economic system in which there is no wasteful competition, unjust distribution or excessive consumption.

Fifth, he will unify the world's religions by accomplishing the mission of Christianity which has always been "to restore the one great world family which God... intended at the creation."[13] In fulfilling this mission he will also become the central figure which all other religions await.

How will the Lord of the Second Advent achieve these goals? As noted above, he will begin at the family level, gradually broadening his mission to the national and world levels. The first step in this process of restoring man to his original position will be the perfection of the individual through the establishment of the ideal family. Prior to the Lord of the Second Advent, all people have been born in sin. They have inherited tendencies toward egoism and self-centeredness which cause them to: (a) disregard God's will, (b) fail to develop loving relationships with their parents, children, brothers and sisters, (c) engage in illicit sex and (d) attempt to dominate their fellow man. The Lord of the Second Advent will abolish man's sinful nature by establishing an ideal family in which people are brought up with the proper attitudes toward God, self and others. They will then be able to understand the Bible correctly, communicate with God through meditation and prayer, and transform society to bring about the Kingdom of God on earth. Since the family is the primary unit through which these transformations will take place, its crucial role in Unification thought is apparent.

What will the ideal family be like? How will it be organized? How will decisions be made? What will be the rights and duties of its members? How will it be related to the larger society? How, exactly, will its establishment lead to the Kingdom of God on earth? At this point a number of issues arise which need further elaboration in Unification thought. Most of these involve the proper relationships between freedom and authority.

Respect for authority plays a key role in Unification thought. According to Unificationists Lucifer fell because he tried to overthrow God's order of dominion. Although he had been created to serve man, he dominated him instead. Cain fell for the same reason. He should have served Abel who was closer to God, but he rebelled against God murdering Abel. Since that time Cain-type individuals can obtain salvation only by finding an Abel-type person and submitting to his will. The story of Abraham and Isaac provides an extreme example of the type of obedience required. Abraham's faith in God was so great that he was willing to sacrifice his own son Isaac. And Isaac's loyalty to his father was so strong that he was willing to do whatever his father asked him. It was because of this loyalty that "Isaac . . . inherited the divine mission from his father Abraham, by obeying him in complete surrender . . ."[14]

The Unification accounts of the fall and Abraham's and Isaac's roles in establishing a foundation for the ideal family presuppose a preordained order of dominion. Some individuals were intended from creation to obey others. Thus children have an obligation of filial piety toward their parents, and juniors one of respect toward their seniors. And although *Divine Principle* does not state the idea explicitly, it seems reasonable to conclude as the *Outline of the Principle, Level 4* does that "Eve was supposed to be under Adam's dominion . . ."[15] It also seems reasonable to conclude that in an ideal family, the father would exercise absolute authority over both his wife and children. However, this is difficult to reconcile with the statements that one of the signs of the last days is that "men have come to pursue the original value of individuality endowed at the creation"[16] and that this may be seen in the "demand for human dignity, equality between the sexes and equality among all people."[17] At what point do children become adults in their own right, owing their parents love and respect but no longer under their authority? Are women to be equal partners in marriage or are they to be under the dominion of their husbands? *Divine Principle* does not speak with an unequivocal voice.

Given the Asian background of *Divine Principle,* it is natural for people trained in the social sciences to look for one of the sources of its teaching in oriental culture. The dominant influence on oriental ideas of the family and society has been Confucianism. The heart of Confucian thinking about the family and society is the doctrine of the five basic obligations of man. These are filial piety, respect for one's elders, devotion to one's spouse, loyalty to the emperor and trust between friends. The most fundamental of these obligations is filial piety.

The Classic of Filial Piety, written sometime during the 4th or 3rd century B.C., and used for centuries in Chinese schools states: "Of all the actions of man there is none greater that filial piety. In filial piety there is nothing greater than the reverential awe of one's father."[18] It also states that "The relation between father and son is rooted in the nature of Heaven and is the principle of the relation between the ruler and the minister."[19] The *Analects* similarly states "Filial piety and brotherly respect are the root of humanity."[20] And the *Tongmong Sonsup,* a book on the history of China and Korea, taught in the Korean schools in recent years, states: "You should serve those who are twice your age as you serve your father. You should serve those who are ten years your senior as you serve your elder brothers. You should follow those who are five years your senior."[21] It also recommends that: "The husband should not speak of inside affairs while he is out. The wife should not speak of outside affairs while she stays at home."[22]

Choi Jae-Seuk, a sociologist at the Korean National University, writing on the traditional Korean family, says: "Filial piety is the guiding principle in the life of Koreans. . . . Parental instructions are considered as absolute, demanding strict obedience. Even though a son believes what he asserts is right, he should not disobey the wishes of his parents. Even though his parents cannot perform their roles properly, it is the son's moral obligation . . . to serve his parents with all sincerity."[23] He also says: "The status of women in Korean families is very low. It is thought an ideal husband-wife relationship that the husband commands his wife well and the wife obeys her husband."[24] In fact, "the wife should devotedly serve not only her husband but her parents-in-law, brothers-in-law, and sisters-in-law."[25] Women are also expected to not marry again if their husbands die.

Choi Jae-Seuk further states that "the Korean people . . . regard society as a huge family and carry their patterns of conduct in family life to social life . . ."[26] And Song Chan-Shik, a historian also writing on the traditional Korean family, says: "It was stressed that the state, too, should be governed on the basis of filial piety. The overriding principle for governing the state was loyalty. Loyalty . . . was . . . an expanded form of filial piety."[27]

The Neo-Confucian view of the family and its relation to the state, which has governed Korean thought, is quite different from the one which has dominated recent western thought. In fact, modern democratic theory which began with John Locke is based on an *explicit rejection* of this type of theory. Thus Locke states at the beginning of *The Second Treatise of Government* that his purpose is "to set down what I take to be political power; that the power of a magistrate over a subject may be distinguished from that of a father over his children, a master over his servants, a husband over his wife, and a lord over his slave."[28]

According to Locke the authority which parents have over their children is only a temporary authority to govern them for their own good until they reach the age of reason. It is grounded in the fact that the parents are responsible for the children's existence and have an obligation to care for them. It ceases when the children no longer need their parents' assistance. Filial obligation rests on the gratitude children owe their parents. It too is limited. When the child becomes an adult he owes his parents respect and assistance, but not obedience. Indeed, if the parent becomes childlike in his or her old age, then the obligation of the child to the parent is similar to that of the parent to the child during childhood.

Political authority is based on an abstract and general contract between subject and sovereign. But parental authority is concrete and particular, grounded in obligation to specific people. It does not rest on respect for principles such as the duty to abide by the constitution, but on obligation to determinate individuals. Filial piety is simliar, growing out of past indebtedness to specific people rather than being the result of assuming an office or role which may be voluntarily terminated. It follows that the kind of loyalty one owes one's parents or friends is quite unlike the loyalty one owes the state. Indeed, to be loyal to the state, one must agree to subordinate loyalty to one's friends and relatives whenever it conflicts with loyalty to the state. The primary obligation of Richard Nixon's aides, e.g., was not to him as a person, but to the Constitution of the United States.

But, if this is true, can the values upon which the family is based, even if it is a family centered on God, be generalized to society as a whole? Are the duties and obligations we acquire from our relations with our parents and friends appropriate for governing urban societies in which most of our interactions with others must be brief and impersonal? What role, e.g., should respect for elders play in government? Should we look upon government leaders as wise parents who know better than all the rest of us what should be done for our own good? Should loyalty to government leaders be placed above all other duties?

Affirmative answers to the last two questions commit one to a basically totalitarian view, for as *Divine Principle* rightly points out: "Totalitarianism is a political ideology which denies the dignity of man's individuality and the freedoms of speech, publication, meeting and association, together with the basic human rights regarding the state and the parliamentary system... it insists that any individual or group should exist for the benefit... of the whole nation or state.... The guiding principle of totalitarianism does not put any authority on the majority but on one man, the ruler. The will of the ruler... becomes the ideology of the whole nation or state."[29]

Although family values are not an appropriate basis for civil government, they can provide an adequate foundation for church government. This is because the church is a voluntary association which one may leave whenever he or she chooses. This isn't true of civil government. Only government which rests on the consent of the governed is legitimate; but whether or not one consents, there is no way for individuals to avoid government. This is especially true today when governments are based on force as much as, or more than, they rest on consent.

If family values cannot replace democratic values, might they not supplement them? Would not people who grew up in an ideal family, also be ideal citizens who would unfailingly respect the rights of their fellow citizens? According to *Divine Principle,* if men were to live in a society based on the ideal family, then because they "have a vertical relationship with God, the horizontal relationship among them is automatically established... "[30]

What, then, if all members of society were products of ideal, God-centered families? Would not government necessarily reflect this? "Naturally, as history draws near its consummation, the will of the people inclines to be Christian-like, and the democratic government following the will of the people is also forced to be changed into that of Christianity. Thus, when the Messiah comes again... he will be able to set up God's sovereignty on the earth by the will of the people... "[31]

How will the Messiah bring this about? What will his relationship to the people be at the second coming? If democratic values are to be maintained it cannot be one of direct political rule modeled on the parent-child relation. If his role is to be that of "true parent," it cannot be political at all. People must follow him because they believe in him and his teachings. They must choose to follow him. Moreover, if the Kingdom of God on earth is to come about, *all* people must follow him.

There has never been a religious leader all people followed and there have never been teachings which were not interpreted differently by different people. As *Divine Principle* points out regarding the Bible: "Differences of interpretation have produced many denominations."[32] Will there ever be one man all will follow? And will there ever be teachings all will accept? I doubt there will ever be. This means that I am skeptical regarding the possibility of the Kingdom of God being realized on earth. But it does not mean that I am unmoved by the vision of *Divine Principle*. The goal of uniting all people in brotherly love is one of the highest man can undertake. It also provides a standard by which all religions may be judged. If one applies this standard to the Unification Church, one cannot fail to be struck by the radical difference between its many projects to unite people of different races, nationalities and faiths, and the practices of other churches. As the Preface to *Divine Principle* states: "Although they teach and believe that all men are descendants of the same parents, many Christians do not like to sit with brothers and sisters of different skin color. This is a representative example of today's Christianity, which is deprived of the life force needed to practice the word of Christ."[33]

Although I am skeptical that the Kingdom of God will ever be brought about on earth, I am certain that if it ever does exist it will be characterized by the kind of brotherly love preached and practiced by the Unification Church. Only if people love one another in this way will mankind ever be one family.

NOTES

1 *Divine Principle*, 5th ed. (New York: Holy Spirit Assn. for the Unif. of World Christianity, 1977), p. 42.

2 *Ibid.*, p. 55.

3 *Ibid.*, p. 48.

4 *Ibid.*, p. 49.

5 *Ibid.*, p. 244.

6 *Ibid.*, p. 250.

7 *Ibid.*, p. 121.

8 *Ibid.*, p. 128.

9 *Ibid.*, p. 129.

10 *Ibid.*, p. 126.

11 *Ibid.*, p. 369.

12 *Ibid.*, p. 30.

13 *Ibid.*, p. 123.

14 *Ibid.*, p. 276.

15 *Outline of the Principle, Level 4* (New York: Holy Spirit Assn. for the Unif. of World Christianity, 1980), p. 53.

16 *Divine Principle*, p. 121.

17 *Ibid.*

18 *The Classic of Filial Piety*, selections in James W. Dye and William H. Forthman, eds., *Religions of the World* (New York: Appleton Century Crofts, 1967), p. 292.

19 *The Classic of Filial Piety*, selections in Wing-Tsit Chan, *et al.*, *The Great Asian Religions* (London: Collier Macmillan, 1969), p. 125.

20 *Analects*, selections in Chan, p. 106.

21 Quoted by Han Sang-Bok, "Village Conventions in Korea," in *Korean Society* ed. Chun Shin-Yong (Seoul: International Cultural Foundation, 1976), p. 106.

22 *Ibid.*

23 Choi Jae-Seuk, "Family System," in Shin-Yong, p. 20.

24 *Ibid.*, p. 21.

25 *Ibid.*

26 *Ibid.*, p. 15.

27 Song Chan-Shik, "Genealogical Records," in Shin-Yong, p. 39.

28 John Locke, *The Second Treatise of Government*, ed. Thomas P. Peardon (New York: The Liberal Arts Press, 1956), pp. 3-4.

29 *Divine Principle*, p. 484.

30 *Ibid.*, p. 470.

31 *Ibid.*, pp. 441-42.

32 *Ibid.*, p. 132.

33 *Ibid.*, p. 7.

CONTRIBUTORS

Na'im Akbar
Clinical Psychologist
Department of Psychology
Florida State University
Tallahassee, Florida

Kenneth P. Ambrose
Associate Professor of Sociology
Marshall University
Huntington, West Virginia

Eileen Barker
Dean of Undergraduates
Department of Sociology
London School of Economics
University of London
London, England

David G. Bromley
Department of Sociology
University of Hartford
West Hartford, Connecticut

Diana Muxworthy Feige
Ed.D. Candidate
Columbia University
Teachers College
New York, New York

Frank K. Flinn
Consultant in Forensic Religion
Religion Editor
Edwin Mellen Press
Toronto/New York

Jane Zeni Flinn
Lecturer, English/Education
University of Missouri-St. Louis
St. Louis, Missouri

Donald Heinz
Associate Professor
Department of Religious Studies
California State University
Chico, California

Gene G. James
Professor of Philosophy
Coordinator, Religion & Society
  Program
Memphis State University
Memphis, Tennessee

Michael Mickler
Ph.D. Candidate
Graduate Theological Union
Berkeley, California

Timothy Miller
Lecturer in Religious Studies
Department of Religious Studies
University of Kansas
Lawrence, Kansas

Anson D. Shupe, Jr.
Department of Sociology
University of Texas at Arlington
Arlington, Texas

Frederick Sontag
Department of Philosophy
Pomona College
Claremont, California

Hugh Spurgin
Secretary Genera, PWPA (USA)
Ph.D. Candidate in American History
Columbia University
New York, New York

Nora Spurgin (M.S.W.)
Director, Family Department
Unification Church in America
New York, New York

Thomas Walsh
Ph.D. Candidate in Religious Ethics
Vanderbilt University
Nashville, Tennessee

Patricia A. Zulkosky
Ph.D. Candidate
School of Theology at Claremont
Claremont, California

Other Books on the Unification Movement

Distributed by
The Rose of Sharon Press, Inc.
G.P.O. Box 2432
New York, N.Y. 10116